THE SCOTT AND LAURIE OKI SERIES IN ASIAN AMERICAN STUDIES

Becoming Nisei

JAPANESE AMERICAN URBAN LIVES
IN PREWAR TACOMA

Lisa M. Hoffman and Mary L. Hanneman

UNIVERSITY OF WASHINGTON PRESS | *Seattle*

in association with

UNIVERSITY OF WASHINGTON LIBRARIES

Becoming Nisei was supported by a grant from the Scott and Laurie Oki Endowment for Books in Asian American Studies.

This publication was also made possible in part by a grant from the Phillip and Estelle De Lacy Endowed Libraries Fund.

Cover and interior design by Katrina Noble
Composed in Cala, typeface designed by Dieter Hofrichter
Maps by Ben Pease, Pease Press Cartography, data compiled by Sarah Pyle 2019
Cover photograph: Teachers, families, and students at the Tacoma Japanese Language School, ca. 1920–35 (Courtesy of Washington State Historical Society, 1989.18.17.1)

25 24 23 22 21   5 4 3 2 1

Printed and bound in the United States of America

UNIVERSITY OF WASHINGTON PRESS
uwapress.uw.edu

UNIVERSITY OF WASHINGTON LIBRARIES
www.lib.washington.edu

LIBRARY OF CONGRESS CATALOGING-IN-PUBLICATION DATA
LC record available at https://lccn.loc.gov/2020015408
LC ebook record available at https://lccn.loc.gov/2020015409

ISBN 978-0-295-74821-4 (hardcover), ISBN 978-0-295-74822-1 (paperback), ISBN 978-0-295-74823-8 (ebook)

The paper used in this publication is acid free and meets the minimum requirements of American National Standard for Information Sciences—Permanence of Paper for Printed Library Materials, ANSI z39.48–1984.∞

For our children, the future, our hope

CONTENTS

Foreword by Gregory Masao Tanbara   ix
Acknowledgments   xi

INTRODUCTION
Becoming Nisei: Spatial Stories and Imprints of Meiji Japan   3

CHAPTER ONE
Establishing a New Community in Tacoma   28

CHAPTER TWO
Struggle and Hard Work: From Physical Labor
to Entrepreneurialism   61

CHAPTER THREE
Japanese American Urban Lives: Spatial Stories
of a Close Community   96

CHAPTER FOUR
Expanding the Mapping of Japanese Urban Lives   127

CHAPTER FIVE
The Yamasakis and the Tacoma Japanese Language School   143

CHAPTER SIX
Ethical Lessons of Meiji Japan Woven into Nisei Stories   173

CONCLUSION
Incarceration, Dispersal, and Erasure: Destruction of a Community   203

Appendix A: Interviewees and Family Backgrounds   223
Appendix B: Tacoma Japanese Language School Faculty   233
Notes   235
Bibliography   253
Index   267

FOREWORD

I was intrigued by the chance to read *Becoming Nisei*. I grew up in Tacoma, Washington, and have lived my whole life here. The book is about my hometown. I had Japanese grandparents who were Tacoma Issei—first-generation immigrants from Japan. My mother was Nisei, second-generation Japanese born in the US, who lived all her life in Tacoma. This book is about Tacoma Nisei. My sisters and I (Sansei, third generation) knew lots of Issei and Nisei people in Tacoma.

I was interested to learn more about the place where my mother and her sisters grew up—the middle of what was Tacoma's Japanese community. Mom and my aunties told us story after story about the time when there were so many Japanese here. Little things about life and people in the Nihonmachi before World War II. Their stories were about everything. I loved hearing them, but always figured they would only be interesting to us who knew Issei and Nisei.

And the book is about the Tacoma Japanese Language School, an important place in my childhood. You see, Mom, Dad, sisters Diane and Susan, and I, through a series of circumstances, lived in what once was the teachers' quarters in that building in the mid-1950s—the same place Principal Masato Yamasaki and his wife, Kuniko, the school's first teacher, lived before World War II. I have memories of that place from so long ago. This book is about that building, the important role it played, and the Yamasakis, all gone now.

I am glad I have this moment to tell you about my experience with *Becoming Nisei*. The interviews in it are wonderful renditions of many of the stories I have heard over the years, and some I had not. I could hear the voices of the Nisei I knew as I read what they tell us. And I have come away with a deeper understanding of the Issei and Nisei people who shaped my early life in Tacoma's post–World War II Japanese American community. My experience with this book has been a very personal one.

For others of you, reading *Becoming Nisei* will also be something special. The work of Lisa Hoffman and Mary Hanneman is about a place, now gone, but returned to you through the voices of people who lived there. Lisa and Mary present these memories and stories amid the world events and social dynamics of the times—US immigration, world war, racism—but with a tight focus on one community and place. That gives the work depth and perspective. It speaks to something we all know—that places are important to people—and reminds us of the changing nature of places and the fragility of their communities.

I want to thank Lisa Hoffman and Mary Hanneman for *Becoming Nisei* and for their other work in this area, *Tacoma's Japanese Language School: An Oral History*, a wonderful collection of recorded interviews with Nisei about the Japanese Language School, their time there as students, and the influence the school had on their lives.

Lisa and Mary were also part of the University of Washington Tacoma's effort to create *Maru*, the bronze memorial to the Tacoma Japanese Language School. It is a marvelous art piece that stands on the university campus. You should visit it when you are here.

Altogether, I am grateful to Lisa and Mary for their work. Theirs is a creative blend of the academic and the compassionate.

I hope you enjoy reading *Becoming Nisei*.

GREGORY MASAO TANBARA
Tacoma, Washington

ACKNOWLEDGMENTS

This project has been a long time in the making and we are sorry that it did not come out sooner so that more of the Nisei we interviewed could have read their stories in print. Our gratitude to those we spoke with cannot be understated. They opened their hearts and homes, met us at public locations, and shared their childhood memories with us—though we were professors, strangers, and younger, white women. Their graciousness was inspiring and we are forever touched by these experiences, the laughter and even tears we shared. The full list of those we interviewed, along with brief family backgrounds, can be found in appendix A—we thank each individual, deeply and sincerely. Yet there are a few people without whom this project would not have been possible. Dr. Ryo Munekata was a leader of the Tacoma Nisei, and generously shared with us lists upon lists of addresses so we could find as many people as possible. He was forever an optimist with an incredible memory; we learned much from him and were saddened by his passing in 2017. Joe Kosai, who ran Kabuki Restaurant in Tacoma and passed away in 2008, was always present and supportive, working closely with the university on the *Maru* memorial for the school (sculpture by Gerard Tsutakawa). He willingly spoke with students about his family history and consistently warmed any room he was in. In Chicago, Kazuo Horita (passed in 2013), whom we met in Tacoma at one of the Nisei reunions, spoke passionately about what mattered and helped organize fellow former Tacomans for interviews. We also want to thank all three of the "Fujimoto sisters"—Yoshiko Fujimoto Sugiyama, Chiyeko Tadaye Fujimoto Kawasaki, and Kimiko Fujimoto Tanbara—for their participation and grace throughout the project. Not only were we in awe of these three elegant women, all of whom have now passed, but we also felt their genuine kindness. It was a blessing to have met them. We especially wish to show our gratitude to Kimi Tanbara and her family, daughters Diane, Susan, and Merilee and son Gregory. Kimi was a staunch supporter from the early days of this project; Greg was a critical player in getting the memorial for the Japanese Language School established. After reading a draft of this manuscript, Greg moved us to tears by talking about his reaction to the narratives, hearing the voices of those he knew so well. We are grateful that he agreed to provide the book's foreword, which is insightful and incisive. We also thank Greg and his sisters for allowing us to include the family photo of their grandmother, mother, and aunt in the Capital Cleaners.

While there were many student research assistants on this project over the years, Sarah Pyle displayed remarkable dedication, hard work, and aptitude for detail, not to mention genuine curiosity and excellent research skills. The pleasure she shared with us upon finding a treasure in the *Polk City Directories* was palpable, and her detailed research led to the maps that are in this book, which so enhance the stories being told. We cannot thank Sarah enough. Misaki Seto, native Japanese speaker and biomed major, was also an incredible asset on this project. She helped us in the UW Special Collections archives, going through pages of documents and working with Mary Hanneman on translations. Her dawning wonder at the power of historical research was exciting to share, and we are grateful for all she provided. Many other students supported this project by transcribing the interviews (notably June Moore, as well as Nadia Van Buren) and performing other research needs. They were all committed and most helpful. We are grateful to Paige Cunningham, Jeff Eck, Neil Grigsby, Beverly O'Dea, Josh Scullin, Arianna Shorey, Kazuaki Suhama, and Rain Wilson. Hope St. John also provided key analysis and literature review and we thank her for these contributions. Lisa Hoffman thanks the students in Pacific Rim Cities in Winter 2020 for their input on a draft of the introduction. Parts of our argument were presented at the Asian Studies on the Pacific Coast meetings in 2019 and the American Anthropological Association Annual Meeting in 2019; we are grateful for those opportunities and the feedback we received. Lisa is particularly grateful to anthropologists Jennifer Hubbert and Monica DeHart for their engagement and continuous support. *Conflux*, the online working paper series managed by

Urban Studies at UW Tacoma, also published two papers on this project, "Tacoma's Japanese Language School: An Alternative Path to Citizenship and Belonging in Pre-WWII Urban America" (2014) and "Re-mapping Tacoma's Pre-war Japantown: Living on the Tideflats" (2018, with Sarah Pyle). That material is incorporated into this manuscript as well.

In addition to conducting interviews in Tacoma and Seattle, we met with the Nisei in Los Angeles, Chicago, and Oakland. The Japanese American National Museum graciously provided space for interviews in LA at no charge. We are very grateful for this support. Steve Winch packed his cameras and equipment and did the taping for all of the interviews. We are grateful for his professionalism and for his dedication to the project. After Steve left the university, Paul Lovelady, also at UW Tacoma, professionally took up the mantle of holding the original tapes, copying them when we needed access, and working with us to preserve these memories. These trips, Steve's time, and funds for student researchers would not have been possible without the financial support from a number of sources. We are grateful especially to the Institute for Ethnic Studies in the United States at University of Washington in Seattle for grant funding in support of the travel expenses. University of Washington Tacoma Founders' Endowment Grant and the Chancellor's Funds also provided early support for the project. Thanks too to Brian Coffey and Ali Modarres of Urban Studies and Interdisciplinary Arts and Sciences at UW Tacoma, which provided funding over the years. Mike Wark in the Advancement Office at UW Tacoma was always deeply committed to memorializing the Tacoma Japanese Language School, and without his advocacy, fundraising, and networking it may not have happened. He also made sure our book project was a part of the UW's Come Together Washington event in 2004. We are deeply grateful for his support. In the final stages of manuscript production Leslie Kinkade helped us find funding as well. Managing student researchers and funding requires on-the-ball administrative help, which Julia Smith and then Abbey Schwarz in Urban Studies provided. Susan Stone provided last-minute quality indexing. Thank you to all.

University of Washington Press always seemed like the right home for this book and we are so grateful for Larin McLaughlin's interest and encouragement and for the support from the whole UW Press team. Hanni Jalil patiently helped us through the final stages of manuscript production, and Anne Canright provided excellent editing. The two anonymous reviewers provided helpful insight and endorsement at the right moment and we thank them for their time in reviewing the manuscript. Tamiko Nimura and Michael Sullivan also read the manuscript and provided helpful comments. We worked with Heidi Betts as well and thank her for her professionalism in pushing us with edits. Of course, we take responsibility for any inaccuracies or failings of this book, some of which we recognize but have been unable to address (e.g., a page number of a quote) due to finalizing the manuscript during COVID-19 quarantine!

Regarding the various images and maps in this book: Ben Pease created wonderful maps, building on the work Sarah Pyle had done. We thank him for his patience and good humor in working with us and producing all the maps we needed in short order. The Nakano family—mother, Yaeko, and children, Stan, Maya, and Hiroshi—allowed us to use the beach outing photo, and the Nishijima family, particularly Stacey Nishijima Ferguson, allowed us to use the photo of her family's Yakima Fruit Company business. These images are wonderful and we are deeply grateful. We thank Tamiko Nimura for the connection to Stacey as well. Densho, Washington State Historical Society, Japanese Community Service of Seattle, Northwest Room at Tacoma Public Library, and University of Washington Libraries Special Collections also provided permissions for their images to be used. CSI Drone Solutions at the last minute provided the image of downtown Tacoma today, and at no charge. A special thank you to Joe Seto for materials related to Nisei in the armed forces; see the Seto Collection at the Tacoma Public Library, Northwest Room. We also want to thank the staff at UW Libraries Special Collections for pulling boxes from remote locations and providing access as we, Sarah Pyle, and Misaki Seto found opportunities to get there. Mariko Kawamoto, visiting librarian from Keio University in Japan, also organized the Japanese Association of Tacoma collection, making it accessible and easy to use. We are grateful to all.

There are many reasons it took so many years to finish this book, including teaching responsibilities, other research projects, and children, but also because of our own losses. Mary's parents, who were born in 1923 and 1926, both passed in 2004. Lisa's mother, born in 1938, passed in 2015, and her brother in 2018. Our parents were born in the same years as the Nisei we interviewed, such that the passing of many of the Nisei interviewees sits alongside our own personal losses. It is only thanks to the support of our families, Bill, John Saul, and Anna Driscoll (for Lisa) and Jim, Davy, and Caroline Allen (for Mary), that we were able to push through and get this done. Lisa also thanks her father, Allan S. Hoffman, for providing a role model of a hardworking and considerate academic, who also knew how to take a break and appreciate family and friends.

As this book looks back and asks us to remember what has been silenced and made invisible, we also look forward. For this reason, we dedicate this book to our children, our future and our hope.

Becoming Nisei

INTRODUCTION

Becoming Nisei

Spatial Stories and Imprints of Meiji Japan

My name is Ryo Munekata and I was born right here in Tacoma.
In fact, from this location[1] I was born one block south at a hotel
with a midwife. That was April 12, 1921 . . . And this area is really
the area [where] we spent our childhood . . . This street here, right
in front of us, Broadway, between 13th and 15th, was, you could
say, not solidly, but the greater majority of the merchants were
Japanese families.

—DR. RYO MUNEKATA (B. 1921)

RYO NARRATED HIS CHILDHOOD MEMORIES OF JAPANESE FAMILIES
and businesses along Broadway in 2003, when we interviewed forty-
two second-generation Japanese Americans (Nisei) about their pre–World
War II lives in Tacoma, Washington. He had a vivid memory of what was
on the street, including a beer tavern on 13th and Broadway called Happy
Days Are Here Again, the Fuji Ten Cents Store, and Japanese and Chinese
restaurants. He was born in the hotel where his family lived and worked,
but he also remembered the Victoria Hotel, the Mayflower Hotel run by
Mrs. Yoshioka, and the A B Hotel further down the street. "Next to the
[A B] hotel was a family named Mori, and they had a cleaning business,
and next to that was a barbershop. The lady's name was Mrs. Kubo. . . .
And next door to that was a lady by the name of Mrs. Jinguji, who [also]
had a barbershop." There was even a food counter that had a back room
where only the adults were allowed. When he was little, "we were told,

3

'No, you can't go back there because it's an area where people like to gamble.'" In his 2003 visit to his childhood city, however, he noted: "I don't see any of [those] structures."

As in many cities where Japanese immigrants and their families lived prior to World War II, the built landscape of Ryo's childhood has been demolished. The structures of his memories—the hotels, restaurants, barbershops, and the Japanese Language School building—inhabited, funded, and constructed by the immigrants, have gradually disappeared in many urban centers. With little attention to preserving histories and memories, these spaces in downtown Tacoma were turned into parking lots, modern office buildings, and a convention center, contributing to the "disassembl[ing of] Japanese American heritage" that began with wartime incarceration (Dubrow 2002, 4).

In contrast to pre-1940s urban Japanese settlements (often known as Nihonmachi, or Japan Town), wartime incarceration camps have received considerable attention in recent years, including recognition in the National Register of Historic Places, thanks to the effective political mobilization by Nisei.[2] This understandable focus on the internment and redress means that the rich social history and built landscapes of prewar Japanese immigrants and their children, such as temples, schools, and shops, have suffered from a lack of attention (see, e.g., Dubrow 2002, 5; Morrison 1994). Even when certain "property types" remain, such as single-room-occupancy hotels, they have not been preserved adequately, owing to "a long history of neglect of Asian/Pacific American heritage" (Dubrow et al. 1993, 52). The disappearance of the businesses and homes of Japanese in prewar Tacoma is a prime example of what may be called structural or systemic forgetting (Connerton 2009).[3] (See figures I.1 and I.2.)

Becoming Nisei addresses this forgetting. Based on interviews with second-generation Japanese Americans who grew up in Tacoma and attended Tacoma's Japanese Language School in the 1910s, '20s, and '30s, this book both elaborates on the early Japanese immigrant experience in urban America and highlights what many interviewees noted as important about Tacoma. The prewar focus also recognizes a need expressed by the interviewees themselves to examine their growing-up years and Nikkei life before the war,[4] a shift away from the scholarly tendency to focus on the trauma of incarceration. The interview narratives accentuated cultural practices and ethics (*shushin*) emphasized by their parents'

FIGURE 1.1. Nihonmachi, 13th and Broadway, Tacoma, ca. 1940. Courtesy of Densho.

FIGURE 1.2. Looking down Broadway from 13th to 15th Street, 2020. Courtesy of CSI Drone Solutions.

generation (Issei) and featured the places and spaces in which they played, learned, and grew up.

TACOMA IN PERSPECTIVE

Tacoma offers a particularly interesting place to examine these experiences. The city, incorporated in 1875, sits on Puyallup tribal land—part of the Coast Salish landscape. This layer of erasure and forgetting sits within what Iyko Day terms "the triangulation of Native, alien, and settler positions" (2019, 19).[5] Thirty miles south of Seattle and a major port in its own right in the late 1880s, Tacoma was the final destination of the Northern Pacific Railroad and seemed on the verge of becoming the region's economic center. As a result, the Japanese Consulate established offices there, encouraging a number of immigrants from Japan to settle in Tacoma. After the railroad extended to Seattle and political and economic activity shifted north, however, so too, in 1900, did the consular office (Magden 1998; Morgan 2003). Nevertheless, Tacoma offered work in industry to Japanese immigrants—railroads, canneries, and sawmills— and later, as in other West Coast urban communities including Los Angeles, San Francisco, and Seattle, developed a robust economy of small businesses like laundries, grocery stores, barbershops, garages, and restaurants. Thus Tacoma continued to attract first-generation immigrants.

Yet Tacoma's Japanese community was smaller in population than in those other locations; it was described by a Japanese government official as having a "gentleness among cities of the Pacific coast" (Otsuka and Fukui [1940] 1986, 7), and the Nisei we interviewed felt it was unique as a particularly "close" community. It also had only one Japanese language school (see chapter 3 and figure I.3), and unlike elsewhere, where language schools were opened by religious groups, such as the Buddhists or Methodists, Tacoma's Japanese Language School (TJLS) was secular.[6] These religious affiliations, along with prefectural associations (*kenjinkai*), tended to divide the community. Tacoma's Japanese Language School, in contrast, brought families together from across religious, prefectural, and even economic backgrounds through the children's activities and the leadership of the school principal, Mr. Masato Yamasaki (b. 1874), and his wife, Mrs. Kuniko Yamasaki (b. 1872), the founding teacher.[7] Under the Yamasakis' leadership, the school was well run and serious in its efforts

FIGURE I.3. Students and teachers taken from side rear of Tacoma Japanese Language School, May 22, 1927. Courtesy of University of Washington Libraries, Special Collections.

to teach the language and instill traditional values in the children (see chapters 5 and 6). In fact, during World War II Tacoma's school was recognized as particularly strong in teaching Japanese language by the US Military Intelligence Service Language School, which was interested in finding Japanese speakers for intelligence work, contradicting some scholarship which argues that these schools were ineffective (Adachi 1979, 129; Ichioka 2006, 44–46). Some interviewees noted, for instance, that during the war the Japanese language competency test was waived for them because they had attended *Tacoma's* Japanese Language School, the military authorities apparently assuming they had strong language skills owing to the quality of the teaching there (see conclusion).

To students of the Japanese American experience, Tacoma is thus both unique and familiar, with similarities and differences to other West Coast cities. The individuals we interviewed shared immigration stories of their parents, tales of daily life in the home, and values emphasized by their parents and in lessons at the TJLS, suggesting that a critical aspect of becoming Nisei was related to Japan's transitional Meiji period (1868–1912). At the same time, the interviews are filled with spatial stories of experiencing the city on foot, through daily paths of walking to public school and then on to the TJLS. Yet like other urban centers, Tacoma also was a segregated city, and many endured discrimination and insecurity in blatant forms. Becoming Nisei, in other words, was embedded in prevailing social and power relations, making these processes complicated and multifaceted. The following chapters examine these issues, addressing the structural forgetting and erasure of prewar lives and histories experienced not only in Tacoma, but in many other contemporary urban settings.

EXPANDING UNDERSTANDINGS OF PREWAR URBAN JAPANESE LIVES: A TRANSNATIONAL AND SPATIAL APPROACH

The emphasis on transnational and spatial aspects of becoming Nisei underscores the complex, contingent, and ongoing nature of identity formation for the Nisei, a process we term "bridging," in contrast to the more typical representation of Nisei as "a bridge" between two distinct locations, Japan and the US. In what follows, we outline what this means.

A TRANSNATIONAL APPROACH

This book embeds the Nisei experience in transnational relations and exchanges of ideas, people, and goods. The fact that Issei parents were "aliens ineligible to citizenship" in the United States, on the one hand,[8] and instruction both in the TJLS and within family settings relied on cultural practices of *shushin* (ethics), on the other, underscore the transnational character of the Nisei's own place in the world. Because US law forbid the Issei from becoming US citizens, Issei remained Japanese nationals—subjects of the Japanese emperor. Absent their connection with Japan, however, they were stateless, such that official connections were maintained via Japanese associations that linked the immigrants with Japanese consulates in the US. In this sense, the Issei and their Nisei children lived in spaces that were relational and dynamic, rather than in spaces either in or between the two distinct points of Japan and the US.[9]

The Nisei experience must also be understood in the larger context of Japan's own transformations in the late 1800s and early 1900s, related to Japan's national effort to become an equal member of the international community in response to the threat of Western imperialist encroachment. This framing is the backdrop to Japanese migration to the US (and elsewhere) in the late nineteenth and early twentieth centuries and is relevant to Japanese language and culture learning in the US and thus to Nisei identity formation. The Meiji Restoration of 1868, which ironically promoted Japan's modernization under the aegis of the most traditional of symbols, the emperor, was an important aspect of this transformation.

At the same time, prompted by concerns over the safety and security of their nationals, and also by a desire to shape a positive popular international image of Japan, the Japanese consular authorities in the US worked actively to keep Japanese immigrants out of trouble and to maintain a respectable national reputation locally. Their greatest concern was that Japan would suffer the same fate as China had with the Chinese Exclusion Act of 1882 and that the US government would bar all Japanese immigration. The legal manifestation of this dynamic between the US and Japan was the Gentlemen's Agreement of 1907–8, which limited Japanese immigration to the children and wives of men already in the US. Part of this process involved Japanese government support for the establishment of Japanese associations in America, including a branch in Tacoma that was responsible for everything from helping those in material need to doing the paperwork for visas and assisting with local matters. Thus, in very concrete terms, the distinct second-generation Nisei cohort experience in cities like Tacoma was structured by immigration policies that allowed wives, "picture brides," and other dependents into the US, but not single men (see Daniels 1992, 434–35), forming families and seeing the birth of a cohort in the early 1900s. Examining Nisei interviewees' stories of the everyday makes its own contribution, then, to broader understandings of national and transnational histories. The politics of international relations help to explain Japanese governmental concern with behaviors of Japanese immigrants in the United States, which certainly affected the Nisei (and intermingled Sansei), highlighting the intersectionality of local and transnational experiences.

Additionally, specific aspects of social control in late nineteenth- and early twentieth-century Japan, such as the symbolic power of the emperor manifested in the Meiji Constitution and the reification of traditional Japanese values in the 1890 Imperial Rescript on Education, strongly impacted the social landscape of Tacoma's Japanese immigrants. The values promoted in the rescript, including the central ideal of filial piety, had informed educational policy in Japan for the Issei themselves; these same ideals provided the foundation for the ethics (*shushin*) curriculum at the TJLS, as well as values and ethics as they were reinforced in the home. Nisei interviewees deeply remembered the school's principal, Mr. Yamasaki, for instance, for teaching those ethics, and even for emphasizing them to their Issei parents. As young people they felt social control through family rules about what they could and could not do, the feeling that everyone in the community would know if they had done something wrong even before they got home, and in part through the watchful eye of Mr. Yamasaki and his emphasis on traditional values, such as *oyakoko* (filial piety, including respect for and obedience to one's parents). Important to note, however, is that our attention to the importance of *shushin* (see chapter 6) is not an appeal to cultural essentialism, but is rather a recognition of the complex and transnational processes that informed Nisei subject formation (see also Foucault 1980, 1988, 2007).[10]

Thus, as Japan experienced its own (national) identity transformation in the late nineteenth and early twentieth centuries, so too did Japanese immigrants in the United States, who negotiated their new surroundings and identities as ethnic and national minorities. In both cases, this process was at least partially self-protective, bound up in the need to shape new identities that would, on the one hand, retain elements of traditional culture, while on the other hand providing strength through the adoption of new, more "modern" elements. Understanding the parallel nature of individual and national efforts at identity construction not only alerts us to the significant ways in which the migrants brought elements of their native land to their lives in the US, but also suggests *why* they did so. The weaving together of these stories enables us to move beyond a false dichotomy of local vs. transnational to understand the fluid process by which each affects the other (see Ono 2005).

Approaching Nisei lives and identities as translocal, dynamic, and emergent is in contrast to an understanding of people *uprooting* themselves from the home country, moving to the United States, and becoming assimilated and "Americanized." A transnational perspective, along with a focus on processes of "bridging" rather than "lack of fit," allows us to consider more complex and messy identity configurations (see also DeHart 2021). Furthermore, situating issues in spaces that are not just "here" or "there" is "a mode of research that brings attention to the contingent nature and multiple causes of specific events" (Ettlinger 2011, 543). By focusing on the urban, this book addresses the "complex interconnectivity" of becoming Nisei "in multiple fields of social practice," what Michael Smith terms transnational urbanism (M. Smith 2005, 2001).

A SPATIAL APPROACH

Our deployment of a *spatial* lens also helps us understand how Nisei had to negotiate multiple positionalities on a daily basis and how identity and place are intertwined, also emphasizing why the erasure of this history in built landscapes may be experienced as an erasure of self. To make sense of the ways in which spatiality shaped the Tacoma Nisei experience, we build on the work of geographers[11] who help us understand space in processual terms, as emergent (vs. finished), as shaped by existing social and power relations, and as made through acts by ordinary individuals as well as power-holders and institutions.[12] City streets, for instance, involve walking, moving, and perhaps a fleeting sense of belonging that may also be recurring, helping to establish a sense of the right to belong in a place. Our interviewees' stories are important pieces of evidence, then, of how movements through space shaped a sense of self and belonging in the city.

The interview narratives are punctuated by specific spatial references: residential and business locations, the homes of neighbors and friends, places the interviewees played and studied, and picnics and other gathering sites. They are social memories rooted in "sites" that help to anchor "memories in place" (Hoelscher and Alderman 2004, 349).[13] As adult memories of childhood, some of the spatial references were exact and specific, while we have supplemented others with additional archival research to locate and identify.[14] Spatial experiences are also collective memories, recited by numerous people, sometimes in group conversations. Recognizing that these collective memories are, as geographer Allan Pred put it, "both acquired and activated through bodily engagement in situated social or economic practices" helps us to interpret these individuals' everyday walks and tasks as embodied experiences that impacted who they became. Pred argued that identities and biographies are "formed, reformed and deformed through the corporeal involvement of women and men in the discourses and activities of everyday life" (1990). Thus, space and place are not simply locations in which social life occurs, or a set of boundaries and census numbers; rather, they are processes and forms of power, and essential components of the social and the subject— indeed, of the city itself.[15]

Moreover, analyzing how Nisei negotiated their multiple positionalities enhances our understanding of the mutually constitutive nature of spatiality and subjectivity. It also emphasizes why the erasure of this history through massive transformation of built landscapes may be not only understood as a result of historic processes, such as incarceration and urban change, but also experienced as a reorganization of the self. The Nisei's spatial stories could then be understood as attempts to *reconstruct* the self and community in one's own terms, even if these reconstructions may produce more romanticized and positive memories of childhood—such as a greater emphasis on happy memories at the language school than of a desire not to attend daily. Additionally, such agentive remembering has the potential, we argue, to unsettle the contemporary urban landscape of parking lots and high-rise office buildings, "undermining linear and progressive notions of urban development" and "pushing up images of the past that had long been buried" (MacFarlane and Mitchell 2019, 819). Flashes of such silenced histories may be able to disrupt current urban growth narratives such that memory may be "mobilized relative to what happens," inserting itself into what exists, "clever enough to transform into an opportunity" (de Certeau 1984, 86; see also Merrill and Hoffman 2015).

We thus understand the interviewees' everyday childhood paths as acts of self-making, whether by foot, trolley car, or private vehicle, as well as processes of space- and place-making. The Nisei were *active* participants in constituting their identities and social worlds as well as in the making of urban landscapes. Space and subjectivity are mutually constituted, in other words, such that becoming Nisei also shaped the urban space of Tacoma. Yet those streets also had police, acts of discrimination and racism, and were subject to rules about noncitizens being unable to purchase land (alien land laws). Coupled with active self-making were then processes of being-made, which were also spatial in nature. Public spaces were not necessarily in an individual's control, and thus were "a possible zone of massive contestation," even as they were a part of the Nisei's daily routines (Connerton 2009, 22). So while we are interested in the Nisei stories as personal memories, the analysis in this book is also always concerned with who may or may not do "what, when and where" (Pred 1984, 289). This reminds us of the profound reality of the lack of power Japanese Americans have had in defining belonging in urban America, as well as the blatant discrimination they experienced, including campaigns to close down Japanese schools, alien land laws, and ultimately registration at

Civil Control Centers after the issuance of Executive Order 9066. Therefore, as this book examines Japanese Americans' claims on belonging, it also examines the Nisei's inability to "escape the cultural inscription of state power and other forms of regulation that define the different modalities of belonging" (Ong 1996, 738). The Nisei we interviewed, for instance, recounted powerful memories of packing personal items before going to camps, giving away belongings they could not pack, and of walking from their homes to Union Station where they boarded trains for Pinedale Assembly Center and wartime incarceration. In the conclusion we return to these issues and argue that not only was the establishment of belonging and identity a spatial process, but so was the destruction of the community, leading to the dramatic reconstitution of identities as "noncitizens." Arrests, removal, incarceration, and then the deliberate *postwar dispersal* of the Tacoma Japanese community underscore that these were spatial processes as well.

The narratives also alert us to heterogeneity in the community, differences of opinion, prefectural identification, class position, and varied experiences of growing up in Tacoma, such that "differences *within* a generation may be as crucial as differences between" Issei and Nisei (Yanagisako 1985, 63, emphasis added). Some commented on the experiences of boys versus girls, with the boys, for example, playing ball, while the girls stayed home to help their mothers. In one family, the brother chose to attend Lincoln High School because it offered an electric shop class and he wanted to be an electrical engineer; his sister chose Stadium High School— what she called a "more exclusive" school—for a more traditional academic course of study. In another family, the girls went to the Methodist church "because they had more fun," while the boys went to the Buddhist church for activities.[16] Other interviewees were explicit about occupational and class differences between families. In one joint conversation, two former students noted class distinctions: one, who went on to own an auto repair shop, self-identified as the son of a peddler who was embarrassed to be seen selling vegetables with his father, while the other, the son of a hotel owner, went on to become a dentist. This heterogeneity and multiplicity emerged in memories of the Japanese Language School as well. While most former students spoke highly of the school and how it brought the community together, others remembered the school for denying them childhood desires.

In addition, as children, the Nisei did not always listen to parents; for example, they might eat while walking on the streets and make excessive noise in their language school classrooms. Subject formation is never complete, in other words; it is contested, and we should expect negotiation rather than the reification of some "essence." Like children and young people everywhere, Tacoma's young Nisei rebelled, sometimes oblivious to the multiple positionalities they were navigating daily. Stories of these daily experiences and of moving through city streets are quotidian and tangible moments in these processes. In this book we aim to hold on to this heterogeneity and at the same time offer some generalizable arguments.

BECOMING NISEI: PROCESSES OF "BRIDGING"

One of the most persistent images of Nisei is as a "bridge", spanning two distinct locations. Our transnational and spatial approach, however, allows us to problematize the dual identity paradigm—the notion of "functioning in two worlds" (Spickard 2009, 82)—as well as the idea of Nisei as having a particular kind of "personality" based on "adaptation" to this twoness (Miyamoto 1984, xiv), a position that informs much of the literature on Nisei identity and that presupposes "lack of fit" in either the Japanese or the American category.[17] This book, however, illustrates that identity formation is fluid, contested, and ongoing, thus giving voice to a more nuanced and intersectional understanding of subjectivity and identity formation, processes that we term "bridging." Bridging suggests agency as well and can be distinguished from the idea of Nisei as a static "bridge" between one place and another. The movement of Nisei lives and identities was not necessarily between *an* American world and *a* Japanese world, nor was it a movement between "victimhood and heroism" (Ono 2005, 1). Such categories, we underscore, have multiple positionings in terms of regional/ethnic identity, class status, and family and gender norms, even as Nisei individuals' worlds were described to them in dual terms. Negotiations over belonging are thus more important than the categories themselves (see K. Anderson 1991). As one Nisei woman remarked, "It's a wonder we weren't all schizos . . . " (in Spickard 2009, 88).

Tacoma's Japanese Language School itself played an important role in Nisei children's negotiation of these multiple positions in prewar urban America. At the TJLS, where the children spent every afternoon,

Mr. Yamasaki emphasized the ideal that Nisei were firmly rooted citizens of the US, who should also possess a strong understanding of and connection to their Japanese heritage. Although Mr. Yamasaki himself used the "bridge" metaphor to describe the young Nisei, we interpret their subject formation in a more dynamic and emergent way with the shift from *a thing* to the more processual concept of "bridging" and a move from a straight line between two points to ideas of "crisscrossing, weaving, exchange, sharing" (Nancy 2000, 150). Our concept of "bridging" thus illuminates what we mean by a situated, spatial, and transnational approach to becoming Nisei. While a bridge can be traversed, and as an infrastructural term suggests something fixed and static with two distinct and polar endpoints, "bridging" provides a more apt metaphor for the interactive, ongoing process of subject formation and a more topological understanding of lived spatiality. It thus provides a way of understanding the development of a more complex, layered, and dynamic Nisei subjectivity in the prewar period, in which both the transnational and the spatial emerge as important.

The notion of *bridging* also challenges assumptions about identity formation embedded in theories of immigrant assimilation and Americanization. Rather than conceiving of ethnic identities as involving a move from there to here, along a trajectory between two distinct points, we understand becoming Nisei as embodying multiple positionalities. Instead of being situated in a "twoness," Nisei children "moved between many spheres and occupied multiple identities," thus making "little sense to argue for an authentic self that somehow was either Japanese or American" (Yoo 2000, 5; see also chapter 5). Historian Lon Kurashige calls this "a historic admixture" (2002, 41), which also draws attention to the multiple layers of settler, alien, and indigenous positionalities and spaces (see Day 2016).

EXPANDING THE MAPPING OF JAPANESE LIVES IN TACOMA

Maps have long been understood as place-making documents, such that what is mapped becomes knowledge and what is left off of the map is silenced and may be forgotten. An influential map of Tacoma's prewar Nihonmachi, originally drawn by Kazuo Ito and published in his volume

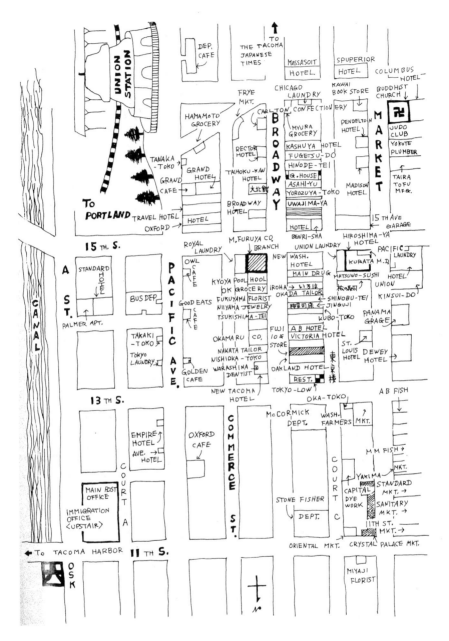

FIGURE 1.4. Map of Tacoma's Nihonmachi by Kazuo Ito, ca. 1920s, published 1973. Courtesy of Japanese Community Service of Seattle.

The Issei: A History of Japanese Immigrants in North America in 1973 (along with maps of Nihonmachi in Seattle; Vancouver, BC; Spokane; and Portland), provided a detailed view of Japanese life in ca. 1920s Tacoma (figure I.4). Ronald E. Magden included this map in his authoritative history *Furusato: Tacoma–Pierce County Japanese* (1998) as well, and it has since circulated as a visual representation of Tacoma's prewar Japanese residential and businesses communities. This and related maps are significant images of Tacoma's prewar Japanese inhabitants and businesses, in a sense "containing" the community within specific boundaries.

In the following chapters we consider the effects of living within a predominantly concentrated community and how that facilitated walking-scale daily lives. Most of the students we interviewed lived in this area, what is now known as downtown Tacoma, making it easy for them to walk home from public school, have a snack, and then continue on to the Japanese Language School. In 1930, approximately 70 percent of Tacoma's Japanese community lived in this neighborhood (HABS 1995, 5; Morrison 1994, 30), meaning that many disciplinary eyes from the older generation kept watch over these children. This tightly centralized settlement of hotels, shops, laundries, restaurants, barbers, and other services between Tacoma and Pacific Avenues and 11th and 19th Streets impacted Nisei experiences of the streets, where belonging was claimed and yet fleeting. The walkability of the children's educational and social worlds, and the spatial practices of their economic and social lives, led a number of the Nisei interviewees to claim that Tacoma was a "close" Japanese community and that the Language School was a central reason for it being so.

And yet our interviews also included mentions of small outposts of Japanese on the tideflats and along South Tacoma Way, as well as of individual families in other locations, such as South 19th and K Streets, and North I Street and the current Ruston Way—which were *not* on the older maps (see map I.1). As we have argued elsewhere (Hoffman, Hanneman, and Pyle 2018; see also chapters 3 and 4), the spatial patterns of Japanese work, residence, and community life in these areas have been erased and forgotten. For instance, of the forty discrete buildings mentioned three or more times by the interviewees, by 2018 thirty-six were vacant or had been replaced by parking lots.[18] This is important not only for Tacoma's history and a fuller accounting of the industries and businesses that shaped the South Puget Sound region, but also because Japanese contributions to

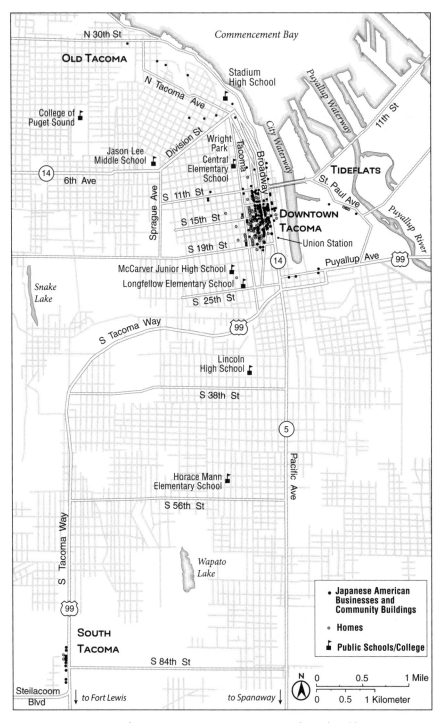

MAP I.I. Overview of Tacoma Japanese community residential and business areas, ca. 1900–1942

early industrial development—such as the lumber industry, illustrated by the documented presence of family housing in Tacoma's tideflats area—are typically overlooked. While these structures may be gone, the interview narratives *revisibilize* and repopulate areas of Tacoma in ways elided by the contemporary built landscape.

While presence on the tideflats indicates most strongly employment in the lumber industry, the South Tacoma grouping of Japanese families also recognizes the "highway" markets that sold fruit, vegetables, and flowers to a largely white clientele. Some locations, such as "Tokyo Beach," where the children would go to swim and play on the tideflats, are difficult to locate precisely based on the interviews. We recognize that these interviews provide memories of childhood from the position of old age and post–wartime incarceration—and we recognize that memories are "not an inert and passive thing, but a field of activity in which past events are selected, reconstructed, maintained, modified" (Said 2000, 185). Thus, while many of the references coincided with Kazuo Ito's map, many others have required additional archival research to locate and identify.

Recognizing issues of memory and power in analyzing our respondents' narratives is not meant to question their authenticity. It is necessary to remap and expand existing visualizations of the Japanese community in Tacoma and to recognize the daily Japanese presence in more locations, not simply as a supplement to the existing focus on the downtown core, but also to allow for rethinking the relationship between urban spaces and identity—especially in regard to the Japanese immigrant community and an understanding of the self in the world. The narratives engaged here stretch the boundaries of what has been depicted as a densely connected, lively Japanese community in the downtown core. Not only does this correct an erasure of ethnic history in places like the tideflats, but it also accentuates Japanese contributions to Tacoma's development, which has typically been written as a white man's history.

Documenting these narratives addresses these erasures. What happens when that which has been structurally erased and systematically forgotten, that which has been made invisible, a situated ignorance (Pred 2007), is rearticulated for others to recognize? As Allan Pred noted, "the past is not dead" (Pred 2004), but it has been "buried and forgotten." For whom is this amnesia most convenient, and for whom is it most costly for this past to be remembered (MacFarlane and Mitchell 2019)? In exploring

Nihonmachi—the prewar Japanese community in Tacoma—then, we are exploring a place where that which has been "collectively forgotten" may reemerge, disrupting the selective memories presented by cities, their makers, and the visible urban landscape. In other words, this project of excavating Nisei narratives through a situated, spatial, transnational analytic might produce a flash of recognition that destabilizes structural forgetting, allowing us *"to interrogate the taken-for-granted* and *to make visible* and legible that which is silenced, providing deeper understandings of the forms of power shaping our lives" (Merrill and Hoffman 2015, 3, emphasis in original). A dynamic, contingent approach to urban experience may thus be more revealing than anticipated.

ADDRESSING ERASURES DIRECTLY: RESEARCH METHODS

The University of Washington Tacoma campus, established in its current location in 1997, identifies itself as an Urban Serving University—an anchor institution in the middle of downtown Tacoma that aims to contribute to the revitalization of the city and the expansion of higher education opportunities for surrounding communities. The expansive forty-acre downtown footprint of UW Tacoma originally included a number of historic structures, including the TJLS building on Tacoma Avenue between 17th and 19th (figure I.5). It was here, at the first educational institution on the future university campus, that from 1923 to 1942 Tacoma's Nisei children were educated in the language and culture of their parents. After numerous conversations, in 1993 UW Tacoma purchased the building from then-owner Chiyeko Tadaye Fujimoto Kawasaki (b. 1921, known as Teddy). She and her two sisters, Yoshiko Fujimoto Sugiyama (b. 1919) and Kimiko Fujimoto Tanbara (b. 1924, known as Kimi), had all attended the TJLS as children, and Tadaye, following her mother's advice, had purchased the building in the late 1940s (see also HABS 1995, 12).

The growing UW Tacoma campus master plan encompassed not only the TJLS building, but other parts of the original Japanese area, Nihonmachi, as well, including the Whitney United Methodist Church and property adjacent to the still-active Tacoma Buddhist Temple on Fawcett. The TJLS building had been owned by UW Tacoma for a number of years before it was finally decided to conduct historic preservation reviews of

FIGURE 1.5. Tacoma Japanese Language School in disrepair, 2004. Author photo.

the wooden structure. The final recommendation was for demolition, the report arguing that major renovations, necessary for safety, would be expensive and conflict with the architectural qualifications for historic preservation status (HABS 1995). In 2004, UW Tacoma demolished the TJLS building. As one of only four remaining structures in the city that had been constructed by the prewar Japanese community in Tacoma, this was a controversial decision.[19]

Prior to demolition, in an effort to work with the community, the university made a campus-wide announcement about the decision and solicited faculty interest.[20] The two of us, Mary Hanneman and Lisa Hoffman, responded. This research project was thus born out of a moment of social and historical loss, conceived as a way to record memories, experiences, and social histories that revolved around the school in prewar Tacoma.[21] As a historian of modern Japanese intellectual history interested in issues of national identity, Hanneman brought an understanding of Japan in the late nineteenth and early twentieth centuries, knowledge about Japanese national identity in the face of modernization, and a decidedly transnational perspective to the project. As a cultural anthropologist interested in relationships between spatiality and subjectivity, Hoffman brought to the project questions about the mutual constitution of places and identities, the simultaneous emergence of geographies and histories, and insights into narrative analysis and city-making. We combined our disciplinary approaches to approach the topic of early twentieth-century Japanese immigrant identity and community formation. To be clear, we are not coming to this project from the more traditional place of ethnic or Asian American studies, or even of US history. Those disciplines have been extremely valuable for our understanding of issues, but we hope to offer something more by providing different analytical approaches and perspectives to shared questions. *Becoming Nisei* is also meant to be a public history project that recognizes the collaborative production of knowledge with the Nisei interviewees.

The core of our research consisted of videotaped and transcribed interviews with forty-two Nisei in their seventies and eighties, born primarily between 1915 and 1940,[22] all but one of whom grew up in Tacoma and all but three of whom attended Tacoma's Japanese Language School as children.[23] Those we interviewed were children in the 1920s and 1930s, and most were not yet active in organizations such as the Japanese American Citizens League. Framed by US immigration policies, notably the 1924 exclusion of all Japanese immigrants, the Japanese American community had distinct "generations" leading to appropriate use of the terms Issei, Nisei, and Sansei.[24]

We conducted almost all of the interviews as a team, though a few were done by only one of us. The interviews took place in Tacoma, Oakland, Los Angeles, and Chicago, in homes, shared spaces, and the Japanese American National Museum in LA. We conducted a number of individual interviews and interviews with small groups, such as a group of three sisters, or a group of twelve TJLS alumni all residing in Oakland, California. While we recognize that group dynamics alter the flow of conversation and the degree of balance between interviewees, we felt this approach offered an interesting, lively way to explore some of the memories and reflections of community, belonging, and identity.[25] Our status as white women and outsiders also certainly played a role in shaping our discussions, and created particular biases in what information was shared and how we interpreted it. Recognizing that representations of others is necessarily a political act, we strove to provide democratic representations, rather than a static, essentializing portrait (Morris 2010; Spivak 1988). The politics of race, gender, and background, indeed the entire matrix of domination that constitutes oppression (see Crenshaw 1991), are always at play in research projects, and while they must be considered throughout the research process, they should not be paralyzing.

Because this project developed in response to the demolition of the building, our interview questions focused on the TJLS. This, along with our general interest in prewar everyday life, shaped the conversations about the school. Nevertheless, the interview discussions ranged widely, covering such topics as family background, family businesses, observations about Issei parents, public school experiences, childhood experiences of discrimination, interaction with the Caucasian community, the onset of World War II, and wartime incarceration, as well as adult reflections back on the lifelong impact of the TJLS on the interviewees and their families. The chapters in this book reflect those topics.

Archival work in primary sources gives added depth and context to the interviews. Although, like the building, a great deal of material related to the TJLS has been lost or significantly damaged, the University of Washington Libraries Special Collections include a wealth of material from the TJLS and the now-defunct Tacoma Japanese Association. From the TJLS archives, for example, we gathered student essays written in Japanese (some by the same students we interviewed), student calligraphy, school notices, student tests, grade reports, and class diaries that students kept about their daily routines.[26] The Japanese Association of Tacoma archives contained business and census records, visa applications, and records of fund-raising activities for the TJLS. Also in the UW Libraries Special Collections are the records of the St. Paul & Tacoma Lumber Company, which allowed us to explore issues related to the economic foundations of some families in Tacoma's prewar Nikkei community, and the Ronald Magden papers, with personal resources related to the prewar Japanese community in Tacoma, including reminiscences written by Nisei themselves. The result is a project that goes well beyond a descriptive look at the TJLS alone, and allows us to consider an array of nuanced questions about Nisei identity.

Few urban histories of the pre–World War II era have recognized the lives and contributions of Asian Americans, including Japanese. S. Frank Miyamoto wrote in the introduction to the 1981 edition of his 1939 book on Seattle's Japanese community that "there is *not*, to my knowledge, any other published study of a Japanese minority community before World War II" (Miyamoto 1981, vi, emphasis added). General understandings of "American" immigration often focus on white and European migrants, rather than those from China and Japan who also arrived in the late 1800s and early 1900s (see Takaki [1989] 1998, xii). If published histories actually included Asian American populations, they were "almost always about Chinese rather than Japanese," and, as Roger Daniels has argued, the representations were "pejorative about nine times out of ten" (1992, 427–28). This dearth of scholarship on prewar Japanese American history has led to the interwar period being treated simply as "an interlude between the . . . 1924 Immigration Act, terminating all Japanese immigration, and the outbreak of World War II and the ensuing dramatic wartime mass internment of Japanese Americans" (Ichioka 2006, 3). Moreover, the literature has focused less on interethnic or interracial relations than on white-minority relations (Iwata 2005).

The literature examining incarceration and the redress movement is vast and rich and understandably has emphasized exclusion, trauma, as well as victimization and docility (e.g., Hosokawa 1969; Kitano 1993), rather than the active participation and agency of Japanese Americans in shaping their own lives. Daniel Lachapelle Lemire, writing of the Japanese Canadian experience, argues that the political movement for redress contributed to a "discrimination" and "victimhood" narrative, which in turn came to "define many Japanese Canadians' sense of identity" (2016–17, 72), while also offering little examination of the prewar period. "Even sympathetic scholars," Roger Daniels has argued, "tended to treat Asian immigrants as, somehow, immune from most of the influences of American life, as *victims of history* rather than actors in it" (1992, 427–28, emphasis added). While the wartime incarceration is undeniably important, little academic attention to the prewar period not only precludes a full understanding of incarceration and the years that follow, but also makes it difficult to examine central themes in Japanese American history.

More recently, in what has been described as the "second phase" of Asian American studies, scholars have addressed "lines of power beyond the limits of a discourse of victimhood and heroism" (Ono 2005, 1). In our examination of the prewar experience, we aim both to contribute to the more recent scholarship of this era (e.g., Tamura 1994; Hayashi 1995; Takahashi 1997; Kurashige 2002) and to emphasize the constructive agency of Japanese immigrants, who "led far richer lives than the pre-redress narrative would have us believe" (Lemire 2016–17, 78). Providing as many voices as possible helps us reframe Nisei as active agents in their own lives, in the constitution of their identities, and in the urban worlds they inhabited (see also Iwata 2005; Fiset 2009; Williams 2019). Another important aspect of this recent literature is a focus on the diversity of racisms and allyship within the non-Asian community (Kurashige 2016).

While some studies exist of Japanese immigrant communities in the Pacific Northwest (Miyamoto 1984, ; L. Tamura 1993; Neiwert 2005; Fiset and Nomura 2005; Fiset 2009; Lee 2011; Lemire 2016–17), the Tacoma Japanese have received less attention, despite the fact that Tacoma's vibrant prewar Nihonmachi, as Tacoma historian Michael Sullivan notes, "was the largest of any American city based on per capita city size," per 1920 census records (personal communication, April 22, 2020).[27] A number of the Nisei we interviewed also felt that Tacoma was a special place to grow up—large enough to provide an urban experience, but small enough that they knew most of the Japanese they saw on the streets and at events (see chapter 3). Ronald Magden's book *Furusato* (1988) remains the primary postwar publication on Tacoma's Japanese immigrants, but Tamiko Nimura, Michael Sullivan, and Justin Wadland have more recently made important contributions to our understanding of prewar life in the Tacoma Japanese community (e.g., Sullivan 2016; Nimura 2016, 2017a; Nimura and Wadland 2018; Nimura and Sullivan n.d). *Becoming Nisei* builds on such work and contributes new information to studies of Japanese Americans and pre–World War II urban experiences more broadly.

FOLLOWING CHAPTERS

The combined transnational and spatial analysis takes us through a number of specific arguments, laid out in the following chapters. Chapter 1 provides a detailed and transnationally oriented account of the founding of the Japanese community, including establishment of the singular, secular Japanese Language School in Tacoma. As such, it examines the late nineteenth- and early twentieth-century Meiji-era Japan from which the Issei migrated, as well as Japanese government involvement in immigrant communities. Chapter 2 explores both family histories vis-à-vis the businesses these families started and the daily grind that sustained these families, who were often at the lower end of the economic scale. Their stories offer evidence of important contributions to early industrial development (e.g., sawmills) as well as services to the city as a whole. Chapter 3 considers what the Nisei described as a notably "close" community in Tacoma and how that is linked with the spatiality of the Japanese immigrant experience. The co-constitution of spatial and social relations, including discrimination, residential segregation, walking-scale daily lives, and Issei expectations for their children's behavior, helps us understand how Nisei negotiated multiple positionalities and thus engaged in bridging.

Chapter 4 focuses on the spatial "mapping" of the Japanese community in Tacoma and calls for an expanded appreciation of where people lived and worked. While recognizing that the majority of Japanese were concentrated in the central area of Tacoma (chapter 3), this chapter revisibilizes the tideflats and the South Tacoma highway as important places for Japanese lives and economic security prior to the war. Chapter 5 explores the central role that principal Masato Yamasaki and his wife, teacher Kuniko Yamasaki, played in the Japanese Language School and in Tacoma's Japanese community in general, teaching the Nisei both to be proud of their heritage and to embrace their Americanness. Traditional lessons were combined with values of democracy and equality, highlighting a processual understanding of identity formation through bridging. Chapter 6 covers the lessons, school activities, and outings organized by the language school, considering them as micropractices of power that led the Nisei to self-manage and internalize expectations. At the same time, the interviews remind us that we are talking about children, and that Nisei did not always follow rules, nor did their parents. Finally, the conclusion addresses experiences of arrest, forced removal, and wartime incarceration in the camps, recognizing that the traumatic destruction and postwar dispersal of Tacoma's Japanese community was also a spatial process. This spatialized trauma is a critical aspect of becoming Nisei.

The Nisei managed multiple positionalities, often on a daily basis. The ideas and practices from Japan and the imprint of Imperial Japanese customs were evident in this concentrated urban community, where young Nisei needed to bow to Issei they saw on the streets. There were daily joys as well as struggles. Nisei felt instability about their status as US residents given the legal barriers their parents faced. Yet they remembered and articulated their lives, the power structures, spaces, and navigation of identity before incarceration from their vantage point of today. Both transnational relations and spatial dislocations—and often lifelong attempts to reestablish security in place—are essential parts of identity formation processes. This book aims to merge these many factors to present the complexity and nuance that entailed "becoming Nisei."

CHAPTER ONE

Establishing a New Community in Tacoma

Our parents were of the Meiji era, which was the golden era.

—JUNICHI TAIRA (B. 1929)

AS JUNICHI TAIRA'S STATEMENT SUGGESTS, TACOMA'S ISSEI COMmunity bore the strong imprint of the values and customs of Meiji Japan (1868–1912). This in turn wielded a strong influence on the community they built in Tacoma, their approach to childrearing, and ultimately, the Tacoma Japanese Language School (TJLS). Not eligible for US citizenship, the Issei occupied a transnational space. They remained Japanese nationals—subjects of the Japanese emperor. Without this connection to Japan, they would have been stateless. Additionally, specific aspects of late nineteenth- and early twentieth-century Japan, such as the symbolic power of the emperor as manifested in the Meiji Constitution and the reification of traditional Japanese values in the Imperial Rescript on Education of 1890, had a significant impact on the social landscape of Tacoma's Japanese immigrants. This chapter explores how these ideas and practices influenced the environment they created for their children, and in turn the identity negotiations of the Nisei. This transnational perspective (as opposed to a cultural essentialist one) is vital to understanding the multiple positionalities of first-generation Japanese immigrants and thus also their children. Important, too, was the Japanese government's role in working with local Japanese associations, including Tacoma's, to shape the immigrant experience, as in the language schools. While much literature on the immigrant experience in the US considers "local and national forces" (see, e.g., Harmon 1998), we argue that it is vital to consider *transnational* forces as well, considering the immigrants' places of origin, their destinations, and the complex relationships between the two.

A transnational perspective that examines the backdrop and influence particularly of Meiji- and Taisho-era Japan (1868–1912 and 1912–25) on immigration and immigrants, along with an examination of Japan's unfolding relations with the West and the US during that period and beyond, offers a more complex and nuanced understanding of the dynamic forces that shaped the Tacoma Japanese community and Issei and Nisei identities. Historians Yuji Ichioka (1988, 2006) and Sucheng Chan (1990, 2005) were early advocates of placing the immigrant experience within a broader transnational context, with scholarship on Chinese migration in particular contributing much to the development of this perspective. Eiichiro Azuma notes that the "divorce" of Japanese American history from Japanese history emerged out of the Asian Americanist demand, begun in the late 1960s, that Asian American voices be incorporated into the "hitherto Eurocentric narratives of US national formation . . . *within* the US history field, but not beyond it." In his corrective, Azuma urges "more nuanced treatments of ordinary women and men, who often posed alternative visions to the bounded meanings of state and nation" (2008, 1189, 1191). The interplay between Japan and the US, like subject formation for Japanese American identity itself, was dynamic, ongoing, and contested.

Identity formation for Nisei in pre–World War II urban America must be understood in the context of the Japan the Issei had left and Japan's rapid transformation and modernization in the mid-Meiji period as the nation emerged on the international stage. The impact of these forces, however, was not static. Meiji Japan's efforts to gain acceptance in the international community manifested in a wide variety of ways, including attempts to closely monitor and mold the image of Japanese abroad. This meant ongoing involvement with the Nikkei community in the US.

One of our interviewees, Joseph Kosai (b. 1935), commented on the impact of Meiji Japan on his parents' generation:

> I think—again, this is just my feeling—that our parents were raised in the so-called Meiji Era. Because of the 1924 Exclusion Act, there was

very little communication from Japan after that, so most of our parents that came before then really grew up in the Meiji Era, and some in the era after that, which was a short one. I'm not sure of the name of it [Taisho Era, 1912–25]. But in Japan you were taught that the government is always right. Even in those days, they didn't even look up as the emperor passed by; they bowed their heads, they didn't even look at [the emperor].

In Japan's modernization effort, the leadership ironically utilized the most potent traditional symbol available to them as a way to rally people around the new national goals. That potent symbol was the emperor and the "unbroken" imperial line. The position of the emperor in Japan's modernization was secured in the Meiji Constitution of 1890, which granted him vast power, including the authority to declare war, conclude treaties, legislate by edict, and dissolve the legislature. The Imperial Rescript on Education, issued in 1890 in tandem with the new constitution, presented a reification of traditional Japanese values and was intended to serve as an anchor amid the changes of modernization. The Meiji emphasis on the emperor and the accompanying impact of the imperial system on Japanese educational practices were clearly manifested in Tacoma's Japanese Language School. The context in which parents and teachers grew up is therefore directly relevant to the shaping of Nisei children's sense of self and place in the world.

The Meiji-era social and political transformation coincided with the initial migration of Japanese to the US; the Issei generation thus emerged out of this liminal period in Japan's history. Not only did they bring to the US a formed set of traditional Japanese cultural beliefs, but they were also grappling with the social, psychological, political, and economic impacts of a native land in deep flux. Harue Kawano Ozaki (b. 1928) referred to the effect these changes had on her mother, who was raised in Japan by her aunt and uncle and later became a teacher at the TJLS:

They [the aunt and uncle] wanted to have all the children develop on their own and they sent my mom to—they called it a Normal School . . . I guess the Western influence was coming in hard and fast at that time, and they trained all these people to know the way that such a different world handled people, meaning training them for school teachers.

The Meiji-era generation of Japanese immigrants to the US also experienced a lingering, though rapidly disappearing, sense of regional identification and loyalty, as well as an incipient identification of self as "subject" of the newly powerful emperor and the imperial state.

As Japan engaged more directly with the Anglo-European powers at the end of the 1800s, it began to use immigration policy and ongoing involvement with Japanese immigrants in the US to help redefine its national image abroad. Japanese government officials and intellectuals around the turn of the twentieth century viewed immigration abroad as an instrument of national policy, allowing for peaceful expansion of Japanese influence. Kanai En, a professor at Japan's leading Tokyo Imperial University, wrote of the state's role in the immigrant endeavor in 1903: "The two most critical responsibilities of the modern nation are social policy and foreign policy. By foreign policy I mean establishing ideal relations with the powers and achieving an imperialist policy of sending migrants overseas" (in K. Pyle 1973, 54). Accordingly, Japanese policymakers in the late nineteenth and early twentieth centuries encouraged "transplantation of ordinary Japanese to the western hemisphere," as a result of which "the superior qualities of the expansive nation would allow Japanese immigrants to compete successfully with other races in economic endeavors, especially agriculture, on the frontiers of the New World" (Azuma 2008, 1194).

In the 1890s and early 1900s, Japanese government immigration policy engaged directly with Japanese immigrants in the US via the Japanese associations that began to emerge, a chapter of which was established in Tacoma in 1892. These local and regional associations of Japanese were organized by the immigrants themselves in areas with large enough concentrations of Nikkei. They were overseen by Japanese consulates, which provided assistance with visas, registration, picture brides, education, and other issues. The connection between the Japanese associations and the Issei was vital to both the Japanese government and to the Issei themselves. On the one hand, the Issei constituted a tool for shaping Japan's positive national image overseas; on the other, the associations provided access to the Japanese government, without which the Issei would have essentially been stateless persons. The Japanese government was one of few potential allies for protecting Issei in the face of a discriminatory legal environment and anti-Japanese sentiment in the US.

While in the early twentieth century exclusionists in the US claimed this ongoing Japanese governmental involvement with the immigrant community was part of a larger Japanese plan of aggression and domination, with immigrants being used to infiltrate and exert control in American society, the immigrant experience should be placed within a more varied historical frame, one that recognizes not just Japan's later military aggression as it sought to become the dominant power in East Asia, but also its more diplomatic quest for international equality. During the early twentieth century, Japan and the US were engaged in ongoing negotiations regarding the status of Japanese immigrants in the US, as well as, more broadly, Japan's status in the international community. Ultimately, Japan's pre–World War II quest for equality failed. This is evident, for example, in the 1908 Gentlemen's Agreement that limited Japanese immigration to the US, and in the Exclusion Act passed by the US Congress in 1924, which, by ending new Japanese immigration, constituted a turning point in Japanese American history. At the international level, Japan's quest for equality met defeat in 1919 with the rejection of the racial equality clause in the League of Nations charter. When the League of Nations was founded in the aftermath of World War I as part of the Treaty of Versailles, the Japanese delegation requested a clause specifying "equal and just treatment in every respect making no distinction, either in law or in fact, on account of [member nations'] race or nationality." Although the majority of the participating nations voted in favor of its inclusion, the US and Australia pushed back. US President Woodrow Wilson declared that unanimity was necessary in such an important decision, which overturned the majority vote. The clause was not included in the charter, representing a humiliating defeat for Japan and underscoring the role racism played in international relations. Not until the late 1920s and early 1930s, seeing that its efforts to gain international equality had failed—and had failed due in large part to Western racist attitudes—did Japan turn to aggressive policies in Asia in a misguided and ultimately disastrous effort to protect and expand its national interests and "prove its worth" internationally (Hanneman 2001).

Thus, in a symbiotic and dynamic process, immigration law and immigration policy not only affected the migrants themselves, but exerted a strong impact on Japan's international relations in the pre–World War II period.

MEIJI JAPAN IN THE WORLD: SYMBOLISM
OF THE EMPEROR AND EFFECTS OF REFORMS

East Asia's early encounters with the West were a catalyst for chaos and change. For Japan, initial interactions with the US and the European nations would result in wholesale changes to the Japanese system, in turn contributing to the opening of Japanese migration to the West. China's 1842 loss to Great Britain in the Opium War and the subsequent unequal treaties that China was forced to sign in the 1840s and 1850s sounded a warning bell for Japan. As a result, when American ships appeared in Japanese waters in the 1850s Japanese leaders recognized that military resistance would be not only futile, but dangerous, and reluctantly signed a series of unequal treaties, first with the US, and then with other Western nations. In 1868, grappling with how to leverage their country's disadvantaged position vis-à-vis the Western nations and indeed fearing for the very existence of their country as a sovereign state, a group of young, radical samurai staged a coup that toppled the 250-year-old Tokugawa military government (1603–1868). This event, the so-called Meiji Restoration, brought an end to over two centuries of national isolation and resulted in the "restoration" of direct imperial rule under the young Emperor Meiji. Endeavoring to meet the challenges posed by the West, the new Meiji government launched the country on a deliberate, comprehensive program of reform aimed at building a "rich country and strong army"[1] along Western lines via industrialization and military modernization. By so doing, it was hoped, Japan would escape the humiliations and limitations imposed by the unequal treaties, restore national pride, and take its place as an equal power in the community of nations. Only equality with the West could provide protection from the West and preserve Japan as a sovereign and independent nation.

The political, social, and economic reforms adopted by the new government included eliminating the traditional class structure, dismantling the political structure of feudal domains, and instituting compulsory military service for all men. Government leaders adopted Western suits and required members of the former samurai class to dispense with the proud markers of their previous elite status: their distinctive topknots were to be cut off and swords relegated to storerooms or, worse—a new necessity for increasingly impoverished families—to pawn shops. The government also created a system of compulsory public education for both boys and girls to prepare the population for active participation in the country's modernization (Hanneman 2001, 3–12).

Vital to the success of all these reforms was political and national unification. Under the Tokugawa system, Japan had been divided into some 250 feudal domains controlled by regional warlords, *daimyo,* who had pledged allegiance to the Tokugawa house but who enjoyed great autonomy, for example collecting taxes that remained at the domain level and maintaining private armies of samurai warriors who were loyal directly to them. As a result, "Japan" during the Tokugawa period was a very loose concept, with loyalty—and identity—remaining essentially regional. According to Japan's indigenous Shinto belief system, the imperial line had descended unbroken from the central deity, the Sun Goddess, and so strong was this connection that the Japanese imperial dynasty had never been overthrown. Instead, challengers to power (such as the Tokugawa) merely co-opted imperial authority, governing as delegates thereof.

While national unification was a critical prerequisite to the success of the Meiji government's modernizing reforms, it did not emerge naturally. Instead, unification had to be engineered, and the essential ingredient in this effort was the emperor. With all due pomp and circumstance, the Meiji emperor (sixteen years old at the time of the Restoration) was presented to the people as having taken direct control of the government and nation. The new Meiji leaders who were in fact the powers behind the throne sought to create and reinforce national unity and national identity through a series of reforms and public relations efforts. These included both "modern" and "Western" approaches, including the adoption of a constitution and a parliamentary political system, and more familiar strategies, such as the creation of State Shintoism, which boosted the political power of the emperor by reinforcing his traditional spiritual role. These efforts to unify the country by enhancing the authority of the emperor made true imperial subjects out of the Japanese people. In its quest for equality, the Japanese leadership emulated the West; but while they captured the outward forms of Western society, they did not capture the foundational principle of democracy—the new Japanese did not become *citizens* of the state, but remained *subjects* of the emperor.[2]

By eliminating the Tokugawa government and investing direct rule in the most potent symbol of tradition—the emperor—the Meiji-era effort to modernize the country produced one of the great ironies of modern Japanese history. The emperor (or at least the *idea* of the emperor—he was rarely seen in public life) became a daily, if shadowy, presence in the lives of the Japanese people, as symbol of the nation: his portrait hung at the front of every classroom and governmental policies were issued as though directly from the emperor himself. The Issei brought these norms with them to the US. In turn, this orientation provided a foundation for commemorative events, such as celebrations of imperial birthdays, which played a prominent role in the communal life of the Tacoma Japanese.

Many former students remarked on the various ceremonies held at the TJLS. Harue Kawano Ozaki, for instance, remembered the community's New Year's Day ceremony and the symbolic presence of the emperor:

> I could remember so vividly [TJLS principal] Yamasaki-*sensei,* he would put on his formal frock, on New Year's Day, which is the most important holiday in the Japanese culture, and he would have us congregate in our best of clothes, and we would see him go through the procedures like they would in Japan. And to be able to do as they did in Japan about enhancing and reading the Declaration of the Emperor of Japan. And I think that activities like that, and experiences like that, is something very memorable, that each one of the people you interviewed, I don't think they would forget that.

The influence of the imperial system is also apparent in the ritualized phraseology of formal communications from the Tacoma Japanese Association, as in the following excerpt:

> (Mr. Yamasaki read the following proclamation):
> "We wish to express our humblest condolences on the death of Her Majesty the Empress Dowager of Japan on April 11, 1914. Our grief knows no bound. Our grief will travel with her as she enters the far western heaven." Dated April 12, 1914, s/s Masato Yamasaki, Representative, Tacoma Japanese Association. (Otsuka and Fukui [1940] 1986)[3]

As noted earlier, the adoption of the Meiji Constitution in 1890— granted by the emperor as a "gift" to the people—codified the symbolic authority of the emperor and invested tremendous formal power in him. To create a political framework to undergird the modernizing reforms, the Japanese leadership had determined that Japan must adopt a constitution as a way to centralize governmental authority and enhance the status of the new Meiji government on the international stage.[4] The Meiji Constitution demonstrated the Japanese government's sensitivity to its image in the Western eye and its willingness and ability to adopt policies that would influence and shape that image. Along with the promulgation of the Meiji Constitution in 1890, the emperor (that is to say, the government) issued the Imperial Rescript on Education. This document was designed to serve as a conservative counterbalance to the constitution, which, although it invested great power in the emperor, was seen as a radical ("Western-style") document. As Japanologist Klaus Antoni writes, the rescript was "intended mainly to regulate the pedagogical foundations of education in Japanese primary schools by laying down the primary principles for an obligatory moral instruction (*shushin*). . . . The Rescript presented the moral foundation of the late Meiji state" (1991, 159–60). The Imperial Rescript on Education reinforced the traditional Confucian values of

Filial piety: "Ye, Our subjects, be filial to your parents, affectionate to your brothers and sisters; as husbands and wives be harmonious; as friends true";

Self-discipline and education: "bear yourselves in modesty and moderation; extend your benevolence to all; pursue learning and cultivate arts, and thereby develop intellectual faculties and perfect moral powers";

Duty, loyalty, and self-sacrifice: "always respect the Constitution and observe the laws; should emergency arise, offer yourselves courageously to the State; and thus guard and maintain the prosperity of Our Imperial Throne coeval with heaven and earth." (deBary, Gluck, and Tiedemann 2006, 108)[5]

From 1890 until the end of World War II in 1945, students throughout Japan recited the rescript daily, while bowing to the emperor's portrait at the front of their classrooms. While students at the TJLS did not emulate this practice, the lessons of the Imperial Rescript on Education nevertheless impacted Tacoma's Japanese Language School as well. Principal

Yamasaki followed a curriculum that included "ethics based on the Japanese moral code" (Asato 2006, 90), and he was known to have recited the rescript in full at formal events, such as the emperor's birthday celebration, as documented in Tacoma Japanese Association minutes (Otsuka and Fukui [1940] 1986, 46). Throughout the interviews, former students referred to the values taught at the Japanese language school (see also chapters 5 and 6). As Ryo Munekata expressed it, the TJLS emphasized "filial piety to our parents, honesty, endurance, perseverance. I think these were essentially taught to us, not just the language, but within the language."

In an interview in Oakland, Yoneko Aochi (b. 1918) and Anon Male B (b. 1919) discussed the importance of core Japanese values in their experience of the Japanese Language School. Others in the group, including Yoneko's younger sister, Katsuko Aochi Harano (b. 1923), and Teiko Kawano Peterson[6] and Kunio Shibata (b. 1923),[7] agreed with their observations.

ANON MALE B: So my experience of Japanese school was very good because I learned a lot of Japanese so-called . . . that word I use, *shushin* [ethics]. I think that's the main thing

KUNIO: More than the language and everything, I thought it was very important.

KATSUKO: Respect and all that, you know . . .

TEIKO: Filial piety . . .

KUNIO: Is that what it is?

YONEKO: Is that what it is in English?

KUNIO: What is it, now?

TEIKO: Filial piety. The meaning of life . . .

KUNIO: That's the word.

YONEKO: How do you spell it anyways? Filial piety . . .

YONEKO: . . . Respect.

KUNIO: Yes.

ANON MALE B: Humility.

YONEKO: Respect. Any elders. Respect.

These cultural and political influences contributed to the larger set of characteristics the Issei brought to bear as they negotiated their identities and position in their new land. Thus it is important—and useful—to understand the Issei generation (and the influences they passed on to their Nisei children) transnationally, not just in the historico-cultural context of "Japan" writ large, but also in terms of the historically specific Japan from which they migrated as well as the crisscrossing and weaving of these places transnationally.

CULTURAL CHANGE AND JAPANESE NATIONAL POLICY: SHAPING THE JAPANESE MIGRANT IMAGE

Japan's relationship with the Western international community in the Meiji era was asymmetrical: Western countries were clearly dominant vis-à-vis Japan. Even as Japan adopted various reforms aimed at strengthening the nation, the Japanese leadership understood that attaining the status of "rich country, strong army" alone would not move Japan into the ranks of the powerful nations. In order to resist Western hegemony and renegotiate the unequal treaties it had been forced to sign, Japan needed to be seen by Western powers as legitimate, which led to the adoption of new forms of politics and policies. This in turn required thoroughgoing cultural change. Hence, in addition to the social, political, and economic reforms of the 1870s, '80s, and '90s, Japan underwent a "cultural revolution," adopting aspects of Western philosophy, education, arts, and media in an effort to become "civilized" on a par with Western standards.[8] For Japanese leaders at this time, "civilized" meant in particular the adoption of parliamentary government, but other trappings of the West such as dress and etiquette figured in as well.[9] Bureaucrat Kido Koin, who was part of the Iwakura Mission, a diplomatic and study mission to the West in the early 1870s, wrote, for example: "Our people are no different from the Americans or Europeans of today; it is all a matter of education or lack of education" (in Jansen 2000, 356).

This perspective did not recognize the racial elements in US policy toward Japanese immigration. Instead, the Meiji government blamed the migrants themselves for American discrimination. Because Japanese leaders considered most emigrants to be from the "lower class," they attributed discrimination as arising not from "white racism, but, rather, [from] the appearance and behaviour of Japanese emigrants" (Geiger, 2007–8, 39). In response, the Japanese government tried to manage Japan's international image in part by strictly controlling the issuance of passports to would-be migrants. In the late 1800s, for example, any Japanese applying for permission to migrate to Hawaii as a contract laborer, a practice that began in 1885, was required to be a "bona fide farmer . . . between 25 and 30 years of age . . . a single person or married couple with no dependents." Additionally, no "female who is more than four months pregnant . . . [or individual] suffering from chronic or hereditary diseases" was permitted to emigrate. These requirements, which varied over the years, meant that on average only 10 to 40 or 50 percent of those who applied were granted passports (Spickard 2009, 18–19).

The general failure of the Japanese government to apprehend the international effects of white racism lasted into the early twentieth century—at least until the Russo-Japanese War of 1904–5—and helps to frame Japan's active role in immigrant affairs in the US as it tried to shape Japan's image. The modernization narrative, which held that education broadly conceived would lead to cultural equality, was expressed in the Issei belief that "their national civilization and racial characteristics were fundamentally on par with those of their white American counterparts . . . [and] their activities—especially farming—in the western frontier were not dissonant with America's manifest destiny of 'conquest' and 'progress'" (Azuma 2009, 27). Yet this attitude was not generally shared in the West, as reflected, for example, in a July 1900 letter to the London *Times* from A. B. Freeman-Mitford, who opined that "European civilization rested on Japanese society only as a thin veneer and . . . underneath the Japanese were equally as dangerous and wild as the Chinese" (in Jansen 2000, 416). Such attitudes demonstrate why for the Issei, education and avoiding public "shame" (*haji*) may be understood as mechanisms of self-protection in a threatening environment.

While government bureaucrat Kido's view that education (in the broadest sense) was the key to Japanese being accepted as equals, in the actual Issei experience discrimination and disrespect were often the norm. Nevertheless, several methods emerged on the Japanese side to try to "teach" immigrants about Western ways. With the growth of labor-contracted Japanese emigration to the US, for example, entrepreneurs in Japan began producing guidebooks for would-be migrants on how to successfully navigate the potential pitfalls of life in their new home. One such publication, *Kitare nihonjin* (Come, Japanese, 1886), provided instruction on such things as American food and table etiquette; it also advocated general adoption of a strategy of conflict avoidance, with a strong dose of collective responsibility not to make waves: "Do the right thing. If you don't, all Japanese will suffer" (Flewelling 2002, 20)—a message reinforced in lessons at the TJLS and within Nisei families. Japanese policy-makers believed "citizens who went to the US and the West [must] be people whom the government deemed worthy of representing a growing and important imperial presence in East Asia. Put another way, they should categorically not be 'low class' or 'densely ignorant'" (Sawada 1991, 342; see also Geiger 2007–8; Kurashige 2002, 35). This amounted to a national version of young Nisei being told at home to monitor their behavior so as not to "bring shame to the family," a phrase repeated by many interviewees.

In 1893, the SS *Tacoma* arrived in the Port of Tacoma bringing 96 passengers from Japan and 142 from China (Flewelling 2002, 20–21). That the Japanese migrants had studied their guidebooks seems evident given commentary published in the *Tacoma Daily Ledger,* which, while recognizing the new arrivals' preparation, is expressed in racist and essentializing terms, particularly in comparison with views of Chinese immigrants:

> Polite fellows are these Japs, and the inspector was more than once embarrassed by the profound bows and graceful flourishes of arms. They were all neat and genteel looking and were minus the "smell" so noticeable among the Chinese immigrants. . . . A great difference is noticeable between the Japanese and Chinese immigrants. The Japanese came dressed in American costumes throughout, down to their very shoes. . . . They try to adopt American ways even while on the ship before they arrive, and consequently watch the actions of the Americans closely. The Chinese, however, are all dressed in their quaint garb and are as completely Chinese in America as they are in China. (in Flewelling 2002, 21)

Japan's goal of equality with the West seemed to come into reach around the turn of the twentieth century. Between 1894 and 1905 Japan fought—and won—two wars, apparent proof of success of the Meiji reforms of industrialization and military modernization. Japan's victory in the Sino-Japanese War (1894–95) marked its emergence as a colonial power, as China ceded the island of Taiwan to Japan in the peace settlement. Although Japan's victory came as a surprise to most international observers, China at this time was, after all, a weakening Asian power. Thus it was Japan's victory over Russia in the Russo-Japanese War just ten years later that was considered the truly epoch-making achievement. Japan's win in this war, slim and hard-fought, led Western nations to cast a wary eye on Japan. US president Theodore Roosevelt mediated in the peace negotiations between the two powers, and when the resulting treaty gave few gains to Japan, the Japanese people erupted in a riot of resentment against Western powers, feeling their nation had been shut out and disregarded. Former bureaucrat and newspaper owner Ito Miyoji expressed these sentiments to a German friend, saying, "Of course, what is really wrong with us is the color of our skin. If our skins were as white as yours, the whole world would be rejoicing at our calling a halt to Russia's inexorable aggression" (in Baelz 1932, 243). Novelist Arishima Takeo wrote, "Granted that it was inevitable that Russia, having become the enemy of Japan, should have felt animosity toward Japan, it is obviously also true that the peoples of the countries of Europe as a whole felt jealous of Japan's successes because the Japanese belonged to a different race and religion" (in Keene 2002, 612). Within days of the signing of the Treaty of Portsmount, Japan took Korea as a protectorate, securing Japan's status as a colonial power. Amid these gains, though, signs of Japan's emerging strength in Asia contributed to a growing exclusionist movement in the US that helped to fuel the Gentlemen's Agreement of 1908, with significant impact on Japanese immigration to the US.

EARLY TWENTIETH-CENTURY US IMMIGRATION LAW AND JAPAN

After the initial glow of victory in the Russo-Japanese War had receded, Japan found itself and its people increasingly subject to racist policies imposed by Western countries, particularly the United States. In May 1905, for instance, the San Francisco School Board voted to segregate Asian students in the schools, and in October 1906 ordered that all Japanese students must attend a single school in Chinatown. President Roosevelt himself stepped in to mediate and persuaded the San Francisco agitators to withdraw the segregation ordinance, in exchange for an agreement to negotiate with the Japanese government to suspend or limit further Japanese immigration to the US (Neu 1966, 440).

The negotiations ultimately led to the so-called Gentlemen's Agreement of 1907, in which the Japanese government agreed to limit their number of emigrants by stopping the issuance of passports to skilled and unskilled laborers, "prevent[ing] anyone other than parents, wives, and children of men already in the United States" from migrating to the US (Nimura 2016; see also Daniels 1988, 125–26; Daniels 1992, 433; Takaki [1989] 1998). The Japanese government accepted these discriminatory regulations in order to forestall the humiliating possibility of official legal action on the part of the US (Daniels 1988, 125).

In Japan, the popular response to the Gentlemen's Agreement was immediate, resentful, and angry and seriously damaged relations between Japan and the US. Articles and editorials denouncing the order appeared in all the major Japanese newspapers, and the Japanese government lodged a formal complaint with the US. Ironically, however, because it allowed wives (including "picture brides") and children to enter the US, the Gentlemen's Agreement unintentionally led to an increase in the Nikkei population in the US. This brought an end to the male-dominated "frontier phase" of Japanese settlement (Spickard 2009, 33–34) and "helped transform Nikkei society into a settler period" (Asato 2006, 80), or what some have called an "immigrant community phase,"[10] in which families and family-oriented institutions were established in the US, including Japanese language schools and Japanese associations.

In Tacoma, Yoshiko Fujimoto Sugiyama, the eldest of the three Fujimoto sisters, recalled how her parents met and came to the US:

> One of our dear friends was a go-between and had seen my mother working in a hospital in Fukuoka, Japan, and interested her to come to the States, much against her family's wishes. But she was rather headstrong, and wanted the adventure also. And she came on a boat, and she was the only one, she tells us, on the ship that was not seasick. So she took care of all the ladies. And when they landed in Tacoma, one of the officers [having seen her intended husband] came to her and said, "He's a bit too old for you. You have to go back to Japan." (*laughs*) But she wanted to fulfill her dreams.

The anti-Japanese sentiment that had led to the Gentlemen's Agreement flared again after World War I and by 1924 had resulted in enactment of the Exclusion Act, also known as the Johnson-Reed Act after its two leading sponsors. Albert Johnson, US representative from southwestern Washington, had lived in Tacoma from 1898 to 1907 and served as editor of the *Tacoma Daily News*. It was during this time that Johnson, as he put it, "began to call attention to the situation [of Japanese labor in the Puget Sound region] in every way I could. . . . How could I know that . . . I would be elected to Congress, with the restriction of immigration as the chief plank in my platform" (in Hillier 1945, 195). The bill effectively ended Japanese immigration to the US, marking yet another phase in the history of the Nikkei. These restrictive practices shaped the generational structure of Japanese American communities such that "many Nisei had a sense of their shared status *as a generation*" (Yoo 2000, 5, emphasis added; see also Daniels 1988, 1992; Spickard 2009).

JAPANESE ASSOCIATIONS IN THE UNITED STATES

In addition to closely controlling the issuance of passports, Japan regulated its image in the West via government outreach to and involvement with the Japanese immigrant community in the US, primarily through consulate-sponsored and -supported Japanese associations. These began to emerge on the West Coast in the 1890s and early 1900s, and received an additional boost from the 1908 Gentlemen's Agreement. According to Ronald Magden (1998, 110), the "Tacoma Japanese Society" (TJS) was founded in 1892 by Japanese merchants battling criminal gambling and prostitution run by some area Japanese, while *History of Japanese in Tacoma* dates the launch of the first Nihonjin-kai (Japanese Association) to 1891.[11] A subsequent version, the Tacoma Japanese Association, was established in October 1908, led by president Tokuhai Kawai and vice president Kumataro Takahashi (*History of Japanese in Tacoma* 1941, n.p. [123]). Other associations later appeared in communities near Tacoma, including Fife (1916) and Sumner (1936) (*History of Japanese in Tacoma* 1941, n.p. [151, 159]).

The Japanese associations were "the most important organizations of the Japanese immigrant generation in the United States" (Ichioka 1977, 409), serving as instruments of the Japanese government to oversee and "manage" Japanese immigrants in the US and "... function[ing] as critical intermediaries between the Japanese government and its consulates, and the diverse Japanese immigrant population" (E. Anderson, n.d.). For Issei, who remained Japanese nationals despite long residence in the US, the Japanese associations were key to helping them maintain their legal status. In 1894, president of the Tacoma Japanese Society Yukino Eijiro noted the community's need for official Japanese representation when he lobbied for a Pacific Northwest consulate in Tacoma, writing in a letter to Foreign Minister Mutsu Munemitsu that the Japanese could "not count the number of cases where we are deprived of our rights" (*History of Japanese in Tacoma* 1941, n.p. [224–25]).

Japan's first government office in the United States was its consulate in San Francisco, opened in 1870 one month before the Japanese embassy opened in Washington, DC—a testament to San Francisco's position at the center of early Japanese migration to the US. San Francisco's Greater Japanese Association was launched in 1891 by Sutemi Chinda, Japanese consul in that city from 1890 to 1894. Its mission was "to increase friendly intercourse among Japanese residents, to provide mutual aid, and to safeguard the Japanese national image" (Chinda quoted in Ichioka 1977, 411). The founding in 1900 of the Japanese Deliberative Council by Japanese residents of San Francisco also demonstrates not only the agency of these immigrants, but also the importance of immigrants as an element of foreign policy; as its charter stated, its mission was to "expand the rights of Imperial subjects in America and to maintain the Japanese national image" (in Ichioka 1977, 412).

From 1909 to 1926, Japanese consulates headed a system of regional and local Japanese associations (Ichioka 1977, 410). In Washington and Montana, such associations fell under the aegis of the Northwest American Japanese Association, established in 1913 by the Japanese consulate in Seattle. The associations provided aid for newly arrived immigrants, organized against exclusionist activities, and engaged in a variety of social and educational programs (Ichioka 1977, 409).[12] By 1923, Seattle had fifteen Japanese associations (Ichioka 1988, 157). Emblematic of Tacoma's smaller size and what we interpret as the cohesion of the Japanese community, Tacoma had only one.

In its cooperation with the consulate in Seattle, the Tacoma Japanese Association performed a number of functions such as registering births, deaths, marriages, and occupations, certifying identity, and issuing residence certificates, along with processing visa applications and supporting documents. Records of the Tacoma Japanese Association, for example, show that between 1913 and 1924, the association managed over one thousand visa applications.[13] The Tacoma Japanese Association, like others on the West Coast, was also an official conduit for maintaining ties between Tacoma's Japanese community and Japan. These continuing ties were demonstrated by the association's activities, which included collecting and sending donations to Japan for such things as the construction of the shrine for the Meiji Emperor after his death in 1912, the celebrations for the accession of the Taisho Emperor, the marriage of the future Showa Emperor, and relief for victims of Japan's 1923 Kanto Earthquake.[14]

Soon after the Japanese associations were founded, however, they came under attack by exclusionists in the US, who accused them of being agents of Japan's imperial reach. By playing a direct role in the immigrant community, these critics argued, the associations were "forcing all immigrants to be obedient 'subjects' of a foreign government" (Ichioka 1977, 409). According to Ichioka, Japanese immigrants tended to discount this characterization, asserting that there was "no relationship whatsoever—either political or financial—with the Government of Japan." The Japanese government likewise disavowed any role of the Japanese associations as "organs of Japanese propaganda." As Ichioka observes, "That the organizations had a connection with the Japanese government is an indisputable historical fact," yet Japanese government influence was neither as strong as the Japanese government may have wished, nor as nonexistent as the immigrants insisted (Ichioka 1977, 409–10). In 1920, Japanese ambassador to the US, Baron Shidehara Kijuro, testified that the intent of the Japanese associations was to promote "educational work among [Japanese] nationals with a view to familiarizing. . . settlers with American manners and customs." The associations, Baron Shidehara said, "were largely responsible for the improvement which had recently manifested itself in the relations of personal intercourse between Japanese settlers and their American neighbors in many rural districts of California" (Daniels 1988, 129).

For the Issei, then, this ongoing connection with Japan and the Japanese government was necessary and indeed vital: as Japanese subjects, their legal status in the US "made the Japanese Government responsible, more or less, for the behavior of its subjects, all of whom were 'aliens ineligible to citizenship'" (Daniels 1992, 434). Japan was, moreover, the "only sovereign entit[y] that could speak out and stand up for their . . . interests and welfare in America" (Azuma 2009, 26). This transnational relationship had a significant impact not only on the Issei, but also on their children.

ISSEI IN TACOMA: ESTABLISHING NEW
SOCIAL SPACES IN THE IMMIGRANT CITY

Japanese migration to the US began in the 1880s, and the first Japanese began arriving in Tacoma in the late 1880s and early 1890s. By 1891, according to a study by Japanese Consul Sutemi Chinda in the San Francisco consular office, some 90 Japanese were living in Tacoma (and 250 in Seattle) (Flewelling 2002, 21).[15] In light of the growing Japanese population in the Pacific Northwest, the Japanese government considered the possibility of opening a new West Coast consulate. The Tacoma Japanese community received a tremendous boost when in 1895 the Japanese government selected Tacoma for that honor, part of the international outreach that characterized the early Meiji years.

Members of Tacoma's Japanese community had lobbied intensely for their city to host the new consulate. In the above-mentioned letter to Japanese foreign minister Mutsu Munemitsu, Tacoma Japanese Society president Yukino Eijiro emphasized Tacoma's important position in international trade, writing, "As the number of Japanese here increases and considering the potential trade advantage of this location, it becomes clear that establishment of a Japanese Consulate here should be one of the highest priority [sic] of our country" (*History of Japanese in Tacoma* 1941, n.p. [224]).[16] Magden (1998, 9) suggests that Tacoma was selected because its Japanese residents were deemed "virtuous" in contrast to the "gamblers and prostitutes" of Seattle, Portland, and Spokane. Four years earlier, Sutemi Chinda, San Francisco consul general, had sent consulate secretary Yoshiro Fujita to conduct a study of Japanese communities in the Pacific Northwest. Fujita reportedly found that "in Seattle, all but 10 of the 250 Japanese residents [were] deeply involved in illegal (but tolerated) prostitution and gambling," while in Tacoma "all of the 50 Japanese inhabitants were 'enterprising young men' following legitimate occupations" (Daniels 1988, 104–5).[17]

Part of Tacoma's "clean bill of health" may have originated in the 1891/92 founding of the Tacoma Japanese Society, initially formed to deal with criminal elements in Tacoma's Japanese community and the "unexpected appearance" of a group of Japanese "prostitutes and pimps" from San Francisco, who "established themselves in dens of iniquities and plotted ways of parting hard earned money from Japanese and Caucasian males" (Magden 1998, 10). TJS leaders appealed to the mayor and city council to contain those identified as "virtueless" in a small area in the Opera Alley area of downtown Tacoma, on the north end of what became the main core of the Japanese community.

The TJS leaders' action appeared to contain the problem: the Tacoma community had a "clean" image of itself, as illustrated in an early community history which states that Tacoma was "known for its gentleness among cities of the Pacific coast. For example, those common laborers who went to taverns usually did not just wear a shirt, but put on collars" (Otsuka and Fukui [1940] 1986, 7). In tandem with lobbying by Tacoma Japanese residents, these efforts to appear socially presentable may have helped influence the Japanese government to select Tacoma as the site for a new West Coast consulate in 1895 (Magden 1998, 13).

In 1896, however, Tacoma's fortunes changed when it lost out to Seattle as the terminus for Japan's largest shipping company, Nippon Yusen Kaisha (Magden 1998, 13), reflecting the growing importance of this urban center to the north. By the turn of the century, Seattle's Nikkei community, numbering nearly four thousand and constituting about 5 percent of the city's population, had eclipsed Tacoma's in size and importance. As a result, in 1900 the consulate was relocated to Seattle (Asato 2006, 80). These losses came as "major blows to the progress of the Tacoma Japanese community" (Otsuka and Fukui [1940] 1986, 7).

Although it lost the Nippon Yusen Kaisha, Tacoma did become the terminus for Osaka Shosen Kaisha, Japan's second largest shipper, in 1909; this helped to "make Tacoma one of the world's leading seaports" (Otsuka and Fukui [1940] 1986, 1). By 1910, Seattle's Japanese population had risen to 6,127, and Tacoma's to 1,018 (Fiset 2009, 3; Magden 1998, 185). Regardless of which population number one accepts for Tacoma's Japanese population in 1890—50, 70, or 90 (see note 15)—the following twenty years brought phenomenal growth, as well as the development of a thriving Japanese business district, sometimes called Nihonmachi or Japan Town, at the southern end of downtown (see chapter 2).

Owing largely to the Gentlemen's Agreement and the onset of the "settler period," by 1910 Tacoma's Japanese community had experienced another transformation too, with the integration of more women and children. This in turn created a need for community institutions, including a Japanese language school (Spickard 2009, 69).

ESTABLISHING A JAPANESE LANGUAGE SCHOOL IN TACOMA

Tacoma's Issei community came together at the end of the first decade of the 1900s to discuss the establishment of a nonsectarian Japanese language school for local families. While Seattle and Fife[18] had opened schools earlier, in 1902 and 1909 respectively, Tacoma's was established by 1911. Seattle's 1902 Japanese language school was the first in North America and "one of the oldest non-religious Asian language schools . . . in the United States" (Asato 2006, 80). The San Francisco Japanese Language School opened five months later, but it was associated with a religious institution. Although Tacoma's Japanese Methodist Church offered to house Tacoma's school free of charge, TJLS organizers declined, pursuing instead their vision of a neutral, independent school unaffiliated with and unconstrained by the Buddhist, Methodist, or Japanese Baptist churches (Asato 2006, 90; Magden 1998, 70). This nonsectarian approach made both the Seattle and Tacoma Japanese language schools unusual on the West Coast and in Hawaii, where the majority of the early language schools were founded by Buddhist temples (James 1987, 12).

Although it is not clear from existing accounts exactly why Tacoma turned down the Methodist church's offer, Asato writes that the religious affiliations of Japanese language schools provided fodder for exclusionists, with schools linked to Buddhist temples in particular becoming targets of anti-Japanese agitation in the 1910s and '20s (Asato 2006, 56–58 and passim, 2003a). Exemplifying the potentially divisive nature of religious affiliation within Japanese communities in the US, during the 1910s the Japanese in Hawaii became embroiled in a discussion over the appropriateness of the language school–church connection, a debate seen by many as "an undeclared war between the Christians and the Buddhists"

(Onishi 1943, 16). Later, many Christian churches also established language schools. Spokane's Japanese language school, for example, was run by the Methodist Church. As Paul Spickard notes, "By World War II, 22 percent of first-generation Japanese Americans were Christians" (2009, 18)—though this figure is itself complicated, with some leaders of the Japanese American Christian movement arguing that "national belonging [in the US] necessitated adherence to Christianity" (Williams 2019, 106).

In 1908, Seattle's Japanese Association School Affairs Committee chose to call their school the *Kokugo gakko*, or "national language school," as opposed to the more common *Nihongo gakko*, "Japanese language school," a decision perhaps suggesting that "the Japanese spirit, traditional values, morality, and the nurturing of a sense of identity as Japanese were an integral part of language instruction" (Harrison 2005, 6). Indeed, for these first-generation immigrants, coming to the US was not about an "intentional break with . . . family" and nation (Modell 1968, 77). In an October 1901 publication called *Nihonjin* ("Japanese People" or "The Japanese"), put out by Seattle's Japanese Association, local leaders still contended that "the Japanese have no plan to live permanently in the United States, and it goes without saying that we recognize the necessity of providing our children with a Japanese-style education. We are in another country where we differ in terms of racial background, language, culture, and customs. Consequently, we must carefully evaluate the current situation in which we rely on foreigners to provide elementary school education for our children" (in Harrison 2005, 1).

Another important motivator in the founding of the school was fear that anti-Nikkei discrimination would limit Japanese community members' options in the dominant society. In short, Issei wanted to prepare their children to make their livelihoods within the Nikkei community or in Japan (Modell 1977; Miyamoto 1984; Yoo 2000; Kurashige 2002; see also chapter 2). As Ryo Munekata noted,

> In those days, I recall my father saying, "If you're going to go to college, I'll send you through college, and if you need the money, I'm going to pay for it." But he would show me an example of some of the fellows—when they graduate, there's no jobs available, and what do they do? They work in fruit stands with a college degree. And he says, "If you're going to do that, that money I have to spend for you to go to

college, I'll give it to you right now. Get started on something."...
My dad said, "If you want to go to college, take or major in something
where you can be your own boss." And that's when I decided I could
go into dentistry, have my own practice. I would be my own boss.

The Issei believed that providing language education for the second
generation would enable young people to conduct business with the
Japanese community both in the United States and in Japan and would
help ensure "close rapport within the family, including relatives abroad"
(James 1987, 20). At the same time, however, Tokichi Tanaka, the Japanese
consul in Seattle, pointed out that while the Issei were barred from obtaining US citizenship, in most cases their children were born in the US, and
so were citizens; as such, they embodied the community's future in the
United States. Tanaka's comments in 1908, in the wake of the Gentlemen's
Agreement, thus represent a shift in the attitudes of Nikkei in the face of
hostile immigration policies and rising exclusionist sentiment. In 1909,
Hawaii's consul general, Ueno Senichi, likewise remarked that "children
born in the United States are American citizens, so it is natural for the
American public to fear providing these children with an education not
dealing with the United States. . . . It is the duty of farsighted immigrants
to raise children who are loyal to America and yet are familiar with Japan's
situation" (in Asato 2006, 16).

In Seattle, Consul Tanaka cited the soundness of the US public school
system and rejected earlier qualms about "rely[ing] on foreigners to provide elementary school education for our children." But he also believed
Seattle's *Kokugo gakko* should "inculcate the Japanese spirit" in its students.
"This would give them a sense of identity as Japanese, and enable them to
overcome the ill effects of exclusionism and the myriad of other difficulties
they encountered in their lives in America" (Harrison 2005, 6). Much later,
historian Gail Nomura quoted an early Tacoma Issei as she reflected on
the attitudes during this period: "'These children, born in the United
States, are given the rights of citizenship with all the rights and privileges
of a Caucasian, and can be another Wilson'" (Nomura 1986).

Immediately after World War I, however, the anti-Japanese exclusion
movement was gathering momentum (see Daniels 1962), and its focus
began to shift from the Issei to their American-born children, in particular
toward "ousting Japanese language schools" (Asato 2003b, 140, 147). Both

Hawaii and California passed legislation (in 1920 and 1921 respectively) that allowed for some state control over the language schools, particularly after the 1919 Federal Survey of Education in Hawaii that Asato argues was "a pioneering effort of nativist Americanizers" and "created the foundation for an anti-Japanese language school movement" across the West Coast (2003a, 45, 1). In 1921, Washington State passed similar legislation, mandating that "aliens and disloyal persons" be barred from teaching in public and private schools. In an example of Issei agency, the passage of this bill in the Washington State Senate by a vote of 37 to 2 "prompted Nikkei leaders and parents to voice their opposition at a rally," perhaps as a result of which the bill never moved out of the House Education Committee and was never enacted (Asato 2003b, 146). At the same time, however, the agitation over this bill led the Issei in Fife to close the Fife language school, as a way to "ease anti-Japanese sentiment in the valley" (Magden 1998, 61).

After the 1924 Exclusion Act barred further Japanese immigration to the US, the number of Japanese language schools in the US grew, providing new spaces of belonging for Nisei and their families, along with ways of reinforcing the second generation's connection with Issei parents. Asato and others speculate that because they would not have been able to return to the US, many Issei decided to stay put at this point, thus heightening the need for language schools to help reinforce their children's Japanese identity and promoting language skills that might otherwise fade away (Asato 2006, 99). In Washington State in the prewar period, a total of twenty-four Japanese language schools were in operation (Asato 2006, 100), illustrating the importance of these institutions for Japanese communities and families. In the South Puget Sound alone, Japanese language schools were established in Firwood (1915), Sumner (1923), Alderton (1925), Eatonville (1930), Pacific City (1936), and Olympia (1940) (*History of Japanese in Tacoma* 1941, n.p. [93–99]).

In Tacoma, a meeting of the Tacoma Japanese Association in 1911, recognizing the growing number of children locally, elected a committee to study the feasibility of opening a language school. Some of the concerns of the TJLS founders may be seen in the unpublished 1941 manuscript *History of Japanese in Tacoma* (n.p. [43–44]): "Language is very important (essential) for racial cultivation. If nothing is done about the inconsistency in language, it will become a spiritual half-breed. Unable to belong to any nation or to associate themselves with their races, thy [sic] will become a [sic] anomalous breed. No doubt the danger in the future will be for the children lost in such a maze. . . . [T]hrough teaching their children the Japanese language . . . [communities are] making an effort to implant morality, civilization and culture in the NISEI." The emphasis on "morality" and "civilization" echoed the Meiji Imperial Rescript, and can be identified in TJLS lessons as well. As Mitsuo Takasugi (b. 1928) recalled,

> they used to celebrate [the] Meiji Emperor's birthday. You know, he [Principal Yamasaki] would get up there and read the Imperial Rescript on Education, and it was quite a, almost a religious ceremony. He wore his long tails, and he would bow, and like, you know—it was something. Oh, of course, none of us ever knew what it meant, I mean because, you know, it was in very—what is—stiff Japanese language. I read translations of it much later. It's ridiculous! (laughs) The whole school [would attend]. They would call everybody into the auditorium. And it was a solemn ceremony.

Masaye Jinguji Fujita remembered:

> I still remember to this day we sang at the school . . . April 29th was the emperor's birthday and all the children would meet at the school and we would sing "Emperor's Birthday" . . . During the emperor's service there would be a little stand there and there's an attendant that rolls the emperor's flag—the picture—down . . . they say "bow to the lowest." And we all had to bow, and then the principal . . . would read the emperor's words. All that time we had to have our heads down . . . When we would raise our heads, the emperor's picture was rolled up, and we never saw [their] picture . . . That is another experience that all the Japanese schoolchildren remember.

"Due to the increase in the number of children," noted an early history of the Tacoma Japanese Association, "it was decided to take a census of the numbers of children, their sex and their desire to learn the Japanese language" (Otsuka and Fukui [1940] 1986, 12). This informal census identified thirty-three Japanese children; of these, only seven were of school age, and the remainder were ages five and under (Otsuka and Fukui [1940] 1986, 54)—again reflecting the recent transition from a male-only to a more family-oriented immigrant population, a sign that the community was becoming more permanent. Some in the Tacoma Japanese Association were concerned that funding a Japanese language school would divert funds needed for other (primarily political) efforts (Magden 1998, 70). But in November 1911, a small committee consisting of five men—Totaro Kawasoe, Yonezo Okamoto, Kumatoro Takahashi, Hiroshi Yano, and Naoshi Yoshida—was created to pursue the idea of opening of a language school (Otsuka and Fukui [1940] 1986, 55).

Interviews with former students consistently suggested that the non-sectarian nature of Tacoma's language school contributed strongly to the central role it played in the Japanese immigrant population. As Joe Kosai put it, the school "was a focal point, bringing all Japanese in the community together. [There was] no religious segregation." (See also chapters 3 and 5.) This community solidarity was especially important, Joe noted, "because of discrimination prior to World War II. [We] couldn't mingle socially with whites." Similarly, Junichi Taira commented that "the non-sectarian aspect of the school kept an already close-knit community even more closely knit." This community-building role was similar to that afforded by the Buddhist temples built by immigrants in Hawaii and North America. These "were more than just religious sites: like the Christian churches and Jewish synagogues of many European immigrants, they became centers of social and cultural life that addressed the practical needs of a growing and increasingly more settled community. This socio-cultural dimension of Buddhism set the stage for a dynamic process of identity formation, both religious and national" (Williams and Moriya 2010, 2). The nonsectarian nature of Tacoma's school likewise contributed to the dynamic formation of community.

Throughout the life of the school, Principal Yamasaki strictly adhered to religious neutrality, meticulously inviting leaders of each of the community's religious institutions to attend all school functions (Magden 1998, 70; see also chapter 5). He reached out to all members of the Japanese community as well as the local Caucasian community. As Yoshiko Fujimoto Sugiyama remembered, "For school activities, Mr. Yamasaki always invited our public school principal and the superintendent. They're all in the picture, really. We had a good relationship with the school system." Tacoma journalist Shuichi Fukui described the role of the TJLS in helping Nisei children to "compete in America":

> Although . . . the school building . . . [is] important, we must also consider the spiritual aspect of the school. The objective of the school was different from the other usual schools because the children of Japanese immigrants would first go to American public school and then go to the language school after that for one hour [actually two hours] per day. Primarily the children were taught the Japanese language, literature and other Japanese cultural subjects which together will help the students compete in America. Public schools taught mathematics, scientific subjects, and arts as its principal objective. The language school mainly taught Japanese reading, writing and calligraphy. Japanese songs were also taught. (Otsuka and Fukui [1940] 1986, 58)

Soon the education committee appointed an additional ten members to assist with fundraising (Otsuka and Fukui [1940] 1986, 55).[19] First, the group canvassed the local community and established that parents were willing to pay monthly tuition fees of two dollars for each elementary school pupil and fifty cents for each kindergartener. The Nihonmachi area of town was then divided into quadrants and men from the committee invited community members to donate, using a standardized written appeal dated "Meiji 44, 3rd Month" (March 1911) (figure 1.1):

> *To Whom It May Concern;*
>
> *We have just decided to establish a Tacoma Kokugo [national language] School. Therefore, we wish to raise funds to establish it.*
> *Training children's social manners and behaviors is as important as knowledge for children.*
> *Therefore, to improve our countrymen's learning and work, we must not neglect the advantages of educating our children.*
> *Therefore please contribute to this common good.*
>
> *We ask for your support,*
> *Tacoma Japanese Association[20]*

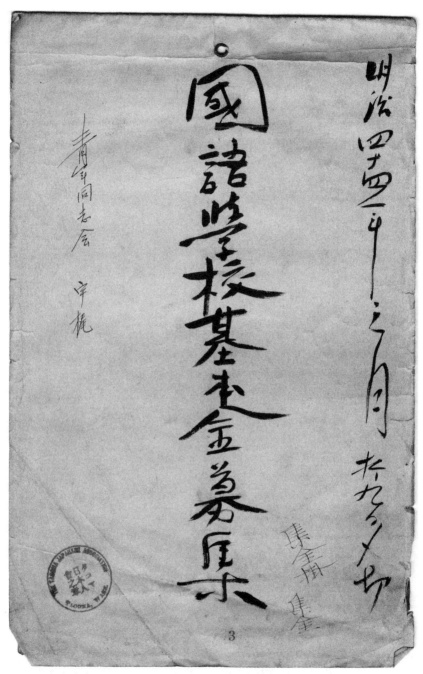

FIGURE 1.1. Notice soliciting funds for establishing TJLS: "Accepting donations for the language school endowment," March 1912. Courtesy of University of Washington Libraries, Special Collections.

The fundraising effort met with early success. The Maruoka Grocery distinguished itself by becoming the first donor, making a pledge of $200 (*History of Japanese in Tacoma* 1941, n.p. [65]). Tacoma's language school movement got a significant boost when the Japanese consulate agreed to grant the fees it collected for "various certificates and documents" to help fund the school (Otsuka and Fukui [1940] 1986, 55). By the end of 1911, thanks to this infusion from the consulate, the Nihonjinkai had rented a small house at 411 South 15th Street (Otsuka and Fukui [1940] 1986, 55; Sonnier 1993, 2).

In 1912, the Tacoma Japanese Association's education committee issued an offer to Kuniko Yamasaki of Seattle to come teach Tacoma's Japanese children (Otsuka and Fukui [1940] 1986, 55; Magden 1998, 70). On May 21, less than nine months after the original discussions were launched, the "school was opened with appropriate ceremony." A gala celebration marked the "wonderful, auspicious occasion," with speakers from the Japanese consulate and from the local Methodist and Baptist churches. Teacher Yamasaki welcomed her new pupils, who when the school opened its doors the next day numbered a mere thirteen (Magden 1998, 71; Otsuka and Fukui [1940] 1986, 55–56).[21] To improve these numbers, the president of the TJLS committee, Totaro Kawasoe, recruited students by visiting their families, and within a couple of months the school's population had doubled, in part owing to an influx of new Japanese residents to the area (*History of Japanese in Tacoma* 1941, n.p. [45]). Some parents, however, preferred to send their school-age children to Japan for education, a sign of continued strong ties with their homeland (Magden 1998, 71; Modell 1977).

By early 1913, members of the Japanese community began to consider the feasibility of buying land and constructing a new building to house the school. This issue, however, caused a division within the Tacoma Japanese Association, as a vocal portion of the group again argued that their efforts should be focused "in the political arena" (Otsuka and Fukui [1940] 1986, 56). Of particular concern to the association in the early 1910s was a variety of discriminatory bills introduced in the state legislature, most significantly the Alien Land Laws—ultimately passed in 1921 and 1923—which would bolster existing legal restrictions on aliens ineligible for citizenship from owning or leasing land. Demonstrating Issei agency, in 1913 the Tacoma Japanese Association had hired a Caucasian attorney to lobby against the passage of these bills. At this time, association members expressed concern that the language school's affiliation with the Tacoma Japanese Association might make it a political target of exclusionists, or that the language school would itself be "used to make political statements" (Asato 2006, 90; *History of Japanese in Tacoma* 1941, n.p. [46]). In 1914, not wishing to defile the "'holiness' of education" with these squabbles (Otsuka and Fukui [1940] 1986, 57), a special School Support Society was created, separate from the Tacoma Japanese Association.[22] As an interim measure, in 1916 the school relocated to a house at 510 South 15th Street, saving $3 per month on rent (*History of Tacoma Japanese* 1941, n.p. [46]; Otsuka and Fukui [1940] 1986, 57).

As the student population increased—by 1913, 27 students were enrolled; by 1920, 62; and by 1923, 101—the push for a permanent facility intensified (Otsuka and Fukui [1940] 1986, 54; Asato 2006, 91). In 1923, amid projections that the student population might quadruple over the next several years, fundraising for a new building began. Other groups, including the Tacoma Japanese Association, the Osaka Shosen Kaisha shipping company, and the local *ken* (prefectural) associations, soon stepped up.[23] Parents contributed as well, purchasing ten-dollar school bonds (Magden 1998, 74). Ultimately, over the course of a year more than $15,000 was raised (Magden 1998, 74), an impressive amount in a relatively short period of time. Harue Kawano Ozaki commented that fundraising within the community could be remarkably effective, particularly because of *tanomoshi,* the customary system of money pooling (see chapter 2). Harue said:

> Oh, you don't understand the way you can do that quickly. It's through that cooperation . . . [T]he Issei would formulate the gathering of every family in contributing to make a so-called—they took turns in being able to use a pot of accumulated money for their own use, whatever it is. I can see how easy that was.

Nevertheless, as Akiyoshi Hayashida points out with regard to Hawaii's Japanese language schools of the early 1930s, the financial commitment for a "class of people rather low in economic status" to support a language school was considerable. "The older Japanese people are scrimping and saving, denying themselves all luxuries, in order that they may send their children to the Japanese language schools" (Hayashida 1933, 1). Linda

Tamura (1993, 121) reported that in the Hood River, Oregon, community, some families stopped sending their children to language school for financial reasons and instead "purchased books from Japan" to try to provide education at home. In our interview with the three Fujimoto sisters, Kimiko and Tadaye recalled that there were indeed class differences within the community and that tuition was a barrier for some families:

> KIMIKO: . . . because the Japanese school was a private school, they had to pay tuition, and there were a lot of families that could not, even if the tuition was very minimal. They wanted the kids to come to school, so apparently my father paid a lot of the tuitions for . . .
>
> TADAYE: We didn't know that until the first reunion—you know, Tacoma had the Japanese school reunion—that's the time some of the elders told me about it, and then I told them (*indicating her sisters*) that Dad used to help so many families.
>
> KIMIKO: See, we were kind of fortunate, because my folks owned a business, that we were able to do that, you know, whereas a lot of the other people couldn't do it. So we happened to be very fortunate.

The successful fundraising effort meant that land could be purchased (Magden 1998, 74). Because Issei were legally prohibited from owning land, the community turned to three white Tacomans with whom they had worked previously—attorney Joseph H. Gordon,[24] Baptist Mission teacher Electa A. Snyder, and accountant Jonathan M. Walker—as well as two unidentified Issei, to incorporate the language school organization and purchase the land for the school (Magden 1998, 74–75). They acquired a double lot at the corner of South Tacoma Avenue and South 19th Street for $1,600 (*History of Tacoma Japanese* 1941, n.p. [67–68]). The School Support Society then hired Frederick Heath, of Tacoma's leading architectural firm, Heath & Gove, to draw up plans for the new school building. Heath was the official architect for the Tacoma public school system, having designed seventeen schools for the district. In addition to repurposing the Tacoma Land Company Hotel as Stadium High School, Heath designed Lincoln High School and Mount Rainier National Park's Paradise Inn (HABS 1995, 7).

The choice of Heath, and the resulting design for the Tacoma Japanese Language School as a boxy, wood-framed clapboard construction devoid of any Japanese architectural design features (although two cherry trees from Japanese stock were later planted out front), accords with what architectural historian Gail L. Dubrow argues regarding Japanese American identity and the urban built environment—that is, that even when it came to architecture, "Japanese immigrants adopted a strategy of blending into the American cultural fabric in an effort to ward off racist hostility from exclusionary federal immigration policies, restrictive state land laws, and discriminatory city ordinances." By "abandon[ing] or mask[ing] outward signs of ethnicity," Dubrow maintains, Japanese immigrants were not displaying assimilation, but rather responding to the pressures of racism (Dubrow 2005, 120–21).

By January 1922, the construction company of N. H. Hylen had completed the building and it was ready for its formal opening (Magden 1998, 75; Morrison 1994, 13–16). Various former students described the physical building and its location. Here is Yuriko Lily Korin Harada (b. 1931):

Well, this school was built on a hill, if I remember correctly, and so the first level was their [the Yamasaki family's] residence and a great big hall, which was used as an auditorium [see figure 6.1]. And the stage was there, I remember. And then the second lower level is where all the classrooms were. I remember a teachers' room, a bathroom. And I was thinking about this last night. There are five classrooms. And then we go down some more stairs, and it's the play area outside. I remember that.

The TJLS building became the site of a robust educational mission, as demonstrated in part by this list of "teaching equipments [sic] and furnishings":

Chart of names, map, Chart of Chinese characters, Chart of Japanese reading books, Chart of Japanese history, Chart of Ethics, Records for reading, various specimens, Fruits for use of nursery children, Movie projector, Health scale, International Eye Chart, Mimeograph Machine, 2 Pianos, Organ, 5 Orchestra instruments, One set of record-player, Three records, Fire-Extinguishers, Three Black Boards, Ping

Pong Table, Two Bulletin Boards, Frames, Three Electric clocks, One Thermometer, Eight Chronicle Charts of Japanese History, Eight sets of Desk and Chair, Chairs, Books, 5300 Literary Exhibition Equipments, Sports Equipments, Stove, 19 Cases of First Aids, Fire-Alarm, Three Fire-hoses. (*History of Japanese in Tacoma* 1941, n.p. [62–63])

In its permanent building the TJLS became a focal point for the community. The school was the culmination of complex efforts to create some security in the immigrants' lives while also safeguarding values and ethics and imbuing them to the next generation. It also embodied the far-reaching effects of the Meiji era's efforts to engage with Western nations, including emigration. Moreover, the Issei, in their status as residents but not citizens of the US, with children whose future remained uncertain, influenced the school's creation and thus its role in linking the community together. The TJLS was integral to the transnationalism that helped shape the understanding Tacoma Japanese had of their world, the ways in which the Issei forged a place for themselves in the city, and the ways in which the Nisei navigated these spaces.

CHAPTER TWO

Struggle and Hard Work

From Physical Labor to Entrepreneurialism

> I guess my mother was probably more entrepreneurial than my
> father, and she saw a chance to lease a hotel, a small hotel down-
> town. And so, she ran the hotel, and my father worked in the saw-
> mill. And that was really a life-saver . . .
>
> —FUMI SATO HATTORI (B. 1921)

L IKE FUMI, A NUMBER OF NISEI INTERVIEWEES REMEMBERED
their parents dividing labor along gendered lines to help their families
survive and prosper. As wives and "picture brides" arrived in the US and
families were started, primarily after the Gentlemen's Agreement of 1908,
some men shifted their economic activity to support new family needs
(e.g., away from running billiard halls), and women worked in family businesses or even started their own (e.g., barbershops). The narratives of Fumi
and the other interviewees illuminate the daily grind that sustained these
families, often at the lower ends of the economic scale, and some of the
pressures and opportunities that shaped Nisei childhood experiences.
With parents working hard predominantly in the ethnic economy, learning Japanese was both culturally relevant and pragmatic. The skills they
honed afforded them the opportunity to work within the community when
dreams of other occupations were thwarted by racist discrimination
(Bonacich and Modell 1980; Kitano 1981; Kurashige 2002).

These Nisei stories of hard work bring statistics and aggregated immigration histories to life, while also providing localized examples of migration experiences that were shaped by immigration policies as well as industrial growth in the Pacific Northwest in the late 1880s and early 1900s. Overall, the majority of Issei migrants were farmers, merchants, and students, and they tended to come from select prefectures (*ken*) in Japan, with few coming from the major urban centers such as Tokyo.[1] Our interviews showed that many families had a father who worked in the sawmills, though many of these men transitioned out of physical wage labor into entrepreneurial self-employment in the ethnic economy. Those venturing into business grew and sustained their enterprises through the pooling of resources and the close proximity of kin and close friends whom they could hire. With the caveat that the stories incorporated here are childhood memories, these interviews expand our understanding of how families survived and also how their labor contributed to regional development. We also consider how the daily practices of sacrifice, hard work, and obligation by the Issei parents reflected lessons taught at the TJLS.

LABOR AND THE SOCIAL CONSTITUTION OF COMMUNITY

Many Japanese immigrants to the United States did not assume that they would remain permanently; rather, they considered themselves sojourners who would work for several years, make money, and return home—a practice called *dekasegi* (going out to work), distinct from *teiju* (emigrating permanently) (Spickard 2009, 22). Yet Issei did settle in the United States, including in Tacoma, Fife, and the Puyallup Valley, significantly contributing to the region's early economic development and agricultural production. Issei came to the US for a variety of reasons, including economic opportunity, working to support family in Japan, or following or accompanying other family members (Yanagisako 1985, 27–62). The economic roles and occupational experiences of the Issei have been shown to be important for identity formation, not only for the Issei but also for their children (e.g., Bonacich and Modell 1980). The Issei parents became integrated into local economic relations—thus constructing an ethnic economy (Modell 1977)—to achieve some financial security in the face of many anti-Asian policies, and this economy also included their children, who at least had the "security" of being US citizens These stories thus not only animate pre–World War II urban immigrant experiences, but also help to clarify the various positionalities of the immigrant parents and their Nisei children.

Previous scholarship has argued that Japanese immigrants "moved quickly out of body labor and into small business, whether urban or agricultural" (Spickard 2009, 2; see also Takaki 1988, 188), and that this trend from wage labor to small business was a part of the "aggregate history" of the Issei (Yanagisako 1985, 64). Why this was the case is complicated, and below we consider a variety of factors. Most of our interviewees told us that their fathers had worked in the lumber industry at some point, especially when they first arrived in the US but also strategically, to complement the mother's labor in a small business, as in the case of Fumi's parents. Discrimination excluded them from many other occupations and professions, and also from unions; and some of the business services in which Japanese immigrants participated, such as cooking and deliveries, required minimal training and capital. Prefectural associations (*kenjinkai*) helped people get started by pooling money in a rotating credit system (*tanomoshi*) (Miyamoto 1984; O'Brien and Fugita 1982; Spickard 2009). Thanks to these practices, Japanese were able to move into small business more efficiently than other immigrant groups. The Japanese-run businesses not only provided needed services to the Japanese community, but also to white customers (Modell 1977): many of the laundries, hotels, and barbershops in Tacoma "served a largely western clientele" (i.e., white), especially men in the lumber and railroad industries (Morrison 1994, 34).[2] The establishment of these Japanese businesses and residences in the downtown core "contributed significantly to the development of the city during the period 1890–1930" (Morrison 1994, 3). Map 2.1 shows the extent and density of the Japanese businesses and lodgings along Broadway between 13th and 15th Streets before 1941, as gleaned from our interviews, Polk City Directories, and other historical sources (Pyle 2019).[3]

Small businesses within the Japanese community often exploited kin and close community relations for low-paid labor, "provid[ing] steady work—for long hours at low wages—for family members and *kenjin* [persons from the same prefecture]" (Spickard 2009, 48). In addition, many of the businesses worked directly with other Japanese businesses; for example, Japanese farmers worked with Japanese distributors who in turn were connected with Japanese markets (figure 2.1) (Modell 1977; O'Brien and

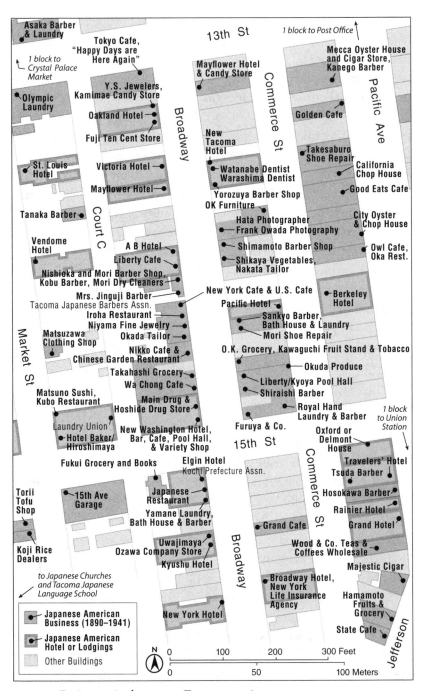

Asaka Barber & Laundry

1 block to Crystal Palace Market

13th St

1 block to Post Office

Tokyo Cafe, "Happy Days are Here Again"

Mecca Oyster House and Cigar Store, Kanego Barber

Mayflower Hotel & Candy Store

Olympic Laundry

Y.S. Jewelers, Kamimae Candy Store

Oakland Hotel

Golden Cafe

Broadway

Commerce St

Pacific Ave

Fuji Ten Cent Store

New Tacoma Hotel

Takesaburo Shoe Repair

California Chop House

St. Louis Hotel

Victoria Hotel

Watanabe Dentist Warashima Dentist

Good Eats Cafe

Mayflower Hotel

Yorozuya Barber Shop OK Furniture

Tanaka Barber

City Oyster & Chop House

Court C

Hata Photographer Frank Owada Photography

Vendome Hotel

A B Hotel

Shimamoto Barber Shop

Owl Cafe, Oka Rest.

Liberty Cafe

Shikaya Vegetables, Nakata Tailor

Nishioka and Mori Barber Shop, Kobu Barber, Mori Dry Cleaners

Mrs. Jinguji Barber

New York Cafe & U.S. Cafe

Berkeley Hotel

Tacoma Japanese Barbers Assn.

Pacific Hotel

Market St

Iroha Restaurant

Sankyo Barber, Bath House & Laundry

Niyama Fine Jewelry

Okada Tailor

Mori Shoe Repair

Matsuzawa Clothing Shop

Nikko Cafe & Chinese Garden Restaurant

O.K. Grocery, Kawaguchi Fruit Stand & Tobacco

Takahashi Grocery

Okuda Produce

Wa Chong Cafe

Liberty/Kyoya Pool Hall

Matsuno Sushi, Kubo Restaurant

Main Drug & Hoshide Drug Store

Shiraishi Barber

Royal Hand Laundry & Barber

1 block to Union Station

Laundry Union

Hotel Baker/ Hiroshimaya

New Washington Hotel, Bar, Cafe, Pool Hall, & Variety Shop

Furuya & Co.

Oxford or Delmont House

15th St

Fukui Grocery and Books

Elgin Hotel

Kochi Prefecture Assn.

Commerce St

Travelers' Hotel

Tsuda Barber

Torii Tofu Shop

15th Ave Garage

Japanese Restaurant

Hosokawa Barber

Yamane Laundry, Bath House & Barber

Rainier Hotel

Grand Cafe

Grand Hotel

Koji Rice Dealers

Uwajimaya

Wood & Co. Teas & Coffees Wholesale

Ozawa Company Store

Kyushu Hotel

Majestic Cigar

to Japanese Churches and Tacoma Japanese Language School

Broadway

Broadway Hotel, New York Life Insurance Agency

Hamamoto Fruits & Grocery

New York Hotel

Japanese American Business (1890–1941)

State Cafe

Japanese American Hotel or Lodgings

Jefferson

Other Buildings

N

0   100   200   300 Feet

0   50   100 Meters

MAP 2.1. Businesses in downtown Tacoma, ca. 1890–1941

FIGURE 2.1. Tommy's Produce Stand run by the Inouye family in the Sanitary Public Market, 1108–14 Market Street, Tacoma, 1922. Courtesy of Tacoma Public Library, BOLAND 6594.

Fugita 1982; Fugita and Fernandez 2004). In an extensive study of economic activity and occupations among Japanese Americans in Los Angeles, Edna Bonacich and John Modell (1980) used the term "middleman minority" to describe their position in between.[4] Not only were they in a "middle position" in terms of moving goods and providing services, but they were also "middling" in terms of social stratification, including the predominance of entrepreneurial activity in small, independent enterprises that drew on kin labor and resources (e.g., *tanomoshi*, the rotating credit system). Similarly, Lon Kurashige (2002, 21) emphasizes the notion of Japanese maintaining "autonomy within racially segregated spheres," suggesting that the "modern racism" that Issei experienced resulted in an independence that in some instances allowed monopolies in certain industries (see also Bonacich and Modell 1980).[5]

What is compelling about the "middleman minority" concept is the attention it gives to the interactions between economic activity and community formation for Japanese Americans. For instance, drawing on kin labor and working with other Japanese businesses both helped keep businesses afloat and reinforced community bonds, helping to "glue Japanese communities together" (Spickard 2009, 48). In Tacoma, moreover, where there was only one Japanese bank (Pacific Bank), the community established "a private 'mutual finance association'" that made loans to Japanese businesses; it also created a number of business groups, such as the Barbers' Association and Grocery Association, that provided welfare and financial support for members (Otsuka and Fukui [1940] 1986, 163, 170–74). Lon Kurashige's (2002) study of "Nisei Week" in Los Angeles's Little Tokyo also raises questions of belonging and identity in the context of economic and occupational factors. The work Issei parents did and the spaces in which the Nisei grew up—in the hotels or behind the markets where their parents worked—were important shapers of identity. Recognizing the role of economic relations underscores that ethnicity and ethnic identity may not be experienced only in naturalized, *a priori*, or even racial terms. Rather, considering immigration stories, middling economic positions, and entrepreneurialism among Japanese immigrants helps us understand ethnicity and ethnic communities as socially and economically constituted. Accordingly, Kurashige argues that Nisei identity is not "an issue of articulating primordial dispositions or remaining true to a fixed strategy of adaptation or resistance," but is rather about "fluidity and contingency" (Kurashige 2002, 43).

ENTRY EMPLOYMENT AND WAGE LABOR IN THE NORTHWEST LUMBER INDUSTRY

When official emigration from Japan to the US began in 1885, most Japanese immigrants ventured to Hawaii and California, and businesses in the Pacific Northwest had to compete for labor with their counterparts in these locations. By the end of the 1890s, however, labor contracting firms, such as Tacoma Construction and Maintenance Company and the Oriental Trading Company of Seattle, both founded in 1898, gave western Washington industries a means for recruiting Japanese workers (Ichioka 1980, 329–30; Takaki [1989] 1998). These firms employed Issei foremen or "bosses" who helped provide workers to industrial businesses, liaise with the English-speaking employers, and even manage salaries. While the majority of Japanese laborers went to work on the railroads, most of the rest were absorbed by the lumber, cannery, and agricultural industries (Nomura 1989).[6] So influential were these labor contractors that by June 1900 "almost half of the 12,635 Japanese admitted to the country entered through the Pacific Northwest" (Fiset 2009, 2). By the first decade of the 1900s, sawmills in Washington and Oregon employed some 2,200 Japanese workers (Fiset 2009, 3), who by 1909 accounted for 4 percent of mill workers (L. Tamura 1993, 71). In 1917 in Tacoma alone, the approximately fifty sawmills employed some 1,300 Japanese workers, who earned over $1.4 million in wages. By 1922 the number of Japanese employed in the Tacoma area sawmills had increased to over 2,000 (Otsuka and Fukui [1940] 1986).

This Japanese labor was an integral part of Tacoma's history and development. While much of the attention on Tacoma's prewar Japanese community has been focused on the downtown core, the presence of these Japanese families in urban industrial spaces such as Tacoma's tideflats is important to acknowledge, in part to counter systemic forgetting and historical erasure (see chapter 4).[7] A majority of our interviewees (25 out of 42) discussed the role of Japanese immigrants in the lumber industry, and a number said that their own fathers had worked in a sawmill at some point. The St. Paul & Tacoma Lumber Company, mentioned specifically by eleven interviewees, was a key employer of Issei in the tideflats. Japanese also worked at the Wheeler-Osgood Lumber Company, down the street from St. Paul & Tacoma (Otsuka and Fukui [1940] 1986, 100), as well as the Pacific National Lumber Company and Mitchell Lumber Company (*History of Japanese in Tacoma* 1941, n.p. [41, 42]). Some interviewees also mentioned the Point Defiance sawmill.

Tacoma was a key player in lumber industry development in the region, with the first sawmill opening in 1852 and an additional sixteen sawmills and shingle mills opening along the Tacoma waterfront during the 1880s (Magden 2008). By the 1920s, "Tacoma was lumber's leading producer" (Morgan and Morgan 1984, 113), which made it a destination for many new immigrants. In a group interview, sisters Yoneko Aochi (b. 1918) and Katsuko Aochi Harano (b. 1923) remember their parents' work:

YONEKO: My name is Yoneko Aochi and I'm the oldest of the five [total siblings in the family]. I have my brother and sister here with me. They could help me with all the questions. I was born August 11, 1918. I'm eighty-five years old. And I was born in, what is it, 4733½ Gold Street, someplace in Ruston Way . . . Then they turned it—changed it to 4618 Waterfront Way. But when I was born it was 4733½ Gold Street . . . My father was working for the sawmill, and my mother was a housewife.

KATSUKO: They had a hotel, too.

YONEKO: Yes. And then, I don't know how long my father was working for the sawmill, but I remember my father buying the hotel in Tacoma. Was it there on Jefferson Street? It was on the corner someplace.

KATSUKO: Yes.

YONEKO: I don't know how long he had it, but he sold that place and we bought a house right across the street from there, and we stayed there for a while until we got burglarized. And my father didn't like that and then he didn't want his children to be in the city, because when friends call, we—you know, he thinks we have to go out with the kids, with the friends. So we moved back to where we were, where we were born . . . And that's where we stayed for a long time, until the war, wasn't it? . . . That's by the smelter. You know where the smelter used to be? . . . It was right close to that. Now, all the sawmills were right in front and that's where we were living, you know, downhill, in front of the place where we were living. But they're all gone now. Nothing left now.

KATSUKO: My—our father worked at the Point Defiance . . .

YONEKO: Yes, Point Defiance Saw . . . was that the Point Defiance Sawmill, was it?

KATSUKO: Uh-hmm.

By far the largest lumber company in Tacoma was St. Paul & Tacoma Lumber,[8] which over the fifty-year period between 1888 and 1938 "maintained an average of 1000 workmen in its payroll" (Cornwall 1938, 30), including a number of Japanese immigrants. Founded in 1888, the company eventually operated three mills—opened in 1889, 1900, and during World War I—on what Tacomans called the Boot, a marshy, boot-shaped "on-again, off-again island" (Morgan 1982, 258; see also Cornwall 1938). Yet although St. Paul & Tacoma Lumber was considered one of the better companies (along with Simpson and Weyerhaeuser), the "greatest problem was labor," in logging camps as well as sawmills, where the work was

"rough and sometimes dangerous . . . the hours were long, the pay low . . .,
even by the industrial standards of the day, and the authority of the boss
often oppressive." As a consequence, those who labored in this industry
"were men regarded as stronger of back than of mind, the unskilled, the
foreigners, itinerants, 'womanless, homeless, voteless'" (Morgan 1982, 198).

Foremen, or bosses, employed by the labor contracting companies
worked as intermediaries between Japanese laborers and their employers,
negotiating and distributing wages for a fee that was deducted from the
workers' wages (Takaki 1998, 182–83). One such boss was Kenkichi Honda,
a "labor gang foreman" for the Wheeler-Osgood Lumber Company on
Tacoma's tideflats. Honda was "well respected by this company, and he
became the foreman over thirty Japanese workers. He is a good natured,
modest, quiet individual" (Otsuka and Fukui [1940] 1986, 100). Anon Male
B and his friend Fusae Fujii Yoshida (b. 1927) talked about foremen in the
sawmills.

> FUSAE: Wasn't your father involved in another business before the war?
> ANON MALE B: Ya, he [was a foreman] . . . at the sawmill . . . he used
> to take care of the Japanese workers . . . He used to take care of the
> Japanese workers at the sawmill . . .
> [*And what do you mean, "He would take care of them"?*]
> ANON MALE B: . . . Say like sawmill needs some workers, sawmill
> workers—well, he would know somebody that would work in saw-
> mill, like . . . Kosai—do you know [Joe] Kosai? His dad used to work
> night shift, and he used to get Japanese sawmill workers for these
> different sawmills.

The St. Paul & Tacoma Lumber Company Records (1903–18) confirm
the employment of Japanese workers, listing individuals by first initial and
surname, the type of job they performed, and the number of hours worked
each day during a month. The following is an example from the February
1915 night shift (absent hours worked).

K. Adachi	Clean, Shingle Mill
M. Jinguji	Clean, D.C. Carriage, H.S. Carriage, Burner, Sorter
K. Kawashima	Sorter, Clean

T. Asada	D.C. Carriage, Sorter
T. Mochizuki	Sorter, Clean
K. Yueta	Sorter
M. Sumi	Sorter, Clean
M. Yamasaki	Sorter
C. Magi	H.S. Offbearer, Sorter
H. Kadayama	Sorter
M. Kurata	Sorter, Clean
I. Nakagawa	Sorter, Clean
S. Tanaka	Sorter, Clean
R. Doi	Sorter, Clean
K. Okamota [sic]	Sorter, Clean
K. Yoshide	Sorter, Clean

Although these logs list individuals and specific jobs, other materials confirm that employees engaged in different kinds of jobs over time, and even found opportunities for leisure after long, hard days. Here are Shichiro Kumasaka's memories of working at the St. Paul & Tacoma mill, as recorded in Kazuo Ito (1973, 404):

Tashiro Matsui from Shiga Prefecture was the bookman there, and under him fifty or sixty Japanese were working. I labored diligently, making nearly $3 a day for ten hours of work. Since we were young, sometimes we took overtime work and went as long as twenty hours without sleeping. I did all kinds of jobs, including slab-turning. Young Issei worked hard and sent their money back to Japan. There were some who sent as much as $70 a month home.

In the Japanese camp at St. Paul most men were wholesome workers and we played judo, tennis and baseball in our leisure time. Setsuzo Ohta, who held fifth *dan*[9] in Kodokan and was the uncle of Keisuke Yoshida (fourth *dan*), taught us judo. As for baseball, along with some Japanese students in Tacoma we organized the Taiyo Club. Among the players were Kiyoshi Kondo (later professor at University of Illinois), and Hitoshi Okada. We had frequent games with Nippon Club, the center for which was the Tacoma Buddhist Church. There was a tennis court in the camp and on Sundays and holidays the workers used to bat balls back and forth. In the sawmill we spent close to $30 for meals[10] so it was pretty good for the time—as good as having hamburgers for breakfast.

In his memoir, Clinton Butsuda also remembered his father's role in the sawmill, and the feeling associated with being there: "My father used to take me through the mill where he worked with its huge cross-cut saws, the gigantic band saws and the ear-splitting noise of the planer. It was very impressive. My father worked as a foreman and a lumber grader. He would grade the lumber #1-2-3-4 or S for scrap according to its quality as it came by on the conveyor and the men down the line stacked it on different piles according to the grade my father chalked on the boards" (1992, 4).

Physical, wage labor in industries such as lumber was a way to feed oneself and potentially a family as well. It was often grueling work, and because workers were segregated by race and national origin, those from Japan and China found themselves in the most difficult and typically lowest-paying positions. Yet Japanese immigrants did not necessarily stay in these positions. "In early days the Japanese saved their income mostly from labor. Gradually, independent enterprises helped to shape up [the] economy" (*History of Japanese of Tacoma* 1941). These independent enterprises were integral to Tacoma's history, shaping the downtown corridor and contributing to the vibrancy of the city's economy. Small businesses often did not require large amounts of capital to get started, took advantage of kin labor, and survived through "community cooperation," including the practice of *tanomoshi* (Bonacich and Modell 1980, 45–80). By 1925, Megan Asaka (2014, 128) argues, the number of Japanese in the lumber industry had declined, indicating that "lumbering had transformed from a critical source of income for those newly arrived from Japan to a stepping-stone out of manual labor and into independent business such as farming or hotel management" (see also Nomura 1992, 4). This movement to an ethnic economy provided greater independence as well as the ability to avoid discriminatory employers and coworkers.[11] Stories of moving from sawmills to entrepreneurialism highlight not only the fluidity of employment, but for those families that straddled the two, stories of entrepreneurialism also underscore the potential complementarity between wage work and self-employment, albeit often stratified by gender.[12]

FROM SAWMILLS TO SMALL BUSINESS:
GROWTH OF ENTREPRENEURIALISM AND
THE STRATEGIC DEPLOYMENT OF LABOR

Starting one's own business was a way to avoid some of the discrimination and racism the Japanese faced, such that by the early 1940s "small business was the predominant economic mode" for urban Japanese (Bonacich and Modell 1980, 39; Takaki 1998, 180). As Anon Male C explained, even his brother who had a university degree had trouble finding professional work. This made family businesses crucial sites of employment for many Nisei. "We just didn't go out and get the jobs, because we knew that we would be discriminated [against] and so most of us had our own businesses."

The growth of such urban ethnic economies across the west was "sudden and extensive." By 1910 "there were 3,000 establishments and 68,150 Japanese in the western states—a ratio of one business per twenty-two persons" (Takaki 1998, 186), while just before World War II over 40 percent of Issei operated their own businesses or farms, "an amazing economic achievement" for first-generation immigrants (Spickard 2009, 40). Between 1909 and 1929, Seattle experienced a 60 percent increase in the number of Japanese Americans running small businesses (Spickard 2009, 46). In 1941 in Los Angeles, 47 percent of males were listed as self-employed (Bonacich and Modell 1980, 39). Tacoma, too, saw a significant increase in businesses run by Japanese (including dental and medical practices serving the Japanese community),[13] from 63 in 1910 to at least 80 in 1917 (Morrison 1994, 40). By 1920, according to a list of Japanese businesses within the jurisdiction of the Tacoma Japanese Association, this number stood at 168,[14] and by 1940 *History of Japanese in Tacoma* (1941, n.p. [36]) listed 251 businesses, noting that those that "dealt with white people [had] gradually increased."

This "startling change . . . in the pattern of Issei employment" was accompanied by a significant change in "gender demographics" as women arrived and families were started (Spickard 2009, 40). As the transition occurred from single male to family life in the early 1900s, finding work that could support a family and in which women could participate became a priority. *History of Japanese in Tacoma* (1941, n.p. [32–36]) lists (with no specific dates) 54 grocery and markets, 24 hotels, 22 laundries, and 9 barbershops. None of the Nisei we interviewed spoke about their mothers being in domestic work, in contrast to San Francisco where more than 50 percent of all Japanese women engaged in such work (Glenn 1986, 6).

In some cases the small business was additional to the father's continued work in the sawmill. Straddling the lumber industry and the ethnic economy suggests that families made strategic decisions in deploying their labor, which were often gender- and generation-specific (see also chapter 4). Fumi Sato Hattori's father, for example, worked for the St. Paul & Tacoma Lumber Company, while her mother ran the Superior Hotel on the corner of Market and South 17th Streets, between the Methodist and Buddhist churches.[15] The family moved into the center of Tacoma later in Fumi's childhood.

> I guess my mother was probably more entrepreneurial than my father, and she saw a chance to lease a hotel, a small hotel downtown. And so, she ran the hotel, and my father worked in the sawmill. And that was really a life-saver, because there were four of us [children], and my father got killed, so she supported us until my brother went to college. I didn't get to go because I'm a girl. You know, in those days boys, it was more important that boys went to college. So, when I think of it now, I'm just amazed at how my mother did it. You know, four kids, sending them all through school, Sunday school, Japanese school, and she paid for all that. I don't know how. It was just a small hotel, I think 39 rooms or something.

While the death of Fumi's father was an unusual situation, mothers were often responsible not only for raising the children and managing the household, but also for running the family business.

Riyeko Fujimoto (b. 1924) also recalled her father first working for the St. Paul & Tacoma Lumber Company, though later in her childhood he also ran a hotel with her mother, the Vendome.[16]

> What I remember is, my dad worked in the lumber mill. And then we moved to Tacoma, I think right before I started school, and he ran a hotel . . . She [mother] helped with it. My dad still worked in the sawmill . . . In the next block there were a lot of shops there run by Japanese people. There were markets and there was a poultry farm. I mean not a farm, but where they sold eggs and chickens, and a meat market . . . a lot of food stands and vegetables.

Joe Kosai's family is another example of gendered deployment of labor between a father in the sawmill and a mother working at the hotel, the Grand, where the family also lived.[17] Joe's father worked the night shift and helped supply workers from Japan to the sawmills.

> There were a lot of weekly boarders [in the family hotel] because all the people that worked in the lumber industry, especially those who worked up in the mountains, would come in and then spend the week there or whatever. And so we had a couple people that were longtime friends of the family because they lived there. So, my mother ran the hotel. Probably her English was nil, just coming from Japan, but somehow she managed to run the hotel. And my father did work for the sawmill here in Tacoma.

Hiroko Betty Fukuhara Yoshioka (b. 1922) shared a similar story about her father first working for a mill before moving on to a new career. She also remembered that when her mother arrived in the US, she did not know how to cook, so "all the lumbermen had to teach her how to cook! . . . I'm not sure about the year [my father arrived], but I know my father was here first, and then he went back to Japan to get my mother. And he used to work in the lumber mill in Tacoma. And then after that he became a salesman, of stocks." Stories repeatedly emphasized family survival strategies, how gender impacted those decisions, and ways in which parents and children negotiated components of identity variously influenced by associations with Meiji Japan, work as immigrant laborers, and life as young Japanese American citizens.

The family histories of Fumi, Joe, Riyeko, and others emphasized the transition from early employment, often in the Tacoma sawmills—especially for men married and with children—to pursuing opportunities in small business when possible. The shift from the frontier to the family stage of immigration increased the diversity both of needs and of economic security solutions, including new businesses and the strategic deployment of family labor resources. John Modell's 1977 study of Los Angeles outlines an "evolution" of Japanese businesses between 1909 and 1928. The first phase is indicated by pre–family era investments in "billiard halls and express and forwarding companies." When more women arrived and families were started, the billiard halls in particular declined in number;

the following phases included tailor shops and barbershops, restaurants, and professional services, such as law offices, that "catered to the needs of the Japanese themselves." After the alien land laws were passed, making farming inherently less secure for the Issei, common businesses included florists, nurseries, and retail food outlets (Modell 1977, 100, 112–13).

Upon arriving in Seattle in 1906, Perry Yoshiaki Yano's (b. 1931) father started out farming. He then owned a pool hall with a friend, but "after he got married, he didn't," Perry explained. "He thought he should do something more, more respectable, I guess." His father worked on farms in Fife and the Puyallup Valley, including a chicken farm at which Perry's mother would help with the grading of the eggs. "He used to go and, on a truck, and sell vegetables, fruits and vegetables. And he did that for a while. And then, when I was around four or five, he bought, well, he rented a grocery store, and . . . so he did that, he did that for about four or five years. . . . Then the war started." While Perry's sister helped in the market, Perry remembered only that "[I'd] hang out. I remember I used to listen to the radio in the back of the store."

Ryo Munekata commented on the relationship between the kinds of businesses that families opened and the arrival of wives and mothers, reinforcing the image of a tightly concentrated community and the importance of Japanese businesses in shaping social relations.

> Now, Mr. [Jerry] Kikuchi's parents had a hotel . . . [on] Pacific Avenue, between 13th and 15th, right in the middle. And that hotel had an entrance to Commerce Street, and I think two or three doors south of that entrance was where Joe Kosai's parents had a hotel.[18] The convenience of having a hotel was, the wife does not have to leave the business premises to find employment. She could take care of the place while he even worked out[side], you see, one or the other. It was very easy, and I think that's why they ran hotels. And a lot of them did housework, whatever, or worked in markets, and so I begin to think that, "Oh, that's why they had hotels."

Small businesses, especially hotels and barbershops, were seen as places for women to contribute economically to the family. Mrs. Kubo and Mrs. Jinguji, Ryo distinctly remembered, both opened barbershops. "We had quite a few barbershops in Tacoma . . . and most . . . were run by women. And so when I was small, I thought barbers were all women! (*laughs*) There were a few men, but mainly women. But as far as the American community is concerned, it's men folks that run the barbershop." This division of labor also facilitated social relations among the women, Ryo explained: "Between—on Market Street—between 11th and 13th, that's where most of the markets were concentrated, and my mother would go there every day—clean up the [hotel] rooms, and after she's done her chores, she'd take off and go to the market. And an interesting thing—the ladies went shopping at the same time, and they'd get together at one of the stores and have a nice gossip session (*laughs*)."

Kazuo Horita's (b. 1921, known as Kaz) family's trajectory from sawmills to a market is another example of the transition to entrepreneurialism. His father, the youngest in his family and well educated "for the Japanese boys in that age," came to the US in 1906 with his older brother to help make money to send home to their family. Kazuo's father "came over here, worked in—and I'm not quite sure exactly how many years, but only a few years—in a sawmill. And then from there, he established his own produce market. He had that produce market for many years." Another Nisei woman (Anon Female B, b. 1933) told of her father transitioning from work at the sawmill to opening a laundry, where both he and his wife worked. "We lived in back of my parents' business."

Mitsuo Takasugi (b. 1928) was the second youngest in a family of four children. Both his father and his uncle arrived in 1905, working in a sawmill in Nanaimo, British Columbia—which suggests they worked with labor contractors and were sent there. Mitsuo's strongest memory was of the family restaurant in downtown Tacoma. Only later in life did he learn that his father and his father's older brother first worked in a sawmill.[19]

The earliest I remember, you know, my father had a restaurant on Broadway. What I remember was a Chinese restaurant,[20] but on that map that you showed me [Ito's map; see fig. I.5] it has a—he had a restaurant before that, which was a Japanese restaurant.[21] And what I remember is, we had a home on Fawcett Avenue . . . and we did okay, I think, in the time of the twenties, but then the Depression came on and things got very difficult, and my father's restaurant, you know, had to close during the Depression and so forth. Then, things got really hard . . . it was a very difficult time for him. He was a proud person, and, you know, he was Japanese, and he couldn't get, you know, any decent job or anything. So, he did what he could. Later on, I think he went to Alaska to work in those salmon canneries, and he worked out on the farm and things. Whatever he could find, he did. He also worked, I think, as a parking attendant in one place near the movie houses up there on 9th Street and near Broadway, someplace around there.

[In the restaurant], he hired a dozen Chinese cooks. Oh, the first one, I don't know. I wasn't around then, but the second one, the Chinese restaurant, he hired Chinese cooks to cook for him and he had the restaurant going. But I think, if you recall, in 1931 Japan invaded Manchuria, and . . . you know, I think the cooks quit because, you know, they didn't want to work for a Japanese at the time. And so he had to do his own cooking after that, I think.

Although World War I led to a production boom and the postwar period saw many technological advances, this period also had downward trends—and then the Depression hit. Emboldened workers across the US unionized and made demands of their employers. In Tacoma, labor unions started more direct organizing and negotiating, leading to strikes and violent clashes with police in 1934 and 1935 (Morgan 1982, 238–42; Gallacci and Karabaich 2006, 125–27). Despite some successes in organizing labor, this applied to only some workers, although the historical record does mention moments when Japanese workers were allowed into unions. For instance, *The History of Japanese in Tacoma* (1941, n.p. [41–42]) comments that the president of the Pacific National Lumber Company, one of the Tacoma-area mills, "took kindly to Japanese. He did not comply with demands of the Union and employed many Japanese. The Union was successful in ousting Japanese from sawmills in the area. On one occasion, when the Union recommended that Japanese join the Union, seeing the position and future of Japanese, he immediately recommended they join the Union, thereby avoided [*sic*] breakdown in relations." Along similar lines, Ronald Olson, in his 1928 survey of multiple mills in the Northwest, notes that Japanese were "allowed Union privileges" at the St. Paul & Tacoma Lumber Company, "but this is the only instance" (1928, 16).

Hanna Kae Nakagawa Torimaru (b. 1922) recalled clashes between workers and police on the streets of Tacoma. Her parents ran the State

Cafe, a small downtown restaurant many of whose customers were long-shoremen. She recounted:

> I have to tell you one thing, which I have never forgotten, or gotten over the pain. And that was, during the mid-thirties, there was a huge longshoreman strike, and of course curiosity got the best of me. I had to go and see where all of this rioting and all this mass hysteria was going on. And let me tell you, at that time, they were throwing, it looked like little grenades. That isn't what it was, but that's what it looked like to me, and actually I think they were tear gas, gas pellets, that each of them was throwing. The police and the military would be throwing, and then the longshoreman people would throw it back. And they found that didn't work. I mean, we were able to watch that demonstration there, and it's really—a mass hysteria is a frightening thing to observe. People are more like animals, they're not—emotion is so high. But finally, what they resorted to was, the police squad car, on their tail light—what, what do you call that thing that sticks out, the exhaust? The tear gas was there, exhaust. And so, they were going up and down the street, and of course I got caught in that. Wowie, to this day I could remember that tremendous pain, and in your eyes, it just blinded with tears. It's so severe. You wonder, but that's how, it's about the only time anybody's ever said they hardly believed me, because they didn't know they would do such a thing. And yet I know. I saw it. Also felt the . . . the pain."

ENTREPRENEURIALISM IN A CONCENTRATED DISTRICT

As noted above, Issei opened a disproportionate number of small businesses in Tacoma's downtown area. O'Brien and Fugita call growing up within an entrepreneurial ethnic economy in the early 1900s a "situational experience" that "had a powerful effect on the world view of the Nisei" (1982, 199; see also Fujimoto 1975). Economic relations; integration of industries, such as farming and produce markets; and reliance on family labor all shaped Nisei lives. As Bonacich and Modell observed, "somewhat less than half" of the Nisei they surveyed also "engaged in small businesses reminiscent of prewar arrangements" (1980, 5).

As noted in the introduction, Ryo Munekata provided a maplike description of the businesses in the core of Tacoma's Nihonmachi, particularly Broadway between 13th and 15th. His detailed reflections about the sites, the people who occupied them, and his sense of walking through those streets as a boy were remarkable. Here he continues:

Let's see, and next door to that [the Chinese Garden restaurant] was a Japanese confection store, and they also sold Japanese magazines and books. And next to that there was a family named Takahashi that ran a grocery store. And next to that was Rice Bowl—Chinese food place run by a Chinese family . . . And those stores were hitting a building on the corner of 15th and Broadway . . . [And then there was the] New Washington Hotel, and it was run by a family named Suyama. At the very corner, first floor, was another food stand, ice cream fountain, and in the back was a pool room run by a family named Obayashi, I think it was. And on the side that I lived, there were less, but I remember a drugstore on the corner, where we—as a child, we'd go there and buy something and the druggist would give us a piece of candy. And so then when we needed something from the drugstore, we always volunteered. (*laughs*) And then further down the street my father had his New Tacoma Hotel.

And then there were—there was a photographer, there was another barbershop, and next to that there was a tailor shop [owned] by the family of Nakata. Then farther down the street there was a family that had a gift shop. They also sold fishing tackle. And by gift, I mean not small gifts, but they were very elaborate and expensive gifts. And their names—the name was Mr. Niiyama. And then we go down the street . . . there was a market, another Chinese food restaurant, and then there was a shoe repair store that also sold new shoes. And the man's name was Mr. Kawai . . . And then at the corner was a dry goods store, and somewhere in between there, there was a Mr. Fukuyu, who had a weekly Japanese newspaper. That's this one block.

Ryo's own family had moved around the neighborhood several times, running hotels. Earlier his father, Tadajiro Munekata, had worked at the Union Laundry,[22] in an alley off South 15th Street between Market and Broadway, and he attended Central School to learn English. The family started at the Broadway Hotel, on Broadway between South 15th and 17th, where Ryo was born,[23] and then moved to the Traveler's Hotel shortly thereafter, "with the main entrance on Pacific Avenue between [South] 17th and 15th," followed by another move in 1927 to the New Tacoma Hotel, which was directly across the street from the current Murano Hotel on Broadway between South 13th and South 15th Streets. These hotels were home to the Nisei growing up in the city (see figure 2.2). "We did not have any residence," Ryo explained. "It was a hotel building, and my parents utilized a room for the kitchen, another room for living room quarters, and then each one of us had a bedroom—a room . . . And we were not the only ones that lived like that. Many other families lived in the hotel, that's the way they lived. Now, I always envied, when I looked upon some of my friends, where they lived in a home. And it was home to us, but not in the way an ordinary home is."

A study of Seattle's early Japanese immigrant community identified 183 hotels run by Issei (Miyamoto 1984), and they were not "the Hilton or the Ritz" (Spickard 2009, 50; see figure 2.2). As Roger Daniels (1992, 439) noted, the "idiosyncratic business for Seattle's Japanese was the operation of hotels catering to working class white men" (see also Sone 2014). Fumi Sato Hattori corroborated that Tacoma had many hotels run by Japanese families that also had white customers; she remembered specifically that many of the people who stayed at her mother's hotel were longtime customers:

> It was just my mother and the kids, and so we used to help at the hotel, although most of the people at the hotel were steady people. They were there for a long time. They were retired, or, you know, older people . . . no Japanese. Mostly Caucasians . . . They were real good to us. In fact, when we went to camp we needed boots, and I remember writing to this man who lived at the hotel, if he would send me a pair of boots. And so he bought them for me . . . He was really nice. They lived in the hotel for years.

The longtime residents often built strong relationships with the Japanese families running the business. Ryo described some of them as "just perpetual customers":

FIGURE 2.2. Pacific Hotel (owned by Ichitaro Kobayashi), 1340 Commerce Street, Tacoma, February 23, 1923. Photo by Marvin Boland, Courtesy of Washington State Historical Society.

There were people—I remember one Italian man who taught my mother how to cook spaghetti. (*laughs*) And there was another man— I don't know what nationality—he taught her how to make what they call "polenta" or something . . . They were part of the family. They even used our kitchen. In a hotel, you don't have a household thing, so one room was the kitchen. Another room was our so-called living room, where we studied, and the piano was in there, and everything. And then we had our individual bedrooms. The hotel had a large living—not living, but parlor area where the customers just sat down, and I recall Dad playing poker, rummy, with them.

Many of the hotels would work with transporters to bring customers from the train station. Ryo again:

Now, during the Depression years—early thirties—I remember Dad used to take his Chevrolet to the . . . train station on the other side of— just south of Puyallup Avenue, where all those frame structures are. I don't know what it was. I don't remember, but that was a terminal for that train that came from the east. And he'd take his car there and pick up these black porters. And if they wanted to stay at the hotel, the ride was free. If they wanted to go somewhere else and stay, they paid him the fare. And that's how he took in customers for the hotel.

Other businesses also served white customers, such as the produce markets and restaurants. The Kawano family (sisters Harue Kawano Ozaki and Teiko Kawano Peterson) ran a small grocery outside of the main downtown Nihonmachi. Around 1919 their parents moved from Seattle to Tacoma and opened "a mom-and-pop store at 213 North I Street" (near Tacoma's Wright Park). Both parents worked at the store "in an all-Caucasian neighborhood" Harue remembered, until their mother, Teruko Kawano, went to teach at the Japanese Language School in the afternoons.[24]

Many key businesses in addition to hotels and markets served the immigrant community, of course. Sister and brother Michie Taira Hori (b. 1926) and Junichi Taira (b. 1929) explained that after their father worked on the railroad and for a lumber company, he returned to Japan to be married, but the newlyweds then came back to Seattle, where their father worked in a tofu manufacturing company.[25] After Michie and Junichi were born, their parents decided to move to Tacoma. Their first residence was on 15th and Fawcett, but after the tofu business grew they moved to 1546½ Market Street. "I'll never forget that address!" Michie proclaimed. They lived above the shop. The customers were Chinese and Japanese business owners.

JUNICHI: Stores that sold tofu and—

MICHIE: Chinese restaurants. Because they're the only people—we were the only people that ate tofu in those days.

JUNICHI: In those days.

MICHIE: And he used to contract with—or they contracted my dad—to send tofu material, like *age* [deep-fried tofu] and stuff, to Portland I think, once or twice a month. And I don't know how they did this, but I know they used to go by train. (*laughs*)

JUNICHI: But he also did take tofu to the ships when they came in—the Japanese ships.

   [*Did you work in the shop and help with the business at all?*]

MICHIE: No. (*laughs*)

JUNICHI: Ate things that he had there.

MICHIE: Towards my teen years, early teen years, sometimes I used to help Mom a little bit in the store, but not *really* to help the customer.

JUNICHI: Yeah, it's not right, because I can recall turning over the *age* in the pan.

MICHIE: Really?

JUNICHI: Oh, yeah.

MICHIE: Wow . . .

JUNICHI: If you can call it helping. (*both laugh*)

In addition to hotels, small markets, restaurants, and Japanese-oriented businesses like tofu manufacturing, many Issei were involved with laundry and cleaning businesses. This was true for the Fujimoto family, whose three daughters, Kimiko, Tadaye, and Yoshiko, we interviewed. In 1918, their parents started Capital Dry Cleaners at 1124 Court C, between Market and Broadway, behind J. C. Penney's (figure 2.3). As the sisters recall:

KIMIKO: We had a wholesale dry cleaning plant. And we had a lot of Caucasian workers and Japanese workers, too.

   [*Did your mother work in the business?*]

KIMIKO: Well, some of the time.

TADAYE: Not when she was rearing us.

KIMIKO: When we were little, she was at home.

FIGURE 2.3. Mitsu Fujimoto with daughters Kimiko and Chiyeko Tadaye at Capital Cleaners, date unknown (likely late 1940s). Courtesy of Tanbara Family.

TADAYE: She said she used to push the buggy at home, you know, with her feet—and iron. I don't know how true it was. (*laughs*)

KIMIKO: . . . And see, in those days, all the smaller cleaners could not do their own cleaning. They had to send it to wholesale cleaning plant, and that's where—

TADAYE: . . . because it was flammable.

KIMIKO: Yes.

TADAYE: Petroleum.

KIMIKO: So there weren't too many wholesale cleaning plants in Tacoma. But my father's was one of them.

Because of business needs, their family always had a car—in fact, two cars, Tadaye reported: "One for the business and one for whenever dignitaries came to the Japanese School or to the church. Our car was always being used." Their mother also drove, which she noted was very unusual for women at the time.

Takeshi Osada's (b. 1927) family had a laundry business as well, but his mother also "had a barbershop of her own." Takeshi believed the business was called Great Northern Hand Laundry and was "where Jefferson and Market" came together (the family lived at the business location), while his mother's shop was on Commerce between 13th and 11th. The Osadas had a number of other relatives in Tacoma.[26] His grandparents lived just down the street from them at 1728 Fawcett—and after the war the family returned to Tacoma and purchased that very house. Takeshi remembered the man who lived in the house while they were incarcerated: "He was a Caucasian guy. He was a guy from Switzerland, I mean, a guy named Johnny. He lived there during the war and then when they came back he moved. . . . He used to come over to our house and he used to come for Sunday dinner . . . we knew him very well."

Like the Fujimotos, the Urushibata (surname later changed to Shibata) family also owned a car, but son Kunio remembered it with embarrassment, as his father used it for vegetable deliveries, like a "peddler." Kunio's father's first job in Tacoma was at the Grand Cafe.

> He worked there as a busboy when he first started, and this was during World War I. And the owner that owned [the cafe] made—it was during the wartime, so it made some money, and he wanted to go back to Japan—[he] asked my father if he wanted to buy it, so he said yes. So he bought it, and he was a good cook, I believe, but you know those places—if you know how to fry eggs: it was one of those restaurants.

During World War I, Kunio's father took the money he had made at the restaurant and returned to Japan to try to be a rice dealer. He was already married, and his wife and daughter had remained in Japan. Tragically, because of the coming Exclusion, his parents hurried back to the United States, but they had to leave their daughter behind. "[My mother] tried to beat the deadline," Kunio explained. "She had to leave my sister with the grandmother. And she regretted that for her all her life. She was always telling me about that."

When they returned to Tacoma, nothing was left.

> KUNIO: And by that time, all the profit, you know, I mean not the profit, but the business, you know, after the war—nothing. So the

next best thing he did was he—in fact a lot of people don't know about it, but he became a vegetable peddler. He had a Model T, and I think [on] 15th Street you'd buy vegetables, and later on he filled up the car and went to Dash Point and Tide Water and Brown's Point, and then through Wright Park. They had nice people. And Saturday in the summers I had to help him, and to me it was the most embarrassing job. I just dreaded it.

RYO: Oh, I don't think you should be embarrassed. That was one way of making a livelihood. And it was honest.

KUNIO: It's not—it's a clean job, but a vegetable peddler . . . I just kind of figured I didn't want to show it to my father, but I used to go late in the morning, you know, then just go over there. But every time I went through the town, you know, I put my head down like that. (*ducks his head down*) Nobody could see me. (*laughs*)

RYO: I recall a number of Japanese men that took their trucks and drove down the street to sell their vegetables and fruit.

KUNIO: He had a Model T and that made it worse. Going up the hill—19th— the steam is coming . . . (*laughs*) Them were the days! But then his friend, who was also a peddler, sold him a Model A, and he was so proud of that. So I thought, well, it wasn't too bad, the Model A wasn't . . . but I still had my head down when I rode on Fawcett Avenue.

As noted above, Kunio's original family name was Urushibata, but he changed it to Shibata.

It's a real long name, and the reason why I changed it was, my father was always using Shibata. He was in business, but [customers] couldn't pronounce my last name. And so I was still Urushibata until about 1958, I believe, but we started the business, and . . . —I mean, we had a garage and everything, but they, you know a lot of the time . . . on the telephone, they'll say, "Ooh, er, er." I'm on video, so I can't tell you what they said. (*laughs*)

His father agreed to change their name because Shibata is what they were using with customers, but Kunio was sorry he had made the legal change.

I'm sorry I did, because I lost identity. [Urushibata] is a very unusual name. In Tacoma, that was the only name, and when I was in Tule Camp, there wasn't another—there wasn't any. But at Heart Mountain they did have one family we didn't know. And when I was stationed in Japan, in Tokyo, they never heard that name. So it's a rare name.

[*But Shibata is not so unusual.*]

That's why. It's just like Brown or Jones. I lost identity.

Kunio also explained that as the oldest son he had the responsibility to care for the family and thus could not pursue his dream of becoming an electrical engineer.

I could not afford to go to the University of Washington. I was the old-est. Again, my father was old-fashioned . . . He's the head of the family, but I'm the oldest, and if we are rich or have money, I'll get everything—the house—but if you're poor, you have to kind of carry the burden. Quite a burden. And I'm from a big family . . . where you know, *oyakoko* [filial piety] means the family, the head of the family. So I had to quit school. I did go to technical school in Minneapolis. And I studied while I was in camp—engineering. But finally I had to quit . . . because I had the younger brother and a younger sister, and another two sisters. They were still going to junior high school and grade school. So I quit.

Kunio and Ryo reflected on the differences between their families. "See," Kunio said, "you have two classes of people. His [Ryo's] father believed in his son's education, and it was very—he was a kind of a—even a leadership in the Japanese community. My father made money all the time, but he didn't invest like his [Ryo's] father did." Such stories typify many of the identity negotiations, compromises, and exchanges Nisei sus-tained to make a life in Tacoma. Kunio's own frustrations with working as a "peddler" reflected a widespread sentiment among Nisei who felt stuck in the lower levels of the ethnic economy as, for instance, a "profes-sional carrot washer" (Modell 1968, 203). Moreover, the literature has often overlooked class differences among Japanese families, what Kurashige (2002, 7) explains as a "deep, historically precedented class cleavage within the ethnic community" that was a combination of economic and cultural capital (see also Kitano 1969).

As in Kunio's and Ryo's reflections above, social class was a complex intermixing of economic, cultural, and social capital (Bourdieu 1984). This is borne out, too, in Hanna Kae Nakagawa Torimaru's recollections about her mother. Recall that Hanna's parents ran the State Cafe. Yet her mother's great-grandfather had been a physician to the emperor, and other family members had been employed by the Japanese imperial household. Her mother, Hanna said, "had this highfalutin' idea that the majority of the Japanese that came here were illiterate and they were farmers . . . She graduated high school . . . and this was why I never went to the Japanese school, because she was afraid I would pick up the Japanese language [that] was commonly used by them."

Harue Kawano Ozaki's mother also had a prominent background, suggesting complex class and social distinctions among the immigrants:

[She] came from a very proud background in which the mother doted on her, and the father too. And they were one of the town leaders . . . And my mother was like a spoiled woman, a little spoiled girl, according to Mama. And the whole village used to brag so much about my mother that she was sort of elevated like a village princess. So we always called her Princess.

Harue explained that her mother's parents died when her mother was young, so her auntie and uncle raised her and her siblings. They insisted on educating them all.

Oh, she knew how to play the shamisen [or samisen: a Japanese three-stringed guitar-like instrument]. You know, this auntie of hers and uncle had her pursue as a young person to play the okoto [a harp-like stringed instrument] and the shamisen and saw to it that she had all the follow-ups of all the opportunities a young lady could have. And Mama loved all that, fortunately, so she incorporated that in her career as a Japanese language teacher. And that's how the students remember her, and give my mother almost too much credit, I think.

Sadly, Riyeko Fujimoto's mother passed away in 1933 when Riyeko was only ten years old, and her father then sold the Vendome Hotel. He moved with his two children next door to an apartment in another hotel. She remembered that she and her brother "looked after ourselves" and also that "Mrs. Murayama kind of looked after us." Her father's salary from the mill was barely enough to get by on. Riyeko talked a bit about the differences between families and mentioned that someone would come to the house to collect the tuition for the Japanese Language School.

> Now it's open for families to talk about their finances and everything, but I don't know if they ever talked about finances. You just knew . . . I don't know if it was because they couldn't afford it or what, but there were families that didn't send their kids to Japanese school. And then I knew that, after we moved to Tacoma, this family that lived next door to us on Market Street, the father killed all his children, and he died, too. I guess it was because of financial worries. I wouldn't know.

Riyeko had one clear memory of going to see Japanese movies with friends and her father's reaction, his feeling that shame had come to the family.

> They didn't have them [Japanese films] in the theaters, and so somebody would bring them around. And so all I remember is they used to have them at the Buddhist church, and it was understood that you pay whatever you can, or I don't know if there was any set fee for attending it—but I remember that one time my father didn't go . . . so I went to see the movie with a group of girls, and when my father found out, he got mad, because he said he didn't pay anything for it. I said, "Oh, well, it was just me and some girls." He said, "That doesn't make any difference." He'd have to pay something. So anyway, he made a contribution or something like that.

These young Nisei navigated the complexities of social status distinctions, economic capacity of families, and norms that insisted they bring no shame to the family.

Another prominent family in Tacoma was Jack Kazuo Hata's (b. 1921). His father worked in the photography industry and acted as the photographer for the Japanese community in Tacoma, and his mother was a teacher at the Japanese Language School. Jack told the story of how his parents met: "Well, he was a conscript in the [Japanese] army, and my mother used to teach school, and she would be walking down this country road and I guess the barracks were close by and I guess Dad saw her. I guess that's how they met. (*laughs*) That's what I heard from my cousin." Jack's grandfather was a doctor and hoped his eldest son would go to medical school, but he refused. Jack's father, as the second son, was asked to go, but he refused as well. "So the third son finally consented and became a doctor." Jack continued his parents' story: "After his [military] service was over, I guess he decided he wanted to come to the United States . . . My mother used to complain that right after they got married he decided to come to the United States, so my mother used to complain that he left her for six years (*laughs*)."

The Hata family lived across the street from the Buddhist Church at 1722 Fawcett Avenue. Jack, an only child, was born in 1921. Jack's father "was a photographer. He had a photo studio for a while, and then he went to work for a portrait studio called Robert M. Smith studio. I guess it was the best studio in Tacoma and it was a few doors down from Winthrop Hotel. So that would be on Broadway, I think. . . . He was a photo finisher—did all the printing, developing, retouching." He also photographed Tacoma's Japanese community, taking "all the group pictures—the weddings, the funerals, et cetera." Jack thought his father studied photography in Portland and then headed to Tacoma. His mother was home with him when he was little, but after he started first grade she began teaching at the TJLS. "She was there for probably around fifteen years, until the war started," Jack remembered.

Jack's father also was known for his garden:

Well, that was his first love. In Tacoma he entered a contest, a show, and got first award. He used to grow flowers that were this big—beautiful flowers—but he was so meticulous. Every night he'd go out with a flashlight to pick worms off the flowers. And he would line these flowers, and they were just perfectly straight all the way across. And also he loved classical music. When he was listening to the radio . . . I couldn't even drop a pin. He was so fussy. And when we lived in Denver [right after the war] and he worked at this studio downtown, he'd go to the main library in Denver, right downtown, and he took out every album the Denver library had, twice over, just to listen to the music. He loved classical that much. Being born in

Japan, born and raised there, you'd think he'd be more interested in Japanese classics, but it was European classics for him. I think he was probably reincarnated as European. He loved the heavy classics.

SUPPLEMENTING INCOMES

The majority of the stories we heard about families and economic survival were urban-based, whether in the downtown core, the tideflats, or along South Tacoma Way. A number of Tacoma Nisei also remembered working on farms in the summer to make extra money. This is noteworthy not only in itself, but also because Japanese contributions to agriculture in western Washington "may have been greater" than to early industrialization (Fiset 2009, 17); indeed, in the 1920s "Japanese supplied 75% of the region's vegetables and most of its berries and small fruits" and half of "Seattle's milk supply" (Nomura 1989, 124).[27] In order to make ends meet, families sent children to work at other Japanese businesses during the summers, furthering the argument that the ethnic economy reinforced community relationships as well as the potential exploitation of family through low-paid labor and a "middleman" economic form. A survey of agricultural assets owned by Japanese families in 1920 showed that in Pierce, Thurston, and Mason Counties, Japanese families were farming a variety of crops.[28] Ronald Magden notes that by the 1910s "Japanese, who were mostly from Hiroshima, and Kumamoto, farmed 2,000 [Puyallup tribe] reservation acres. Wives kept house, cooked meals, and worked long days in the fields" (1998, 37). The Fife area and Puyallup Valley were important areas for agricultural production, where many Japanese farmed small acreages that they rented from members of the Puyallup tribe, growing vegetables and berries.[29] Similarly, in the Los Angeles region Japanese farmers had "near monopolies . . . in the markets for lettuce, berries, celery, and tomatoes" (Kurashige 2002, 18), based on vertical integration from farming to customer sales.

Takao Jerry Kikuchi (b. 1922) was one who did summer work to help make money for the family. He grew up on Commerce Street between 13th and 15th, near the Munekata family's hotel and next door to the Kosai family. "When I was a kid . . . my parents were poor; they're struggling for their life. So it was a hardship. I grew up in hardship." Jerry remembered working on a farm in the Puyallup Valley "so that we can make some money for when the school started. We can buy our own clothes." He pulled weeds, hoed the fields, and picked strawberries and raspberries. "I did it with my older brother, just the two of us. We lived there for the summer. We cooked our own food . . . we were still maybe about twelve years old, twelve, thirteen, or fourteen." Jerry was deeply affected by his childhood financial situation. "When I was growing up, I felt that in my heart, too. My friends used to go to the grocery store and they used to have money in their pocket, but for me, I never had spare money in my pocket. It was a very tough, tough life. I used to envy all my friends with so much money in their pockets. Yes, I used to envy them . . . my parents were poor, just barely making a living." Many families experienced financial strain, especially during the Great Depression. These powerful memories reinforced lessons of sacrifice for the Nisei children.

Even during the school year, some children worked for markets and businesses in town (all within the extended Japanese community). Ryo Munekata recalled:

> Mr. [Kaz] Horita's father had a market, too. He had two locations, and I worked at their market. But there was a concentration of markets, so it was an everyday thing. There was no big refrigerator, so . . . the ladies went there every day to shop for their groceries and fresh food . . . If we worked, we worked on the Saturday mornings [during high school] . . . Since I lived so close to the market, I would be there by around seven o'clock in the morning, and I'd work, and Mr. Horita used to give us lunch. And there was a market cafe close, between, 9th and 11th Avenue on Market, and we'd have our lunch, and it's billed to Mr. Horita, and then we'd work until around seven or eight o'clock at night because we had to stay to clean up the place. Because once the market is closing, we'd have to haul all that vegetable into the cooler.
>
> [*Would you keep that money for yourself, or would you give it to the family?*]
>
> . . . It was something like $1.50. I don't even remember what I did with the money. (*laughs*)

Yet even someone like Ryo, who told stories of being well behaved in front of the elders in the community, was known to stand his ground. "I remember one year when Tacoma was having their—I don't recall—fiftieth State of Washington anniversary, and they were very busy and they wanted me to stay late to work, and I revolted. I said, 'No, I'm not going to.' And I went home (*laughs*)." Issei worked hard to maintain discipline and influence, but clearly there were limits.

WORK, FAMILY, AND THE EMBODIMENT OF *SHUSHIN*

Our interviewees made it clear that their Issei parents were often just scraping by, and sometimes even working several jobs to make ends meet. As entrepreneurs of small businesses, they were not rich—which for Chizu Tomita Takaoka (b. 1920) explained why they lived in a concentrated area: "Because we were the lowest rung of economic immigrants. So that's where it was. I mean, everybody was trying hard."

The Depression was particularly difficult for some families. Indeed, as Mitsuo Takasugi put it, "The Depression never really ended for us, because we were evacuated off the coast and then we went into the camps." The daily lives of the Issei were also reflected in many of the lessons taught at the Japanese Language School, such as those having to do with hard work and discipline. Mitsuo's father did whatever jobs he could find, while his mother

> went to work for this oyster company, opening oysters (*demonstrates scooping*), you know, where you get paid so much a gallon for the oysters. That was pretty hard work, I think, but at least it was a way to survive. Then [in the late 1930s] we used to go out in the summertime to work, you know, picking berries and peas and so forth out in the country . . . My younger brother and I were too young, we didn't hardly do any work, but my older brother and sister, they worked quite hard, and I think they just contributed to the family.

His sister would also work at a friend's grocery store, and his brother helped park cars while still in junior high school.

The three Fujimoto sisters also commented on economic differences, as well as how their behavior lessons were internalized, reflected in a lack of delinquency among the Japanese. Later in life they learned how their parents stepped in to help others in the community. Kimiko explained:

You know, I did a study when I went to UPS[30] and I went to interview social workers and all that, and there's not a record of delinquency reported among the Japanese.[31] This was before the war. I don't know about now. And then no families ever asked for aid through welfare. From what we understand—and now, our folks never talked about those things, but if a family was in desperate need of help, the community would give them money so they would go back to Japan. Because if they go back to Japan, there's always relatives there, you know, to help them, so nobody went on welfare. But then after the war—because everything was gone, you know, when they came back—some of them had to go on welfare. But before the war, and I think that was partly because of the way our Japanese community, through our Japanese school, our church, were united to help each other . . . And that was very—I was very happy to hear that.

And then my sister remembers seeing a girl wearing the same kind of dress that she used to wear. She came home and told my mother that it was very unusual to see this girl wearing the same dress that she used to wear. And my mother said, "She must have bought it at the same store." She never told us. She never told us who we helped or who we didn't help or all that, you know.

Yoshiko explained, "Our folks used to fill a bag full of food and they didn't say who it was from. They would just leave it on the porch for them." Not bringing shame to one's own family or another family in need remained a critical principle for both Issei and Nisei (see chapters 5 and 6).

All these experiences shaped the Nisei's understanding of themselves in the world. Time and again, hard work and sacrifice were a part of their stories of their Issei parents' remarkable transitions from livelihoods centered on physical labor to entrepreneurial activity. These businesses helped to create a vibrant local economy, enhancing the overall development of prewar Tacoma, as in other immigrant communities all along the West Coast. Many of the small-scale enterprises required little capital to start, relied on resource pooling within the ethnic enclave, and used low-paid kin to keep prices low. These practices not only sustained the businesses, but also reinforced community bonds, despite the spatial dispersal of the businesses (e.g., along the highway in South Tacoma; see chapter 4) and social and class differences among the Japanese immigrants themselves. Yet much of this history—from the built environment to the details of daily lives—was rendered invisible with wartime incarceration and the dispersal of Tacoma's Japanese across the country after the war.

CHAPTER THREE

Japanese American Urban Lives

Spatial Stories of a Close Community

The very process of remembering grows out of spatial metaphors of connection and topography. To remember, says Umberto Eco, is like constructing and then travelling again through a space.

—MICHAEL HEBBERT, "THE STREET AS LOCUS OF COLLECTIVE MEMORY"

THE NISEI NARRATIVES WE HEARD IN OUR INTERVIEWS, AS MEMO-ries of childhood from old age, are spatial stories—experiences of walking from one place to another, trudging up hills in the snow, sledding down hills in the snow, walking to and from the language school, and references to businesses, shops, and hotels on Broadway and 13th, family homes along Fawcett Avenue, or markets along the highway in South Tacoma (see chapter 4). It was on these streets, through these spaces, and in the buildings of prewar Tacoma—most of which are now nonexistent or bear little to no mark of their pre–World War II inhabitants—that communities were formed, children grew to understand their place in the world, and negotiations over identity and belonging were experienced. These were spaces in which the combined processes of self-segregation and overt discrimination were central to the constitution of Nisei iden-tity. "You can't separate the two," as Mitsuo Takasugi noted. The Tacoma

Japanese Language School sat in this matrix, and thus in an ambiguous position as both identifiably different from the rest of the local urban world and a safe and familiar space. And yet the daily intersection of Nisei at the TJLS concretized its role in bringing the community together and enhancing what many interviewees identified as a special closeness in Tacoma. Personal as well as collective memories and identities are often rooted in spatial stories. These stories also traverse, avoid, or engage various forms of power, underscoring the fact that becoming Nisei was processual, ongoing, and situated in prevailing power relations. The urban spaces of prewar Tacoma, in other words, are important parts of the Nisei story, essential components of the contested process of subject formation.

Even as becoming Nisei was spatial, the production of the city itself was also a social process. The interview narratives provide evidence about the "intertwining" of subject formation and spatiality, people-making and place-making, with space understood both as a product of social relations and as productive of those relations. In short, spatiality and subjectivity are *mutually constituted* (Hoffman 2003; Merrill and Hoffman 2015). By examining this intertwining, we may better understand the ways in which Nisei children regularly negotiated multiple positionalities. Their daily paths moved through American public schools, public city streets, home life, parents' working worlds, Japanese school, playground fun, and religious institutions, and in most of these spaces the influence of Japan was felt, either subtly or explicitly. There were, for example, the commemorative events held at the TJLS, such as New Year's celebrations. There were visits to Tacoma by Japanese naval vessels, by Japanese dignitaries and relatives. Some children returned to Japan with their families for visits. Aspects of Meiji Japan, such as ethics (*shushin*) lessons, infiltrated their lives, especially in home spaces and at the TJLS. Negotiations over belonging thus impacted these varied positionalities and emerged in spatial ways, including development of a segregated and concentrated Japanese area. Engaging the spatiality of becoming Nisei, then, helps us push beyond more commonplace descriptions of Nisei as experiencing a "lack of fit" between two singular, static locations of "American" and "Japanese." Spatial stories additionally illustrate the active agency of Nisei children in bridging multiple, often contested, positions.

Yet even as we recognize their agency, it is essential to account for the structural racism that constrained the Issei and Nisei. Like other immigrant communities in urban America, Tacoma's racial-ethnic enclave of Japanese families emerged in relation to discriminatory property and citizenship laws, such as the prohibition against Issei purchasing land. Anti-Asian restrictions, generalized exclusion by whites of many backgrounds, as well as cultural affinities that led to self-segregation shaped the spatiality of Tacoma's Nihonmachi and the city more broadly. In Tacoma, the vast majority of Japanese families and businesses were located in a focused area in downtown Tacoma,[1] although as we explain in the next chapter, there also were significant outposts of Japanese families on the tideflats and along the highway in South Tacoma. Due to this centralized, physical concentration, the existence of structural racism, and the reality that few families owned cars, young Nisei experienced a *walking-scale life*. The streets of the city, then, were especially important spaces—spaces where they could make claims on belonging, albeit claims that were forced to be temporary in the context of alien land laws and a segregated urban world.

A "CLOSE" COMMUNITY

Living in a community large enough to feel like there were many Japanese children to play with, but small enough that they knew many of the families, led to descriptions of Tacoma as a particularly "close" community. A number of interviewees cited the existence of the single secular language school in this characterization, while others talked about living in a district separate from the rest of the city, with its walking-scale, neighborhood-oriented daily life. It is worth noting, in this regard, the connections between population size and the lack of other large ethnic groups living nearby. Kazuo Horita described Tacoma as feeling like a family. After he married a Nisei who grew up in San Francisco, his new mother-in-law asked, "How come you Tacoma people are so close together?" Kazuo explained how he first started to recognize and articulate this closeness, after the war when the Tacoma Nisei were having reunions:

> At one of the reunions I made a presentation or a speech, which in fact was taped, but what I said was, you know, it's great that we're here and all that, but one of the reasons why we are here, I think, is that we— our population wasn't that big; we had knowledge of, even [if] only by

name, of all the families around there, and for, for a reunion, all of a sudden we became a family . . . so that when we said, "We're going to have a reunion," all of a sudden the family was going to be together. Now, contrast that to the other community that I know pretty well, which is Seattle. Seattle can't have a reunion or . . . because, well, why? Because there are groups. In Seattle, there are groups, because they're so big.[2] Eight thousand people, you obviously have groups . . . Now, in Seattle, if one little group says, "We're going to have a reunion,"—well, the people there belong to such-and-such a church or something like that—I think you can accomplish it. But they can't accomplish a big one. Tacoma can . . .

I had many people that came up to me, "Kaz, you're so right. By gosh, we're a family." That's back where we had our first reunion in 1977, the fellow who's the editor of the *Pacific Citizen*, which is the newspaper for the JACL [Japanese American Citizens League], he says, "Kaz"—Harry Honda, is his name. But Harry told me, "Kaz, Tacoma was one of the first cities to have a reunion. In fact, if not the first, I think there's some small communities ahead of you," but we were really the first, you know, fairly major group to have a reunion. And Harry said, "Kaz, why don't you write something about that reunion?"

In that *Pacific Citizen* article, titled "Tacoma Reunion—One Man's View," Kazuo wrote that the reunion

was the start of an abrupt journey into the pre–World War II years. "Hi, remember me?" . . . "Boy, he sure looks just like his father did." . . . "What's happened during these 35 years?" . . . "I thought he was planning to be a minister!" . . . "Can't believe he's a teacher now, he sure gave the teachers a hard time in his youth." . . . "She really looks great, hasn't hardly aged." . . . "My apologies for the bad time I gave you, you know boys teasing girls." . . . "You were such a naughty boy then." There were just so many reminiscent remarks and quick impressions. It was "magic."[3] (Horita 1977, 3)

Comparisons with other cities came up with other interviewees as well, as Nisei reflected on what was distinct about growing up in the smaller, concentrated, more walking-scale Nihonmachi in Tacoma. Some of the comparisons produced stereotypes. Taeko Hoshiwara Taniguchi (b. 1924), for example, said that during their wartime incarceration, the boys from Hawaii were known to be "wild."[14] "Well the funny thing is that, *ano*, the Hawaii boys weren't very . . . well, [they were] kind of wild, you see. So we kept away from them, you know, walked around them. And then when we got to know them, they were really good peop—, I shouldn't say good, but they were very friendly people . . . So we just kept them away, you know, us girls (*laughs*)." Taeko also noticed that in camp, compared to Japanese from other parts of the West Coast, those from Tacoma could speak Japanese pretty well, illustrating the significance of the language school in their lives.

The three Fujimoto sisters also contrasted what they learned about other, larger cities with their experience in Tacoma.

> KIMIKO: I always felt that we were one of the lucky ones, because our community was so united, and we all knew each other and we helped each other. Whereas in California, and even in Seattle, the population of the Japanese was so much larger, that they didn't have that privilege of being united, I don't think. I think we were lucky.
>
> TADAYE: Like they say, it's only Tacoma that could have those big reunions, Japanese reunions . . . Because we're so close-knit. We knew everybody . . . And I thought every Japanese was good. When I went into camp and saw some of them, I thought, "Wow." (*laughs*) They had different kinds, too!

Ryo Munekata, too, thought Tacoma's community was closer than in other cities along the West Coast. "Yes, Tacoma is . . . of course, like I say, there's a few of us left that still remember Tacoma. And I think it was a small community. So it's not like growing up in Los Angeles. It's different when I hear about Los Angeles people getting together, a certain area—district—of Los Angeles getting together, but I get the feeling their reunions are not great like ours. There seems to be a difference."

The three Fujimoto sisters also connected the difference directly with having only one language school in Tacoma.

YOSHIKO: Well, I have heard—my husband is from Sacramento—and I know he says the Baptist school, the Episcopal school, the Methodist school. So they had separate schools.

TADAYE: Oh, Japanese schools?

YOSHIKO: Uh-hmm.

TADAYE: Oh. Well, they had a bigger community, you know.

KIMIKO: Bigger population. We would never be able to have two schools. There weren't enough students . . .

TADAYE: The Methodist school tried to start a Japanese school, but it didn't work out.

KIMIKO: Well, and the way I understood it the community was opposed to that because it would separate into two groups . . . there weren't enough students. It's better to be in one group and do it well, you know . . . There weren't that many subgroups. There's some. A few families went to—what kind of church is that? I don't know the name of the church, but there were certain families that went to a small church, you know, but they all came to Japanese school.[5] So that was the big group, and most of the people in Tacoma were Buddhist, so that was another large group. And Methodists, what would you say, about a third maybe? Not even a third went to Methodist church.

NAVIGATING THE CITY ON FOOT

Though a significant urban community, Tacoma attracted distinctly fewer Issei than cities such as Seattle, San Francisco, or Los Angeles. The physical concentration of the majority of the Japanese community, along with the economic reality that few families owned cars, meant young Nisei traversed their social world on foot or via public transportation.

As walkers, the Nisei children helped to "write" the city in a way that did not necessarily follow official mappings, but instead illustrated "a *migrational*, or metaphorical, city" (de Certeau 1984, 93, emphasis in original; see map 3.1). "Pedestrian movements" and "their intertwined paths," in other words, "give their shape to spaces" (de Certeau 1984, 97). At the same time, the young Nisei's own sense of self was built up in these

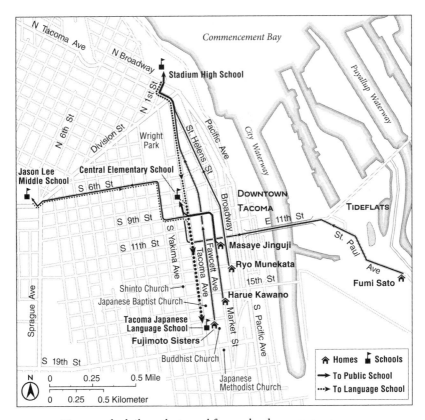

MAP 3.1. Five sample daily paths to and from school, ca. 1920–40

spatial practices. Walking to and from the TJLS after public school, for instance, reinforced both the Nisei's separation from the other children and their identities as Japanese. Taeko remembered, "We just walked and walked and walked." The streets between home and school were playgrounds for the Nisei children, filled with memories of sledding on snowy days, getting into mischief en route to see friends, bowing to members of the older generation, and walking to movie theaters to see a show. These memories underscore that identity formation is "a process rather than an essence" (Harmon 1998, 3), part of ongoing and dynamic spatial and social relations. These everyday movements, then, are not simply memories of childhood, but may be opportunities to reconstitute the self in the face of urban landscapes that no longer exist.

Joe Kosai remembered "roaming" the streets and walking on his own to see movies in the theater. These kinds of memories reflect a sense of belonging and legitimacy in the city.

> Being a kid, you know . . . there used to be two movie theaters on Pacific Avenue—Shell and Cameo, if I remember right. And they used to have Hopalong Cassidy and Roy Rogers. They used to have Flash Gordon movies. And so a lot of times I used to go to the movies by myself. In those days we didn't worry about, you know, what's going on today, where we have to be careful about the youngsters going off by themselves.. . . . And so I roamed the streets of downtown Tacoma. And there was a place on 15th and Commerce on the southwest corner of that intersection. There was a vacant lot, and we played a lot in that vacant lot. In fact, it was vacant until recently. I think they started with the building of the Convention Center. But they never developed that particular corner. That was kind of interesting.

Many of the interviewees commented about traveling between home, public school, and Japanese school. Riyeko Fujimoto recalled taking the streetcar to school and always walking home from school.

> I remember walking home with Sachi Munekata—you know, Ryo's sister? And I didn't know it at that time, but I talked all the way home. And she didn't say a word, and she told me at the end, she said that I had talked all the way home, and she didn't say a word! (*laughs*) I can even remember thinking, "Gee, did I talk that much?" I don't know what I talked about!

Yuriko Lily Korin Harada also told stories of walking to and from school.

> I don't remember at all first grade, second grade. I really don't. All I remember is walking to the school, and Central School had a great big clock, a clock tower . . . I would look at the clock and walk, walk, walk, walk, and the sidewalks would be filled with autumn leaves, and I would have to step on it to go. You know how rain would make them messy? I don't think I really enjoyed that too much, but I hurried on.[6]

"We walked every place because we didn't have cars until the early thirties. And all those hills!" exclaimed Hanna Kae Nakagawa Torimaru. Chizu Tomita Takaoka also recalled trying to walk up the hill to McCarver School in the snow:

> Now I remember a couple of times, you know we, from Market Street, Fawcett, Tacoma Avenue, G Street, J Street—well it was five blocks straight up, and when it snowed, it did a couple of times, we'd take a step and come back, step, and we were all late! I think we had two times, I think it was like that, because you know, in Tacoma it didn't snow like that time. But I remember that. Gosh, we were lined up in the office and we were all late. (*laughs*) . . . And then I remember walking on Fawcett Street. You know there's a horse chestnut, and we used to kick the leaves. And then . . . fog used to be so thick in November, you could hardly see . . . (*holds hand out in front of her face*) I used to love that.

Ryo Munekata had distinct memories of walking on the streets of Nihonmachi and being aware of others around him, who were also watching him. The disciplinary eyes of the older generation on those streets shaped his behavior and his understanding of who he was in the world. He provided a lively overview:

> I remember, you know, we'd go to the public schools—classes start anywhere around eight-thirty, and they would finish around three o'clock. And then between three and four we either had to go home and then go to the language school, or we went directly. And if we did go home, we'd find time to pick up something to munch on. And you'd pick it up, and then start walking to school, and whatever you had in your hand, you're eating it, and I well remember our teacher saying, "It's not proper to be *standing*, let alone *walking*, to be eating food." And so sometimes we'd cheat and we'd put something in our mouth, and walking the street, you'd try not to move your jaws. (*laughs*)
> And when I think of that, like I mentioned, about 13th to 15th and the merchants, the owner of the business would be standing right there in the store, and they would be looking out, and as we walked the street, you see them, and they know you, and I know them. You

must bow your head and acknowledge. You just couldn't walk by without acknowledging each other. So when I went to California, it was nothing for the people of California to walk and see another Japanese American person and not bow, because they're really strangers. But I grew up in a community where we knew each other, so invariably we would bow and acknowledge. And so to me, it was strange when they could not acknowledge each other.

These disciplinary eyes and living in an area that was predominantly Japanese produced a closeness that was normalizing. The main corridor of Japanese businesses, Ryo noted, was "solidly" Japanese:

We were very close, so close to the point where we knew the good things and the bad things of all the families and we all shared our life. I always like to relate my one personal experience, helping at the church in the Sunday School Department. We went to eat out, went to a restaurant to eat. And there was another teacher that lived in the neighborhood, so we walked to this restaurant together up on St. Helens, and after eating we walked back together. Next morning the rumor is all over town saying, "Oh, Munekata is going out with this girl." (*laughs*) You see, that is the kind of neighborhood we grew up in.

Thus, along with wider experiences of discrimination, the Nisei were subject to behavioral expectations from the Issei on a micro level, the watchful eyes of community and parents over everyday activities and responsibilities.

Fumi Sato Hattori also reflected on her movement to and from school and the TJLS (see map 3.1), as well as on a sense of belonging:

Elementary school, don't know, I can't really remember how we got there. I remember when we went to high school we took a streetcar. But then we'd go to Japanese school afterwards. And I knew my girlfriend who lived in town, she and I would walk to her house, and her mother would have baked yams on those stoves, you know, and we would have that and then go out to Japanese school . . . Her name is Yone Nakako . . . And so, we had a good time. We used to sing "Danny Boy" on the way home from high school. (*laughs*) Anyway, so

I think we had a pretty happy childhood. We didn't feel particularly—we didn't really associate too much with Caucasian kids. It just so happened that most of the Japanese lived on one end of town. When we went to high school, we went to Stadium, which is in this end of town [near Nihonmachi]. They sent the boys to Lincoln High School for more work-related kinds of things, drafting and that kind of stuff. They sent the boys over there, and the girls went over here. Except a few, like I think Ryo went to Stadium, and there were a couple of other boys. But most of them went to Lincoln.

Mitsuo Takasugi remembered the children walking together from public school (Central) directly to the language school. "There was no sense in stopping [at home] because there was nobody there. Both of our parents were probably working or doing something like that, so we. . . all walked along Tacoma Avenue, straight from Central School to the Japanese School." The walking-scale character of life—the result of both necessity and the concentrated nature of much of their everyday activities—shaped individual identities, the Japanese community overall, and the human geography of the city.

While walking was the prominent means of travel for the Nisei, some children did take the streetcar. Katsuko Aochi Harano remembered catching the streetcar at "that end of Tacoma Avenue where the funeral parlor was, St. Helen's . . . We'd run up there—it's only about a quarter of a block—but the conductor would always wait for us to make sure we got to school on time." Teiko Kawano Peterson also remembered living near Wright Park and taking the streetcar home after Japanese Language School. The fog would occasionally be very thick, "so when the streetcar came, we couldn't see the streetcar. So . . . the conductor would just ring and ring his bell so we'd know he's coming (*laughs*)."

Not all remembered the small size of Tacoma's prewar Japanese population fondly, however. While Ryo described the Tacoma community as "very warm," Chizu Tomita Takaoka, for one, felt that the Japanese in Tacoma were "clannish."[7]

You see, most of the people associated with people that came from the same part of the country.[8] Now my folks. . . had difficulty, in that we didn't have too many people from Fukushima, except Yamasaki-sensei.

So it was sort of family, too, in that respect. Yoshi [Yamasaki's daughter] and my sister were good friends . . . So, gee, I remember people that have, came from the same Fukushima, from Seattle, but I can't remember in Tacoma. And so with the immigrants, they were pretty well isolated unless they found somebody from their same province or same part of the country. They didn't associate too much. Besides, they couldn't; they were too busy . . . earning a living.

At the time of the interview, Chizu was living in Chicago, which she compared with her hometown:

Well this [Chicago] is a big city, and I think that makes a difference. I know in the Japanese community, you know, and I know some of my friends that came from Tacoma still have that very narrow mentality. And I used to think the old saying, "You could take a, what, what is it, a girl out of the country, but you can't take the country . . . "—well, that was it.

[*What do you mean by a narrow mentality?*]

Clannish . . . I think that's what it is. And I think they felt safe or secure in that little feeling, that you belong to this church, and this organization. But I found—I don't know what's wrong with our family, but we were loners, all of us.

TACOMA JAPANESE LANGUAGE SCHOOL
AS A SPACE OF BELONGING

The predominantly walking-scale character of their community and the convergence of multiple paths at the TJLS building meant that this location, this place, was where their lives intertwined. The fact that TJLS was established as a secular institution rather than as a church-based school is critical. The coalition that started and supported the school itself cut across religious, economic, and place-of-origin lines, pulling the Issei together. As Joe Kosai put it, "I think Tacoma Japanese Language School, as we call it *Nihongo no gakko*, was a focal point of bringing all Japanese in the community together. [There] was no religious segregation there. So that's the reason that so many of our people know each other even though they may have gone to a different church. This really brought the different families together." After its construction in 1923, the TJLS building also served as the meeting place for the Tacoma Japanese Association and other community functions, which "had until then been held in Japanese-American run hotels or in rented halls" (Morrison 1994, 18).

Tacoma was distinct in this regard. Louis Fiset argues that in Seattle, for instance, the "Nikkei community's social structure, for the most part, centered in churches" (2009, 13), and Monica Sone's memoir *Nisei Daughter* (2014) describes *ken* association relationships, neighborhood relations, and community events such as picnics as important sites of community building for the Seattle Japanese community. Paul Spickard also notes that Japanese communities in the US were initially organized largely through the labor boss system that managed Japanese workers in groups, that the *kenjinkai* organized "a person's social life", and that Buddhist temples "alone brought together Issei from different ken and different trades" (2009, 54–55, 56, 59; see also Williams 2019).

While these institutions were certainly important in Tacoma, emphasizing them exclusively seems too limiting. This is not to say that these other affiliations did not matter; they certainly did, especially for the Issei who left Japan when a shared "Japanese" national identity was newly emerging (vs. a prefectural or other local identity; see chapter 1). Rather, it is to underscore the prominent place the TJLS held in the social world of the Tacoma Japanese. The language our interviewees used to reflect this is noteworthy. Sally Someko Shirasago, for example, called the TJLS "a good gathering place *for all of us. All of us* had a place to go. And they had something going on often" (emphasis added). This building and institution, *this place,* was central to articulations of identity and belonging, both for individuals and a collective community. As a dominant theme in the narratives it reflects shared memories of prewar Tacoma and childhood lives. Even though not all Nisei in Tacoma attended the TJLS, the role the school played in people's memories was so strong that some remembered *every* child attending. Takao Jerry Kikuchi, for example, noted: "One thing all the Japanese that lived in Tacoma, they all attended the Japanese school. That's what held all the Japanese community together. But that I remember." Chizu explained that the TJLS "was kind of *like a second home,* that and the temple. That's where *our playground* . . . all us kids used to meet" (emphasis added). Jerry also remembered that the Language School "held all the Japanese people in Tacoma together." One reason for this may have been that the school met each weekday, and often had Saturday activities as well, unlike in other West Coast communities where language studies were often only on weekends. The Nisei children built bonds at the school that transcended other institutional affiliations.

Takeshi Osada was emphatic that Tacoma was "unique" because the TJLS was a *secular* institution. He learned this in the internment camp where those from Tacoma did not divide into Buddhist and Christian groups, and also from his wife, who grew up in Fresno where Japanese instruction took place in religious institutions.

> Okay, now every other Japanese community has a Japanese school, but they all split into Buddhist and Christian. Here everybody came to this one school, and so when we went to camp, we didn't have any Buddhist and Christian [divide]. I have a lot of Christian friends. We used to go to the Christian church for a bazaar, you know, and other communities didn't have that. It was very unique here.

Kazuo Horita said it "was very beneficial for us that it [TJLS] was not church oriented."

> I think it gave us an opportunity maybe . . . See, because when you think about it, here, here's the town, eight hundred total population— you know, that was at the end [right before incarceration in 1942]. Now, I realize that before that it was up to. . . two thousand–something, but it was, it had cut down to where it was about eight hundred or so. And to have qualified teachers for all of that, seems to me that the fact that we had a single entity, rather than a Methodist church, a Baptist church, and a Buddhist church, having its own classes and all that, it was a big benefit to us. I mean, we got a better education, I think, because of it.

Fumi Sato Hattori agreed that the secular nature and narrower focus on Japanese language and traditions meant they learned more. "Tacoma, I understand, had a pretty good reputation. It was supposed to be quite a good school, and I think partly because at Japanese School we weren't Buddhist or Methodists or anything. We were just studying Japanese."

Michie Taira Hori commented that the language school "played in our memory":

> MICHIE: I think it [community closeness] was because of the impact of the Japanese school for one, and a lot of the community, you know, things that went on—the festivals or things like that—the gathering of the community of the Japanese families. I think that had a lot to do [with it]. Because those things are played in our memory . . . So even though we may forget from time to time, it still has an impact on our psyche . . .
>
> JUNICHI: I think Tacoma was small enough, and there were enough Japanese there in a fairly centralized area, that they were pretty close.
>
> MICHIE: Because I don't recall my husband [born in LA] ever saying, "I went to Japanese school, or tried to go to Japanese school." I do know his mother saying, "They were tutored at home," which didn't work out too well. Especially when he's playing football and stuff, you know.

Kunio Shibata commented that those who did not attend the school were somehow separate, reinforcing the idea that the language school was important for the understood "closeness" of Tacoma's Japanese. "There were a very few families that didn't go to that Japanese Language School. There were some . . . we had some that didn't go to there, but seems like they're sort of isolated when we have a reunion because they don't have any close tie after that American school like we do." Kunio also remarked that he and other Nisei "didn't mingle that much at high school. It was the Japanese school that really kind of molded us together."

Special events, such as celebrations of the emperor's birthday, the reading of the Imperial Rescript on Education, as well as children's performances of plays and concerts, also pulled individuals from across the Japanese community together at the language school building (see also chapter 6). Masaye Jinguji Fujita (b. 1917; see figure 3.1) recounted:

> It was the Japanese Language School that brought the community together, because on special occasions, like. . . February 11th [Japan's National Foundation Day] and the emperor's birthday, all the

FIGURE 3.1. Masaye Jinguji Fujita (*far left*) with friends Hatsuye Kurose and Yoshiye Omori, at the College of Puget Sound, November 7, 1939. Courtesy of Tacoma Public Library, Richards Studio D9047-1.

> bigwigs—you know, the doctors, and dentists, and they would all attend, and that made it more a community affair. We enjoyed it together, because some of the well-known leaders of the—of the city would come and attend the . . . services together. And this made the emp—uh, the principal very happy, too. We were very much together, I think . . .

Even as the parents were so busy working, trying to make ends meet, especially during the Depression years, they came together at the school, building connections in and through this place.

Despite repeated comments about the role of the TJLS in bringing children and families together, some of the interviewees maintained that having to attend the school meant they were further isolated from others in the city. The flipside of the closeness, in other words, was segregation. Masatoshi Fujii, for instance, commented:

I think there was one negative aspect of the Japanese Language School . . . The boys couldn't turn out for sports, after-school sports— football, baseball, and basketball . . . because they had to go to the Japanese school . . . And I think it retarded the assimilation of Japanese into the mainstream of the community because we were segregating ourselves all the time. I mean, certain part is okay, but geez, one hundred percent of the time we were segregated, except for the public school. Even in public school I always played with Japanese friends. We had lunch and then we played together. I can't even remember playing with the others. I mean, there were only whites and Japanese in Tacoma anyway. I could only remember one or two Jap—Chinese families. In fact, one girl, Yoko Sang, and she was half—*hapa* [Hawaiian word for "half"]. And she was in my class. But I think she was the only other nonwhite at Central School that I could ever remember.

Thus, even as it was required, "no questions asked," that the children attend Japanese Language School, some interviewees acknowledged their disagreement and mixed emotions. Michie said, for instance, "I think it was just a matter of—because the whole community went—it was just a matter of, 'Hey, this is the thing to do.' I mean, I don't ever remember questioning it. I did resent sometimes having to go on Saturday, but everybody else went, too." Shigeko Tamaki Yoshiwara (b. 1916) personally chafed at the restrictions, but recalled that most students had no viable alternative when it came to extracurricular activities: "Very few of the Japanese students participated in after-school sports, because of their obligation to their parents . . . I got scolded all the time because I did after-school activities and I skipped my Japanese school or went late. When they sent my [TJLS] report card, my attendance was very poor." In *Furusato,* Ronald Magden notes that, "according to twenty-four Nisei interviewed, there were classmates who vociferously objected to going to the language school. Two hours on top of the seven already spent in public schools was too much for them" (1998, 76).

STRUCTURAL DISCRIMINATION, SEGREGATION, AND A CONCENTRATED COMMUNITY

In bringing the Nisei together in a secular space on a daily basis, the TJLS also served as an agent of de facto racial segregation, a situation that was further enforced by the youngsters' immersion in Japanese language and cultural learning in this building. It was enforced also, however, by structural discrimination in the prewar city. As the Nisei children walked through the city, shaping the meaning of those spaces and experiencing the emergence of a self there, their movements were embodied expressions of early twentieth-century social and power relations. The interplay of subject formation and spatiality for the Nisei was thus "historically contingent," linked as it was with hegemonic practices of racism and anti-Asianism all along the West Coast (Pred 1984).[9] Their daily paths, for instance, reflected a segregated city with discriminatory land and citizenship laws, such as those that prohibited ownership by Issei, as well as requirements to participate in the institutional projects of American public education. These embodied inequities and situated spatial practices "determine[d] who—individually or collectively—may or may not do what, when, and where, [and] under what conditions of control or surveillance, if any" (Pred 1998, 636).[10] Joe Kosai in fact made a direct connection between the discrimination and segregation the Japanese experienced and their social world.

> Because of the discrimination at that time, I believe that the two sites, the Japanese Language School and the [Tacoma Buddhist] church, were also a place for socializing, because they [Issei] could not mingle with other people socially. My father worked with non-Japanese, and our hotel residents were all non-Japanese, but that was the extent of it, but not for socializing. All the socializing went on at the two areas. I attended the Buddhist church first and then attended the language school when I became of age. But things that were stressed in the family were that we do not bring shame to our family and to our community.... Sometimes it was difficult to follow those precepts, but I think we all tried very hard, and so we look at the activities at either the language school or at the church.

Thus, while accounting for Nisei children's agency is crucial (that is, *they made decisions* about which routes to take, whether they had a snack on the street, whether they played games that pushed the limits of "proper" decorum), it is essential to recognize that these were constrained choices that cannot be separated from prevailing social and power relations.

The concentrated character of the central area of Tacoma where most Japanese lived as essentially "a racial-ethnic community" (Yoo 2000, 8) meant, for instance, that many children only played with other Japanese. While Japanese families, especially those who ran hotels and lived alongside whites in their hotels, lived among other racial-ethnic groups, Tacoma's relatively small size led to less noticeable ethnic heterogeneity than, say, in Seattle, where sizable Chinese, Filipino, and African American populations lived alongside Japanese immigrants (Fiset 2009, 14–15). Tacoma, however, had violently expelled the Chinese in the late 1880s, resulting in distinctly fewer Chinese in Tacoma (Morgan 2003).[11]

Takao Jerry Kikuchi and Joe Seto noted limited friendships with young people outside the Japanese community, reflecting a divided city, self-segregation, as well as discriminatory laws and attitudes in the surrounding society:

> JERRY: For me, I did not interact with Caucasians. I mean, I was more or less secluded . . . I remember one Japanese friend I had, Sachio—was his name, Sachio Ikeda? . . . He and I were like buddy-buddy. I mean, we grew up together. We did everything together. Outside of that, I didn't have anybody . . . He lived way up, going up the hill somewhere. I forgot the—
> JOE: I think on Fawcett.
> JERRY: . . . He was a track star. I remember he had the big "L" here (*draws imaginary "L" on his chest*)—Lincoln High.
> JOE: He was a broad jumper. He was Kibei [Japanese American who had been educated in Japan and returned to the US], I think.
> JERRY: Yeah, he was Kibei. Yes.[12]

The reality of ethnic and racial segregation before World War II meant Nisei children had few non-Japanese playmates, as the Taira siblings discussed.

> MICHIE: I played with just my classmates more or less, you know, and they were all Oriental—Japanese friends. There was no mingling of the Caucasian "others," you know. It was just with us playing on the rings or jacks or something like that. I never thought of it, but that's true. That's the way it was.

JUNICHI: I recall intermingling with some. Still remember [some non-Japanese friends], with David Mata or something like that. Yeah, like Michie says, we'd get together and play.

MICHIE: Ya, I don't remember doing that, except I had one Caucasian girlfriend who, I don't know why, she seemed to be a loner, and her name was Sydney. I'll never forget that. Her home was not too far from the elementary school. So one day she invited me to come for lunch, which was very unusual, and I was scared because I had never been in a Caucasian home. But she said it was okay with her grandmother, and so I remember going there one time for lunch. And she gave me a beautiful little scrapbook when we parted. I remember that.

[*Why do you think you were afraid to go to her home?*]

MICHIE: Well, I think part of it, for me anyway, probably was not being in a Caucasian home ever before, one, and this idea of discrimination is still kind of in the back of your head, you know. Because other friends who wanted—when I invited, they couldn't come to my home.

[*Caucasian friends were not allowed to come to your home?*]

MICHIE: The girls were willing, but the parents were not.

JUNICHI: I don't think not allowed. When you say not allowed, do you mean by our parents? I don't think that was true.

MICHIE: I meant the Caucasians. Like, Irene's parents didn't let her come.

JUNICHI: I never had that experience. I don't remember that at all, although we never had . . . I never went to a Caucasian home [or] had them come to our house.

Joe Kosai reflected on the effect that segregation—the combined forces of overt, institutionalized discrimination and a tendency toward self-segregation—had on his social world:

The only thing I remember about living downtown was, I didn't have any non-Japanese friends. There were about six families that lived on the same block we did between 13th and 15th and Commerce Street, and so they were the people I played with . . . and all the other business establishments in that neighborhood there were people who had homes elsewhere so their children didn't come down there. So when we went to school, we kind of hung around with our Japanese friends, the people we knew.

These stories about whom they did and did not play with tacitly acknowledged the central role of race in their subject formation. Yet not all Nisei had only Japanese friends. Hiroko Betty Fukuhara Yoshioka, who did not attend the TJLS, remembered some of her childhood playmates:

> One was Donna May Tjaden, who became Janis Page. The actress? She was in my class. Then in high school, the Latin class, we were quite close. So I had a lot of Caucasian friends there. The first time I went to a Caucasian house for dinner, was to a classmate in Latin. And I remember I told the teacher, "I don't know about my manners when it comes to an American home." And she told me, "Don't worry, you just follow what I do and you'll be all right." So, I went there—it was a classmate, Jane Elder. And I think she lives in Chicago [now], or in the suburbs someplace. But I got along; they treated me very well.

Harue Kawano Ozaki and her sister Teiko Kawano Peterson lived outside the central Japanese area when their parents ran a store on North I Street. It was a predominantly white neighborhood, and Harue remembered playing with Caucasian children.

> When I was a little girl, not only did I go to Japanese school and have an environment of my fellow Japanese-American friends at the language school, but then when we came home, we came home to a white neighborhood and all my chums were playmates that were, that were non-Japanese. They were all white, Caucasian friends. And I still keep in contact with them too, by the way. And uh, so I always thought that my father, who was very nationalistic, you know, always ingrained in us that it's so important to know who you are. I always knew who I was, and that certainly, I think, was the reason why my brothers and sisters and myself, we were more or less like leaders in the neighborhood. And they always followed us in all the kids' games, they'd always be coming to our backyard and getting us out of the house.

And we went to each others' homes, and were just something that, just was so natural.

The oppression created by racist policies, many of which were developed in California in the early twentieth century and subsequently taken up by politicians and community leaders in Washington State, has been well documented (e.g, Daniels [1962] 1977; Hata 1978). In the late 1800s, too, Tacoma had implemented the "Tacoma Method" of violently driving Chinese out of the city, a fact that Clifford Uyeda described as "a dark past that haunted [Tacoma's] memory" (2000, 10).[13] The early 1900s were a tense time, in other words.

And yet Tacoma also had "sympathetic" politicians, such as Harry P. Cain, who took office in June 1940 and served as Tacoma's mayor at the time of Executive Order 9066 authorizing the incarceration of persons of Japanese ancestry—and became one of just two West Coast officials to publicly oppose it (Nunnaly 2016). This left an impression on some, who noted that he was different from other virulent anti-Asian politicians in places like California. Fumi Sato Hattori, for instance, commented that Tacoma Japanese were not "as discriminated against as they were in California," explaining that "people who farmed near railroad tracks were accused of being ready to blow up the tracks or something, you know. People didn't treat us that way in Washington. And we came here [Los Angeles], and we found out that Californians really are a little different. And I think I was lucky to grow up in Washington." Shigeko Gay Tamaki Yoshiwara specifically mentioned the role of Mayor Cain—both as a sympathetic leader and as the one who arranged a meeting between Tacoma's young Nisei community leaders and Eleanor Roosevelt in the mayor's office on December 12, 1941, barely a week after Pearl Harbor (figure 3.2). Shigeko remembered that Mrs. Roosevelt had come to "bolster our feelings in that it was not anything that was our fault or, you know, something that we could control. But she didn't sound like a politician's wife. Very sympathetic." She went on to explain why she was selected to be part of the small group meeting with the First Lady:

SHIGEKO: Well, it happened to be—I was a member of JACL, the
Japanese American Citizens League, and like I said, we had a

FIGURE 3.2. Shigeko Gay Tamaki Yoshiwara (*left*), Shigeo Wakamatsu, Waichi Oyanagi, and Ted Nakamura with Eleanor Roosevelt, December 1941. Courtesy of Tacoma Public Library, Richards Studio D12299-11.

sympathetic mayor, Mayor Cain. And you know, that's always the situation. Depending on the community, if you have a sympathetic leader, you know, it makes all the difference. She—he called the group together and said, "You get a chance to meet Mrs. Roosevelt. She wants to talk to you people."

KUNIO: Wow . . .

SHIGEKO: It was in the mayor's office. And like I said, it was because Mayor Cain was sympathetic. He called us, and I happened to be on the board of JACL at the time. So they called us and had our picture taken. I still have mine framed. (*laughs*) But she was very down-to-earth.. . . I used to admire her columns that used to come out in the paper.

FUSAE: What was it called? "My Day" or something?

SHIGEKO: Yes . . . As I said, Mayor Cain had a lot to do with it.

MASATOSHI: He became a senator later.

YONEKO: I think so.

SHIGEKO: On the West Coast, he was just exactly the opposite of some of the politicians in California that were making a lot of noise. He was very—we were very fortunate to have him as a mayor.

Eleanor Roosevelt followed up the meeting with her "My Day" column of December 16, 1941.[14] In it she specifically referred to "the situation on the West coast for the American-born Japanese":

> The great mass of our people, stemming from these various national ties, must not feel that they have suddenly ceased to be Americans . . . If we can not meet the challenge of fairness to our citizens of every nationality, of really believing in the Bill of Rights and making it a reality for all loyal American citizens, regardless of race, creed or color; if we can not keep in check anti-semitism, anti-racial feeling as well as anti-religious feelings, then we shall have removed from the world the one real hope for the future on which all humanity must now rely. (Roosevelt 1941)

Nevertheless, racial politics and confrontational racist actions did shape Nisei experiences. Susan Morrison in fact attributes the "slow decline" of Tacoma's Japanese community, starting in 1920, to "race based restrictions imposed by both local and federal governments" (1994, 64). Moreover, despite interviewees' comments on "sympathetic" politicians in Tacoma, the Japanese community was keenly aware of the city's ominous history regarding race relations. Finally, neither Mayor Cain's efforts, Eleanor Roosevelt's words, nor the Tacoma Japanese community's own efforts to protect itself would prevent wartime incarceration.

This discrimination led to a social world where belonging and legitimacy were far from secure, such that what belonging the children did claim was more temporary than long-lasting. Michie Taira remembered feeling the need to tactically move through city spaces:

> There was a store called Fisher's on Broadway, and we knew not to go there. That's all I—and I, being a teenager, I went in there anyway one

time thinking maybe I could buy something really cheap. And you know, no one would wait on me . . . And then the dime store, what was that dime store there? . . . Woolworth or one of those. They always had a counter where you could buy things or eat, you know. I couldn't get served there, either. But that was the two times I experienced that. But you know, we were so used to that, we just accepted it.

CROSSING RELIGIOUS BOUNDARIES: ONE SCHOOL, MULTIPLE RELIGIONS

The secular TJLS offered an opportunity for Nisei to develop bonds with children across the community, including those affiliated with distinct *ken* associations and different religious institutions, Buddhist, Methodist, and Baptist. These friendships developed at the TJLS brought young people together in new ways, crossing over the social worlds of their parents in some instances. The school also offered an opportunity for Issei to associate with others outside of the religious or prefectural associations. We thus suggest that Japanese language schools have been overlooked in their role as important sites of community formation.

Chizu Tomita Takaoka said that religious affiliation made no difference in the friendships she formed, pointing out that "Yone, Fumi Sato, Hanna, they were all Christian, but were my friends." Kazuo concurred. "We didn't really care about the difference," he said. "We really didn't know the difference."[15] Some, such as Jack Kazuo Hata, said their family didn't attend church. The interviewees told stories of going from one religious institution to another as children, picking and choosing from the activities offered. "Because we all went to Japanese School," Riyeko Fujimoto explained, "so you knew all the people, all the kids there . . . I think the school kept everybody together."

Masaye Jinguji Fujita reminisced:

In the Methodist church, we had a basketball team. And I know that the Buddhist people had a team also, and we played with each other. And I remember I was a forward, and as short as I was, I made a big . . . point with one hand! (*laughs*) . . . I remember the time the

Methodist girls won the basketball team. (*laughs*) I'm so proud of that! But we were friendly with each other, and we would go to bazaars. They would come to ours, and we would go to theirs, and we [were] friends with each other . . .

I remember more of the Buddhist girl—uh, boys, because, uh, they went to the Japanese school where we would do many things together— singing, and . . . doing skits, and having parties.

. . . We had very smart boys, you know. The one that gave me [a certain letter], he was one of my latest boyfriends. Well, he is from Buddhist church, and he, on a Christmas card, he said that eighty— for over eighty years we have been friends.

She also commented that when there were events at the school, such as plays, everyone would work together: "The principal would be there, and the teacher would be there to plan to make scenery things for the plays, and that included the Japanese, the uh, the Buddhists, and the Methodists . . . all together. We were all there doing the same thing for the same purpose . . . Yes, much, much together."

Takeshi Osada also noted the movement across religious institutions.

Well, they had, like, Japanese movies, you know, and then they had bazaars. They used to have bazaars and so you were intermingled. I went to that Methodist church a lot of times when I was a kid. I was a scout, and when the scout troop was over there we went to the Methodist church . . . Tacoma in the summer, all of us kids went to a Baptist church. It was down on Fawcett over there. This Mrs. Rye took in all the kids.[16] We used to all go there . . . she had projects for us, you know. I don't know why, but most of us kids in the summer went there— Buddhist, Christian, everybody.

When we asked if the parents relied more on the religious institutions for their socializing, she said, "No, because we all got together at school. They knew each other, so I don't think it mattered whether you were Buddhist or Methodist or . . . So whatever social event they had, we'd go to either one."

Kazuo Horita also described going to activities at the Buddhist church with his friend Stogie, even though Kazuo attended the Methodist church.

Masaji is his original name, but Stogie, everyone called him Stogie. But anyhow, Stogie and I were buddy-buddies. He was going to the Buddhist church, and I happened to be going to the Methodist church. He says, "Kaz, why don't you come to the Buddhist church? We've got movies over there! (*laughs*) You know, during classes and all that, we have movies!" And I said, "Yeah, maybe I'll go." So I, I went to the Buddhist church. Well Stogie, a few years later, he goes to the Methodist church. So you can see how I, you know, I, I kind of flipped around. But then I became a pretty, I became a good Buddhist church citizen. Not a religious citizen, but a good citizen, because I was active in the activities—my sports were with the Bussei [Buddhist youth] group, and all of that . . . But all during my school years, all during my time in Tacoma, my friends were just mixtures. I mean, I played a lot of baseball with George Omori, he went to the Methodist church, he was—but a good buddy. My early years, with Mas Jinguji, he was Methodist. But again, lots of my good friends, again, were Buddhists . . . playing ball together and all that kind of stuff.

While a number of the interviewees remembered attending movies at the Buddhist church, Fumi Sato Hattori also remembered events such as funerals bringing everyone together, reflecting what Kazuo meant when he said the Japanese community felt like "a family."

In Tacoma, if somebody at the Buddhist church died, everybody at the Methodist church went to the funeral, you know, and vice versa. It was, uh, it was just something you did. Even our Methodist minister went to the Buddhist funerals, and so it was a community thing. Churches were very active. They . . . I think the kids who went to the Buddhist church, you know, their social life centered around their church . . . But we were a little bit more, uh, connected to the Caucasian churches, so we had that sort of an advantage . . . We were close, you know. We're here [at the Methodist church], and the next block, there's the Buddhist church. And so, uh, of course we saw the kids at school, but now that I think of it, I didn't know many of the younger Buddhist kids, for instance, you know. If they were in my class I'd know them, but otherwise I probably wouldn't know them, because our activities just didn't involve them . . . The Japanese Language

School? (*pause*) It must have played a big part because almost everybody went.

While June Miyeko Shirozu Hayashi's (b. 1940) family was Buddhist, they lived at the Whitney Memorial Methodist Church after the war.

> You know, it is really interesting, because in Tacoma it didn't make any difference where you went. You know, I grew up like that, then I come to California where it makes a difference. You know, it's very interesting because I remember when we—my father tried farming for a while, and at that time I think my grandfather was farming in Fife, and they were kind of, I don't know, somebody else owned the land, but they were working it, and I remember [the reverend] from the Methodist church coming to pick us up by car to take us to [the Methodist] church . . . And we went to the Methodist church. It didn't make any difference.
>
> You know, uh, I think that's kind of how they view religion in Japan. They're not—they just have so many that, you know, it doesn't make any difference. But my father's family were really Higashi[17] Buddhists . . .

In Japan, indeed, "flexibility rather than dogmatism was the watchword" (Spickard 2009, 59) for religious life, something largely true of traditional religion in East Asia generally, where few adhere to the monotheistic approach of Judeo-Christianity or Islam. Scholars have noted that when Japanese arrived in the US, there was a "softening" of differences across religions (Yoo 2000, 44), but there were also increased "feuds" between Buddhist and Christian schools (Asato 2006, 6, 10).

June Miyeko Shirozu Hayashi remembered that she and her sisters did not even always attend the same church as her brother.

> Our family was very, uh, well . . . let me say, "different," in that all the girls went to the Buddhist church. And then I had an only brother, and so he didn't want to come to church with us because there were no boys in our age group. And so, his best friends, Ryo and Frank, went to the Methodist church, so he went to the Methodist Church. It was okay with my parents, as long as we went *some*where. So, he always

remained, not Buddhist, but not really Christian either, but just kind of, you know . . . and we all accepted it . . .

They planned lots of activities for us because we could not really—my age group—did not do anything on the weekends with people at school. We lived two lives: one at school, one on the weekends, because we really weren't accepted . . . well, I was in all the clubs and so forth, but we never saw anybody on just, you know, just personally, just as friends. We were just friends at school, and that was it. So, our church played a really big role in providing lots of activities for us. I had a great, you know, childhood, actually.

Other families also attended different religious institutions. Shigeko, for example, explained that "there was no problem, in terms of religious differences . . . I was raised in a family—and my father, although he was a Buddhist, said, 'As long as you go to a church.' Because the girls liked the Methodist church activities and my brothers went to the Buddhist church. As long as you went to a church it was fine with him. But depends on the family, how strong the religious beliefs were."

This flexible movement between churches did not mean there were no divisions within the community. Nisei we interviewed had conflicting memories about the relationships between churches and the TJLS. For instance, Masaye Jinguji Fujita recollected that the Buddhist boys attended the Japanese Language School, but many of the Methodist boys did not. In her estimation, the fact that they did not attend the language school suggested that they were "not Japanese," that they developed a different—less "Japanese"—identity than those who did. The TJLS was central to the formation of a Japanese identity in her view.

I have no idea why they [Methodist boys] did not go to Japanese School . . . It's amazing how, even to this day, many of the boys are not Japanese. They don't speak too much Japanese either, even though they are Nisei. Mm-hmm. Like, the Buddhist boys—they're more "together," shall I say . . . We didn't have too many Methodist boys in class—in Japanese school. It's amazing . . . , and to this day, I don't know why. You know, we were mostly socializing with the Buddhist boys. I don't know why. (laughs)

The Methodist boys are very strict about some things, I think, maybe. Or . . . they didn't enjoy the kind of things that us girls would enjoy, like dancing and things like that . . . And the boys—Methodist boys—didn't dance, either. (*laughs*) I don't know why. Well, I should ask . . . well, some have passed away already, but I don't know why. Mm-hmm, yes.

Although the "majority of Issei came from Jodo Shinshu (True Pure Land) Buddhist backgrounds" (Yoo 2000, 41), in the US a number of families identified as Christian. According to Riyeko Fujimoto, fewer children from Methodist families than Buddhist attended the Language School, which led to them playing "by themselves." Yet she also noted that those who went to the Buddhist church also "played by themselves. I don't mean they purposely did it, but they would have different activities. So they wouldn't come to school when they had their activities [e.g., a picnic]." She explained that "each church had their own picnic, and then besides that, the Japanese school had their own picnic, too." Sally Shirasago also recognized that their family friends were predominantly Buddhist, but that the children were able to cross these boundaries more readily than their parents: "the kids maybe, but not with the parents."

In the end, not all the interviewees agreed on the significance of religious differences. The churches were, however, important institutions in the community, and "played a role in the lives of Nikkei that went far beyond the numbers registered on membership rolls or in statistical percentages" (Yoo 2000, 67). When discussing if the TJLS brought people together, Jack Kazuo Hata said, "Oh definitely," but then added that, for the Issei, it "was one of the three centers for their being together. The Methodist church and the Buddhist church, and the school. I think [for] the Nisei maybe a little bit less, but still, I don't think the Nisei as a whole, as a group, participated in too much outside activity or whatever. I think the churches and the school just were very important to us."

While the majority of the Nisei lived in the spatially concentrated central district, with its walking-scale mode of existence, structural racism and discrimination as well as self-segregation for economic and social security shaped this neighborhood. For the Nisei children growing up in this urban setting, their daily paths not only shaped their own subjectivity, but also gave meaning to the spaces they inhabited. Subjectivity and spatiality were mutually constituted, producing memories of a distinctly close community in comparison to other Nikkei along the West Coast. The spatial stories they told of moving through the city suggested experiences of belonging through the occupation of space on their own terms. And yet, structural racism, such as alien land laws, and persistent isolation imply their "rights to the city" were fleeting and impermanent. Becoming Nisei, in other words, included "struggles over the use of time and space . . . [and] the production of place" (Pred 1990, 47), such that these ongoing processes of becoming were also *spatial practices*. Their narratives also pointed to the TJLS as a particularly important site for identity formation, as it both provided a safe and reliable space for being Japanese and marked the young Nisei as distinctively different in the diverse urban environment. Thus the spatiality of belonging, whether in games on city streets where Nisei children had momentary "rights" to urban spaces, or in the decidedly marked space of the Japanese Language School, underscores the processual, emergent, and ongoing nature of becoming Nisei.

CHAPTER FOUR

Expanding the Mapping of Japanese Urban Lives

We lived in the tideflats, which was sort of not too upper class, but we didn't know that.

—FUMI SATO HATTORI (B. 1921)

AS WE HAVE SEEN, MUCH OF THE FOCUS OF THE JAPANESE COM-munity was in the downtown core, where the relatively small population was physically concentrated—largely between South 11th and South 19th Streets and Tacoma and Pacific Avenues. This focus is reinforced by the fact that Tacoma's prewar Japanese community has primarily been visualized through Kazuo Ito's hand-drawn map (see figure I.5), which zooms in on just a few blocks. In addition, publications that do exist about the Japanese community during this time deal chiefly with the downtown area (e.g., Morrison 1994; Magden 1998; Norima 2016; Sullivan 2016).[1] Such a focus certainly was for good reason. The main religious and educational institutions of the Japanese community, along with the majority of their businesses and homes, were located in that socially isolated district, creating a sense of "closeness."

Yet not all of the Japanese community lived and worked in the down-town core. Significant findings from our interviews and archival work expand the community beyond the well-documented downtown core, not only providing new information about prewar Tacoma and its Japanese residents, but also correcting for the erasure of Japanese history in the city.

Areas such as the tideflats and South Tacoma were assumed to have strictly European immigrant histories, but we have found that Japanese families and individuals lived, worked, and played in these spaces as well. The interview narratives include childhood memories, for instance, of fishing, swimming, and playing on the tideflats, of parents working for the St. Paul & Tacoma Lumber Company and other sawmills, and of moving to South Tacoma to open "highway" markets. These stories expand our sense of the daily paths traveled by the Japanese community in Tacoma, including movement between the tideflats and the main Nihonmachi area in the downtown core where Japanese businesses, churches, and the language school were located. Stories of working in the highway stands over the summer to earn spending money or income for the family also illustrate the linkages between Japanese business enterprises and the ways in which kin and close friends were relied on to provide an inexpensive labor within an ethnic economy (see chapter 2).

Indeed, as the documentation of businesses and homes by Sarah Pyle shows (see maps I.1, 2.1), Japanese Americans occupied and made their marks in a variety of areas for over fifty years. To represent Japanese Tacoma, Pyle combined Kazuo Ito's map, addresses listed in Morrison's "Tacoma's Nihongo Gakko" (1994) and Otsuka and Fukui's *History of the Japanese of Tacoma* ([1940] 1986), and locations mentioned in our interviews. The interview narratives provided specific addresses as well as descriptions of places in relation to city landmarks. Consultation of several yearly issues of *Polk's Tacoma City Directory* confirmed 400 unique addresses of Japanese businesses, homes, and organizations in Tacoma between the years 1910 and 1942, although many places with no exact addresses or names remained (see S. Pyle 2019). After further analysis, Pyle determined the existence of 340 unique locations, taking into account that one building may have contained three or four different establishments during the prewar period.[2] This filling in of the spatial representation of Tacoma's Japanese prior to World War II not only expands our understanding of the economic contributions of Japanese in prewar Tacoma, but also underscores the extent of historical erasure that began with wartime incarceration and continues to today.

In terms of Nisei identity formation, this more robust mapping of the community illuminates the diversity of spaces that Japanese families inhabited and the extent of their movement patterns. Even though many of their lives were confined to a fairly concentrated area where most Japanese lived and worked, this was not a full picture of everyone's regular, everyday world. Interviewees told stories of people who lived on the tideflats, of outings to Steilacoom and Point Defiance beaches, and of playing in an empty lot across from the Airway Market in South Tacoma. Navigating these spaces and making claims of belonging in them were important aspects of growing up as Nisei.

LIFE ON THE TIDEFLATS

Living and playing on the tideflats, and work in the sawmills and the lumber industry more broadly, were unexpectedly common topics in the interview narratives, mentioned by 25 of the 42 Nisei we spoke with (see also chapter 2). Yet, prominent existing maps of Tacoma's Nihonmachi did not acknowledge the Japanese presence in the area. In particular, several interviewees referred to living in a row of fourteen houses along St. Paul Avenue on the tideflats, opposite the St. Paul & Tacoma Lumber Company sawmill (see map 4.1). UW Libraries Special Collections holds maps identifying these houses, and St. Paul & Tacoma Lumber Company archives (1903–18) confirm the employment of Japanese workers; the Ronald Magden papers, too, provide additional details about life on the tideflats.

The St. Paul & Tacoma Lumber Company was considered one of the best mills to work for because it offered various inducements and benefits. One of these amenities was the "large wholesale and retail general store" situated between the mill and the company offices. The store supplied such merchandise as hardware, work clothing, and general work supplies and was, "for some years, the largest merchandiser in Tacoma" (Morgan 1982, 226). Another benefit the company offered some workers was the four-story, eighty-by-one-hundred-foot St. Paul and Tacoma Hotel, located on St. Paul Avenue. The main floor of the hotel contained "a lobby, reading room and billiard and pool room," as well as a dining room that was used for entertaining various groups, such as the Association of Railroad Tie Producers. The upper floors served essentially as a boarding house for employees who did not own or rent their own homes, leading to the term "Hotel de Gink" (Morgan 1982, 226).[3] Records of this boarding house in the archives of the St. Paul & Tacoma Lumber Company show only European surnames.

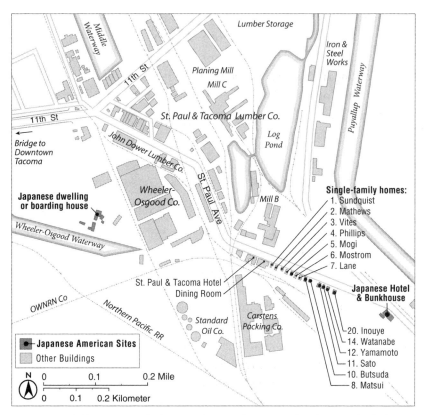

MAP 4.1. Tideflats area, including residences of Japanese families and bachelors

Just south of this hotel on St. Paul Avenue were the fourteen individual houses for families of workers mentioned above. Maps from the UW Libraries Special Collections, such as the 1926 *Metsker's Complete Atlas of Tacoma* and the 1912 *Sanborn Fire Insurance Map of Tacoma*, clearly show these residences, along with a boarding house, the "Japanese Hotel," which we believe was for Japanese workers at the mill. This row of fourteen single-family houses strung between the St. Paul and Tacoma Hotel and the Japanese Hotel (see map 4.1) has not previously been highlighted as residential space for Tacoma Japanese families. In addition, a history of the company by Murray Morgan (1982) does not mention Japanese workers or the individual houses or the boarding house for Japanese. Ronald Magden, in *Furusato* (1998, 1), does mention Japanese pioneers who "found work in sawmills far from towns," but he does not write about the St. Paul & Tacoma Lumber Company or provide much information about working in the Tacoma tideflats. Thus, while the lumber company itself documented the presence of Japanese labor in the mill (St. Paul & Tacoma Lumber Company Records 1903–18), historical literature provides little indication of where or how Japanese mill workers lived or how their working and community lives might have connected.

The one exception is a little-known unpublished memoir by Clinton Butsuda, "Memories of St. Paul Avenue" (1992).[4] Butsuda's descriptions are rich and specific, adding clarity to other comments and memories (including those of our interviewees, several of whom recalled these houses and those who lived in them). When he visited again in the late 1980s, for example, he could almost "hear Mr. Mostrom playing his mandolin on his front porch," and the "children's voices of the past playing in the street and the alley," and "see the willow tree" that his father had planted (1992, 1).

Butsuda remembered the hotel on the north end of St. Paul Avenue as the place where white men stayed on the top floors, "with 100 rooms, billiard and pool rooms, library, and . . . [which] sold cigars, cigarettes and candies for the white laborers. Coming home from school we kids used to go in from one end of the building, race to the second floor, then back to the main floor and scurry out the front door" (1992, 1–2). At the opposite end of St. Paul Avenue

was a dark red and white trimmed two story Japanese boarding house with about 40 rooms for the bachelors.[5] We used to go there to see men engage in Judo and Japanese fencing of kendo with pads, masks, and bamboo swords on holidays and on weekends. . . . There was a large 6' x 10' concrete bath of hot water used for soaking after we washed and rinsed ourselves. (1992, 3)

Siblings Yoneko Aochi and Katsuko Aochi Harano remembered that two different Issei women cooked at the Japanese hotel on the tideflats, including Mrs. Okada.[6]

YONEKO: They used to have a boarding house out where they all used to stay . . .

KATSUKO: It was quite a big boarding house.

YONEKO: Mrs. Okada used to cook for them.

KATSUKO: Yes . . .

ANON MALE B: In the old days there was quite a few Japanese working in different sawmills.

YONEKO: (*nods and smiles in agreement*) Yes, uh-huh.

ANON MALE B: St. Paul, and all around the waterfront. But Tacoma used to be a . . .

YONEKO: . . . lumber port anyway . . . It was a lumber port. And we used to see those big Japanese steamships, is it, that used to come down in front of the sawmill and take lumber out and take it back to Japan.

In addition, the Japanese workers at St. Paul & Tacoma Lumber Company had a "social club" that charged a small fee (50 cents per month) to support "a library with over 200 books, with English and Japanese titles, and a literary publication filled with stories and original poetry" by residents of the boarding house (Asaka 2014, 127).

Between the St. Paul and Tacoma Hotel and the Japanese Hotel, in a single row along St. Paul Avenue, were the single-family homes in which some Japanese employees and their families resided. Clinton Butsuda's memoir provides a summary of those who lived there, Japanese and non-Japanese families alike (quoted sections are his words):

#1 Sundquist Family, "whose older daughter, Iveldell, attended the Japanese language and culture class after the regular school. At the Japanese Festival, the blonde Swedish-American girl in kimono would be dancing with the black-haired Japanese-American friends."

#2, Mathews, no children

#3, Vites

#4, Phillips

#5, Mogi, "who had a son and two daughters"

#6, Mostrom, a large German family

#7, Mr. and Mrs. Lane

#8, Matsui, "with their six sons and two daughters. In their garage was a Hutmobile [*sic*][7] Touring Car that I never saw running."

#10, Butsuda family, "People used to say it was the 'Garden of Eden', for my father grew the best flowers and vegetables on St. Paul

Avenue. . . . Hollyhock, blue bells, cosmos, Irish broom, dahlias of all colors blended in with the green, green lawn. A large stately willow tree shaded the back porch. Our yard was the most popular place to play. It was a fun place to be."

#11, Sato, whose grandson, James Hattori, "is one of NBC's national news reporters"[8]

#12, Yamamoto family, whose "son got the brunt of jokes and pranks. He was the kind of a kid that could take it and laugh about it."

#14, Watanabe family

#20, Paul Inouye family

#21, Asada, whose "father was taken away by the FBI right after Pearl Harbor just because he served in the Japanese Army long ago" (Butsuda 1992, 2–3)[9]

Descriptions of pranks, fun, and hollyhocks and bluebells provide evidence of Japanese in these spaces, building the urban as well as becoming Nisei. Visualizations of these mundane activities offer representations of a population that has previously been not only discounted, but erased from urban histories.

A number of interviewees offered colorful memories of playing, working, and living on the tideflats. Fumi Sato Hattori was the firstborn and the only girl in the Sato family, with its four children. Her brothers were Hidemaru, Masahiro, and Toshiatsu. "My father felt that if he gave the boys substantial names," she remembered, "if they ever became great, you could use the Chinese pronunciation, and it would be very effective. (*laughs*) My name is just plain Fumi. I'm a girl." Fumi's father worked in the St. Paul & Tacoma Lumber Company as a planer in the sawmill. She explained that "he was going to college in Japan, but he came from a, what shall we say, not well-to-do family. So, they ran out of money, so he came over here as a student to go to school here, but he found out that it cost money to go to school here too . . . So he went to work in a sawmill, and that's where he worked his whole career."

Fumi clearly remembered the houses along St. Paul Avenue and the "piles of lumber" across the street from their home. Her mother ran the Superior Hotel in downtown Tacoma, where the family eventually moved— a pattern that reflected the shift into entrepreneurial activities for many Japanese families (see chapter 2). Fumi described the family's situation:

[My father] worked for the St. Paul and Tacoma Lumber Company, down in the tideflats, they called it. And they used to have many, they used to have housing for their Japanese employees, houses numbered from 1 to 14 or something. And my brother remembered that we lived in number 11 at one time, and number 14 at another time.[10] And across, between our house and, oh some distance away, there was a boarding house for Japanese workers at the mill, and my mother used to cook there. And my father was a very reserved man. He never told us anything about his background. All I've learned is from his sister, who lived in New Orleans. And she communicated with her children. So her children can tell more about my father's family than my father did, because my father died when I was sixteen.

By 1937, Fumi's family had moved to the downtown hotel and her father had to walk to the mill every day.

He was coming home from work; he was hit by a car. He was a very healthy person. He used to walk to work and walk home. It was about two miles, but he worked a second shift, and I guess somebody . . . careless driver just hit him, and that's when Mr. Semba . . . he was an insurance man, and he investigated the man who hit him. Of course, in those days we didn't sue anybody, you know, but he investigated, and found that this fellow didn't have any money or anything, so he couldn't do anything.

As children, they played on the block on St. Paul Avenue with the children of other company employees, both Japanese and Caucasian. One such family was the Sundquists, who had girls with whom Fumi played.

Lillian was older than us, and Ivy [Iveldell] was a little bit older than me, but she used to play with one of the Japanese girls, Chio, who lived a couple of doors down from me . . . And the Mostroms, they were mostly boys, but they had one girl, and Paynes—Ruth was a redheaded girl. I remember we always used to play, the whole block . . . We were poor, but we didn't know it. We got along fine, you know, with everybody on the block . . . We had church friends, you know, so a group of us used to go to Japanese school together, so we socialized with them.

And the whole of St. Paul Avenue sort of, we sort of kept an eye on each other. Our activities sort of meshed. We had a happy childhood, really.

Fumi also remembered that they joined the Methodist Church because of a missionary couple who visited the homes on the tideflats.

When we lived down in St. Paul Avenue, which is in the tideflats, there was a Caucasian couple that came down there, sort of missionary I think, I guess, to try to, you know, make sure that we became good Christians and all, and they used to come down. And so that's how we started going to church. And then we . . . they had the Japanese church in town, so we went to that.

Like most of those interviewed, Fumi remembered going to American school, going to Japanese school, and going home (see map 3.1). The day was full, with little time for extracurricular activities. Living on the tideflats added an additional burden, however, as they had to walk the two miles to and from school. On the walk home from TJLS, she recalled,

when it was foggy, my father would come down and meet us, you know, along the way. Because there's a . . . from the time we'd cross the 15th Street bridge there's a long space of . . . I don't know what they had there, but there was nothing there. It was just dark, and so he'd come and meet us . . . We didn't think much of it. There were several of us, you know, my brothers and a couple of neighbors.

The three Fujimoto sisters also remembered those who had to walk back and forth from the tideflats.

TADAYE: I used to walk on Pacific Avenue by myself and never thought anything of it.
KIMIKO: And then, you know, because our home was close to the church and the school, it was easy for us, but some of these students, they lived on the other side of 11th Street bridge, was it?
TADAYE: Tideflats.
KIMIKO: Yes, and they used to walk every day, in the dark, wintertime.

TADAYE: Some of the teachers, too.

KIMIKO: Yes. Some of the teachers did, too. But you know, you don't think about those things when you yourself have it so easy, you know, but some of them had to have a really hard time to go to school.

[*Who lived on the other side? Were they families that had different types of businesses?*]

KIMIKO: Well, no. They were hired by the sawmill? (*looks to sisters*)

YOSHIKO: . . . Sawmill.

KIMIKO: Yes, sawmill . . . I don't know whether it was all sawmill or not, but it was more of them. But a lot of them lived on Broadway, Pacific Avenue. We were lucky, you know. We lived right across the street [from TJLS].

Chizu Tomita Takaoka, like Fumi, remembered playing with some of the children who lived on the tideflats.

I had one friend, now, her name was Iveldell, and. . . she used to live in St. Paul. You know where that St. Paul is, used to be lumber, and then there was a group of Japanese that lived there, and Iveldell was one of them, I don't know what her last name [was]. So that's all the friends she had, too . . . She didn't live nearby, but she was my schoolmate. She was in my same class. The rest of them, eh, cordial, but. . . not a friend.

Jack Kazuo Hata also had memories of the tideflats. When discussing what he did other than go to American school and Japanese school, he remarked: "Just the kid stuff, like in the fall we'd play touch football. In the spring, we'd play baseball. I guess that's about it. And we'd go to the beach and go swimming at the tideflats."

Takeshi Osada recalled playing at a place called "Tokyo Beach":

Oh, we had a lot of happy memories. Every Saturday a bunch of us used to go down to Union Pacific. We used to play baseball down there. On the way we used to play on the logs, you know? I think about it and it could have been very dangerous. You [could fall] and not come up. But everybody came up. And then we used to go, all the Japanese kids my age used to go to this meat market. We used to give him ten cents and the guy would give us four or five wieners, you know? He just gave it to us. Anyway, we'd take that and we'd have a can of pork and beans. I mean, we'd go to this beach that we called "Tokyo Beach" because all the Japanese kids used to go there. It was down at the tideflats down there. We'd stay the whole day and we had a good time.

While some shared these joyful memories of swimming at "Tokyo Beach," others remembered a less bucolic landscape.

ANON MALE A: Well, we used to go to Tokyo Beach . . .
RYO: That's Port of Tacoma.
ANON MALE A: . . . but at that time we didn't know the city sewer came down there. But we were still swimming there. We did see reminders floating down once in a while . . .
ANON FEMALE A: Well, that's all covered now . . .
RYO: Now, I know [you] mentioned about going to the swimming, out Port of Tacoma way where the water was dirty, but during the summertime when we didn't go to summer school, we enjoyed hiking—walking—all the way out there and spent the day out there swimming, and then come home in the evening. We either hitched a ride back home or walked all the way back. But one of our favorite foods was potato and a can of pork and beans. And before we started the fire we would dig the sand and bury all the potatoes under there, and then build a fire—cover it with sand—and then build a fire over it, and then when we were ready for pork and beans, we'd just put it on the fire. And then if we wanted a potato, we'd dig around the side and get the potatoes out . . . I think we were going to—we were in junior high school and high school. And we never thought about, shall we say, being kidnapped or some adults hurting us. It didn't dawn on us. It was just living in the community like any other person, and we had no fear, and evidently our parents didn't have that fear either . . . And once in a while when the parents are free, they'd come after us . . .

That was fun. But if I knew what was there at that time, I don't think we would have gone there. (*laughs*)

Ryo elaborated in an interview with Kunio Shibata:

> There was a beach out there. We called it Tokyo Beach. And why was it named Tokyo Beach? In that area, the . . . what is it? The lumber mill . . . had a number of Japanese residents on their property. And when they—naturally they took the rail system, was it a streetcar? And that's where they all got off. So, the conductor decided to call it Tokyo. And when he would say, "Tokyo!" they all went to the front of the car and got out. (*laughs*) And the beach area was called Tokyo Beach. And that's where we used to go and spend our summers swimming. And the water, like Kunio was saying this morning, wasn't really clean water. There was a lot of sewage in there. (*laughs*)

Japanese immigrants and their Nisei children occupied spaces across the tideflats—whether for working, living, or summertime playing—a fact that should reconfigure maps of prewar Tacoma.

HIGHWAY MARKETS IN SOUTH TACOMA

The historical erasure of Japanese in Tacoma is also apparent in the businesses at the "intersection of [the] highway and roads with heavy traffic"— in other words, the markets and fruit companies of South Tacoma (*History of Japanese of Tacoma* 1941, 30–31; map 4.2). A number of interviewees mentioned these shops and the families that ran them, and some even worked there during the summers (see chapter 2). These markets included the Airway Market, Hayashi Grocery, Henry Horiuchi Fruit, Liberty Florists and Market, Kubo and Son Fruits and Grocery, and the Yakima Fruit Company (figure 4.1).

Sally Someko Shirasago (b. 1923) was the second to youngest in a family of eight children, three boys and five girls. She was born in Fife, where her father "had a farm, big farm," and lived there until she was in sixth grade, including a year in Japan to visit relatives in 1935. When the family returned from Japan, they moved to Tacoma and lived in town until they found a market in South Tacoma.

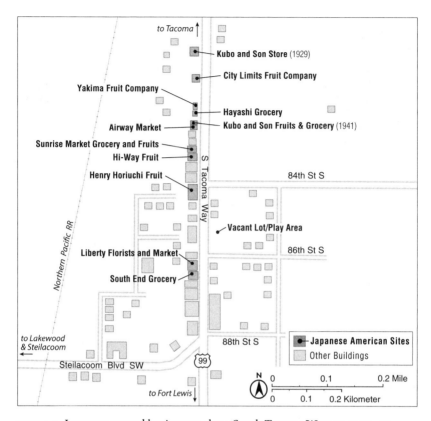

MAP 4.2. Japanese-owned businesses along South Tacoma Way, ca. 1920–40

I guess they didn't want to go into farming again, so we went into Tacoma and did a little grocery store,[11] and then we had bought a, one of those markets on the highway. Do you remember? There were about eight markets on the highway there . . . South Tacoma . . . vegetables and stuff. We used to have one of those. I think they were all Japanese people . . . Airway Market, I think. I think that was it, I can't remember. It's all . . . (*shrugs*) Whenever they were busy, we used to help.

The Polk City Directory (1928, 18) confirms the existence of an Airway Market, registered under the name Kimiko Kimura, that sold groceries and fruits at 8224 South Tacoma Way. Ryo Munekata also remembered that the Kimura family had many children, and that they had a market on South Tacoma Way that "was mostly for people in that area or travelers."[12]

FIGURE 4.1. Yakima Fruit and Produce (Nishijima family business), 8104 South Tacoma Way, ca. 1936–41. Courtesy of the Nishijima Family.

Ryo's comment, and the location of these markets away from the centrally located Nihonmachi, suggest that these businesses were not solely for the Japanese community.

Interestingly, Sally was the only one of her siblings who attended the Japanese Language School and the Tacoma Buddhist Church. She took the public bus back and forth, and her memories of the travel were of getting "used to it" and that it didn't bother her. Her older sisters "joined the women's club—ladies' club—and they used to go to different towns for conventions and things like that," but her older brother was playing football, and the oldest, "well, he . . . already left home because he got married." Young Nisei women were exploring social worlds unknown to their parents' generation, such as dating, moviegoing, and dances.[13] New social clubs also emerged to extend the daily paths of the young women.

Across the street from the Airway Market was an empty field, Sally remembered, where there were organized activities for the community.[14] She also recalled one of her brothers trying to make money selling flowers along the highway:

I know there in the springtime, when we used to have the market, my, uh, brother used to get a bunch of his friends, and they used to sell

flowers like daffodils and stuff like that on the highway . . . they paid
the kids to help. Uh-huh. So, it was something for the young people to
make a few pennies. Yeah, I think they enjoyed that. The flowers were
pretty. (*laughs*) They have a lot of daffodils during the springtime . . .
Because there in springtime they have a daffodil parade, like they
have rose parades here, and so it's a pretty big thing.

Others we interviewed, such as Chizu Tomita Takaoka, remembered
working in one of the markets along South Tacoma Way during the
summer.

When I was around, oh gosh, I can't remember . . . maybe about thirteen? I used to, Saturday I used to work in the, oh, market. All, they
all had market, food stand, market stand, flower shop, those are the
kind of places I used to work in. For ten hours for two dollars . . . my
older sister, myself . . . the three of us . . . In the summertime, I used
to go working; they had a mar-, these people that had, uh, came from
the same part of the country as my father. And they had a highway—
you know South Tacoma? There used to be a highway market. I used
to work there, and right, uh, second day after [school] ends, I was
there, and then I came back Monday before the [summer] ended. But
I never knew how much I made because Mr. Kumasaka would come
and give it to my mother, and she took it. Period.

The Polk City Directory (1933, 854) shows a Liberty Florist and Liberty
Fruit Stand registered to a Mr. Kumasaka, coinciding with Chizu's
memories of flowers and food at the markets. Kazuo Horita also referred
to the produce markets on the highway.

Yuriko Lily Korin Harada was not sure why her family had settled in
Tacoma, but many people came from Hiroshima to Tacoma, so her father
"must have either followed them or they followed him." She explained that
her father "was not a farmer. He was a merchant. He was working for a big
wholesale Japanese food merchant and he would take orders and deliver
to the outskirts of Tacoma to the farmers. That was his job." The Polk City
Directory (1933, 390) notes that Mr. Masayuki Ayako Korin was a salesman
for M. Furuya Company, the largest grocery in Tacoma and a major
trading company with branches in Tacoma, Portland, and Vancouver, BC,

as well as two offices in Japan (Nomura 1989, 125; Takaki [1989] 1998, 168–88). Yuriko remembered that he loved cars, buying new ones regularly, including a "brand new light green Buick" when her youngest brother was born, which made her father "so proud." Later the family bought a market on the "outskirts" of Tacoma, and her mother's younger brother, who lived with them, helped at the store and with driving. Yuriko explained:

> Those days a market was not a market. It was a roadside market, and the folks would stay in their car. My parents would have to go running up to the car and take their orders, bag them, and take them back to the car. That's the kind of store they had. And so my mother was very busy.
>
> [*Was it near downtown?*]
>
> No, it was outskirts, because I remember open fields and just houses here and there. I remember that, so it was not in the city. Outskirts . . . I had to take a bus to go home from Japanese School; I couldn't walk home. I had to take a bus . . . [We lived] right behind the store, right behind the store.

Yuriko did not remember other Japanese families near where she lived and noted that she and her brother were the only Asians at Horace Mann Elementary School. Before the family moved to the "outskirts," however, they lived in town, at 1345 Fawcett Ave (Polk 1933, 390), near the Japanese Language School, and she attended Central School, like many of the other Japanese children in Tacoma.

While the history of Japanese immigrants in Tacoma has generally been understood in terms of its downtown area, the tideflats and South Tacoma are two urban spaces that have been made doubly invisible. Hardworking Issei and their Nisei children claimed belonging through playing at "Tokyo Beach," planting flowers in yards along the tideflats' St. Paul Avenue, and through running businesses that largely served a white clientele. The Nisei narratives shed light on histories that have been erased, on memories of places that shaped adult lives, and on the wider spaces that they inhabited.

CHAPTER FIVE

The Yamasakis and the Tacoma Japanese Language School

> To me, the emphasis should be on the two teachers, Mr. and
> Mrs. [Yamasaki] . . . It should be centered around their interest in
> educating us to . . . become, shall we say, good citizens not only
> of the United States, but good citizens of the world.
>
> —RYO MUNEKATA

W HEN TACOMA'S LANGUAGE SCHOOL OPENED IN 1911, KUNIKO
Yamasaki was hired as the school's first teacher, and soon thereafter
her husband, Masato Yamasaki, was appointed to serve as principal (see
chapter 1). Together the couple, who lived with their three children in the
TJLS building itself after its construction, shaped and guided the
development of the school from its founding in 1911 until its closure in
1942, exerting important influences on the Nisei children as they
constructed their identities at home, at play, and at school. Ronald Magden
notes of the twenty-four former students he spoke with: "All of those
interviewed who attended Tacoma Nihongogakko [TJLS] attested to the
lifetime imprint on their development by the Yamasakis" (1998, 76).

Virtually every former student we interviewed also singled out
Masato and Kuniko Yamasaki as being the very core of the school, and
as such, leaders in the Tacoma Japanese community itself (figure 5.1). As

FIGURE 5.1. Group portrait of teachers, families, and students at the Tacoma Japanese Language School, ca. 1920–35. Courtesy of Washington State Historical Society, 1989.18.17.1.

Anon Male A remarked, "The Principal had such a magnetic personality, that kept us all together." Highly respected and sometimes feared by the students, Mr. Yamasaki shaped the educational philosophy of the TJLS, and in turn exerted tremendous influence on the development of identity among Tacoma's Nisei children. He did so through daily micropractices of subject-making such as ethics and language lessons,[1] discipline, influence on the parents, and activities and events. In this way the children internalized behavioral expectations "as second nature . . . the active presence of the whole past," in what Pierre Bourdieu refers to as *habitus,* or "embodied history" (1990, 56; see also chapter 6).

The Yamasakis emerged out of the Meiji era, a transformational moment in Japan's modern history, and as immigrants they brought with them to the US the defining values of that time. As Japan turned its back on centuries of isolation and sought to establish itself as an equal member of the international community, Japanese themselves faced the challenge of forging an identity that was both modern *and* Japanese (K. Pyle 1969). The Yamasakis, like all Issei, confronted their own version of this as they carved out lives in their new home. How could they be good residents of the United States while still maintaining Japanese practices, traditions, and allegiances? Duncan Ryuken Williams examines this question as it relates to Japanese American Buddhists in the prewar period, looking at "those who, even as their loyalty was being questioned, insisted on the right to be Buddhist and American at the same time" (2019, 4). These issues, and the ways in which the Yamasakis grappled with them, formed the very basis of the Tacoma Japanese Language School and the lessons that were taught there. Accordingly, the Yamasakis' curriculum centered around *shushin*, the traditional values encoded in the Meiji-era Imperial Rescript on Education, but also incorporated a mix of American values such as equality and democracy.

The Yamasakis were both "children of Meiji" whose lives in a transnational context contributed to shaping the educational philosophy they developed for the TJLS. They in turn were influenced by early twentieth-century views of Nisei education in the United States, largely formulated around the concept of the Nisei as a "bridge" between the US and Japan. Yet the reality of Nisei identity construction was not static, as the "bridge" metaphor suggests, but rather ongoing and dynamic. This chapter examines the Yamasakis' role in the complex processes of "bridging" experienced by the Nisei.

KUNIKO AND MASATO YAMASAKI

The former students painted vivid pictures of both Mrs. Yamasaki, whom they often referred to as *onna-no-sensei* ("lady teacher") or, less frequently, *oku-san* ("wife"), and Mr. Yamasaki—*kocho-sensei* ("principal"), *otoko-no-sensei* ("male teacher"), or less frequently, Yamasaki-*sensei*. The Nisei stressed the central position the two occupied in the life of the school and the community. As Kazuo Horita expressed it,

> It seems to me the important part of [the TJLS] was maybe the students, but more important in my own mind, is the two that led the school, their contribution. What did they do for us . . . what did we learn from them? We learned perseverance, we learned honesty, these

were things that were instilled. What effect did that have for us? The effect of all of this was that, I hope, to be better citizens. I go out in the world and say, *"I'm a better Nisei than the other people from the other place, because I went to the Japanese Language School."* . . . Somehow or other, we ought to be able to tell people a hundred years from now what the Japanese Americans did . . . And part of that, in my own mind, has to do with the leadership of that school, and how different— how superior, I am going to say—that was to so many others. (emphasis added)

Ryo Munekata concurred, saying: "The Japanese School was what brought the Japanese community together. And within the Japanese School, the principal individuals were Mr. and Mrs. Yamasaki. And I think we all agree that these two individuals, we feel, is the core of our community. And we would like their memory to be permanently engraved in the community." Professor Seiichi Konzo, whom Ronald Magden (1998, 182) identified as "the last living member" of the TJLS's first graduating class to attend the 1977 TJLS reunion, said of the Yamasakis: "Nowhere in Hawaii or on the entire Pacific Coast was there a better qualified sensei than *otoko-no-sensei*. And *onna-no-sensei* was a jewel of equal merit, especially as a teacher of calligraphy" (in Magden 1998, 72; hyphens added).

KUNIKO YAMASAKI

Kuniko Yamasaki was born March 13, 1872, in Aizuwakamatsu City, Fukushima Prefecture, in Japan's Tohoku region, north of Tokyo. Benefiting from the new opportunities for women that emerged in the Meiji period, she graduated from prefectural primary and high schools and then taught in a variety of schools. Female education had been rare in Japan prior to the Meiji Restoration, but in 1872, the same year Kuniko was born, the new government established compulsory public education, requiring two years of schooling for both boys and girls. Soon the requirement was expanded to four years. It was not uncommon for families with girls to limit their daughters' formal schooling to the minimum requirement (if not try to escape it altogether), but clearly Kuniko and her family embraced the new educational opportunities. She then taught in schools in Wakamatsu City, including the Wakamatsu City High School and the Fukushima Prefectural School of Literature, before emigrating to Seattle in July 1910 (Otsuka and Fukui [1940] 1986, 68). Although it is not known precisely when the Yamasakis married, it was certainly prior to Mrs. Yamasaki's immigration in July 1910.

Mrs. Yamasaki was remembered as a "very gentle, kind person" (Junichi Taira), "strict but warm" (Yuriko Lily Korin Harada). The only one of the female teachers designated as *onna-no-sensei*, Mrs. Yamasaki was, like her husband, accorded great respect. As Teiko Kawano Peterson (whose mother, Teruko Kawano, also taught at the school)[2] remarked, "Mrs. Yamasaki was *onna-no-sensei*. (*laughs*) She was really, I think, the background of the whole school, too—the backbone, rather. She wasn't ever visible, but I know that, you know, through my mother's relationship with the two teachers. I could tell that she was really the backbone of the whole school." Teiko's sister, Harue Kawano Ozaki, agreed:

> She never got enough credit, I don't think. [The Yamasakis were] a team . . . and we didn't realize until, you know, a hundred years later how *onna-no-sensei*, who was the principal's wife, was really the power behind the man. As usual. (*smiles*) But anyway, she never received enough credit, in that she was the one who was truly cultured. When the Western influence came into Japan [with the Meiji Restoration], she was a lady who truly was exposed, and embraced much of, I think, the arts and music and all the culture. I think Yamasaki, *otoko-no-sensei*, too, did. The both of them . . . made a good team. Because they both had this foresight that this is what they missed as Japanese people that were confined to their limited kind of culture compared to the opening of the Western world. I think that was one of the main motivations to their whole life.

Ryo Munekata also recognized Mrs. Yamasaki's important role in the TJLS:

> The first person to work for the school was his wife, not him [Mr. Yamasaki]. She was the teacher that had the backbone for education, and then he tagged along later . . . She wasn't one of these outspoken people—not an activist type of an individual, because she would always be behind Mr. Yamasaki and his quiet way—and she was a very highly educated lady, having finished a teaching school in Japan.

According to sisters Tadaye Fujimoto Kawasaki and Kimiko Fujimoto Tanbara,

> TADAYE: [Mrs. Yamasaki was] jovial.
> KIMIKO: Ya. She had a good sense of humor.
> TADAYE: Always smiling.
> KIMIKO: And she used to go around cleaning the restrooms . . . We didn't have that job. We just had to take care of our own classrooms. But you know, that's really something that she really didn't have to do what she did. So we really admire her for that.[3]

In their reminiscing, the Nisei presented an image of Mrs. Yamasaki as a woman of quiet dignity. Chizu Tomita Takaoka called her a "real *ojoo-san*"—a term that can mean "young lady" or "Miss," but which carries the connotation of refinement, elegance, and gentility.

> You know it, like Mrs. Yamasaki—*Oku-*, we used to call her *Oku-san* [respectful term for "wife"]—*Oku-san* came from a family of scholars like that. She was a real *ojoo-san*, see? And then every time I see her, she's down in the basement, or around there, sticking her hand in the toilet, washing. She was a janitress. That's a lady, to me. So we were exposed to that, since we were small kids. How to evaluate that. You don't realize that kind of thing until you're in your forties or fifties. Anyway, I'm slow, so it took me that long . . .
>
> *Kocho-sensei* [Principal], both of them, were such a proud people. That is to say, they had personalities—like I say, here she was washing, sticking her hand in the toilet . . . Then she had the kindergarten, and she could communicate with the kids. But I think if she was presented to the Empress of Japan, she'd carry it beautifully.

Yuriko Lily Korin Harada especially recalled Mrs. Yamasaki's warmth:

> And I remember Mrs. Yamasaki, the lady that—she was a very strict, but warm lady. Somehow I remember her and her two daughters. She had two daughters there helping, and I remember them, too, very playful, but Missus was the warm person, she was. One day I got—not

a black eye or bad injury—but I got hit in the face or eye by somebody throwing a ball, and Mrs. Yamasaki took me right upstairs to her living quarters, because it was right next to the school, and lie me down on the sofa and she would slap on a great big piece of steak on my face . . . I remember that very clearly.

MASATO YAMASAKI

Masato Yamasaki was born in 1874 in Aizuwakamatsu City.[4] In 1902 he graduated with a degree in literature from the Tokyo Special School (Tokyo Senmon Gakko), the forerunner of Waseda University, one of Japan's preeminent private universities. After graduation, Mr. Yamasaki taught at the Fukushima Prefectural Teachers School, but he resigned this position in 1908 and emigrated to the US, entering via Seattle in March of that year. He worked a variety of jobs in Seattle, including as a "common laborer in a Caucasian home, where he worked for five years" (Otsuka and Fukui [1940] 1986, 99). The historical record contains no reason for his decision to emigrate, but an early Tacoma history speculated that although he was "popular with both the staff and students . . . perhaps [Yamasaki resigned] because he had so much drive that he was not content to teach at one normal school" (Otsuka and Fukui [1940] 1986, 99). In 1912, when Mr. Yamasaki's wife became the Tacoma Japanese Language School's first teacher, hired to teach "Japanese language, history and ethics," the couple relocated to Tacoma (Magden 1998, 72).

Masato's original family name was Nakane, according to Chizu Tomita Takaoka, whose father was from the same prefecture, but he had been adopted by Mrs. Yamasaki's family, which apparently had no sons, as a *mukoyoshi*, or adopted son-in-law, a traditional practice in a family without male heirs. In this way, they could continue the Yamasaki family name. Chizu explained: "Now Fukushima [the Yamasakis' natal place] was noted, I found out; the lord encouraged education to the people. So he [Mr. Yamasaki] was there, and Mrs. Yamasaki's ancestors were the teachers of the lord of the province. And I think they got that. Anyway, so the two became . . . they carried on the name of Yamasaki."

The Yamasakis themselves had three children, a son, Shuji, and two daughters, Tetsuko and Yoshiko. Starting in 1916, the family lived in what was the second building housing the language school, at 510 South 15th Street (*History of Japanese in Tacoma,* 1941, n.p. [46]). After construction of the permanent school, the family lived in residential quarters along the south side of the building's upper floor (because the building was situated on a hillside, the main floor was at street level, with two levels beneath it) from the time of its opening in 1922 until incarceration in 1942.[5]

If Kuniko Yamasaki was the TJLS's "backbone," Masato Yamasaki was its public face. In addition to his important role as principal and teacher, Mr. Yamasaki served in a variety of other capacities in the community, including at various times as president, secretary, and board member of the Tacoma Japanese Association (*History of Japanese in Tacoma* 1941). As the association's executive secretary, Yamasaki led the unsuccessful fight to keep Tacoma as the main port of the Osaka Shosen Kaisha shipping company when, in 1915, it announced its intention to shift its business to Seattle (Magden 1998, 49). Another local issue Yamasaki involved himself in, this time as association president, was the problem of picture brides being forced into prostitution upon arrival in Tacoma (Magden 1998, 49–51). "These women should be properly counseled and advised," the association noted (Otsuka and Fukui [1940] 1986, 17). Yamasaki was also a kendo instructor and an advisor to the Tacoma branch of the North American Butoku Kendo Association (*History of Japanese in Tacoma* 1941, n.p. [206]). As a community leader, too, he occasionally gave public talks, such as one titled "The Races of Ancient Japan" delivered at the inaugural meeting of the TJLS alumni association in January 1934 (*History of Japanese in Tacoma* 1941, n.p. [85]).

Masato Yamasaki's prominent position in the local community is evidenced by his selection as the first of ten prominent Japanese "Men of Distinction" from Tacoma and Fife in a poll conducted by the publishers of Tacoma's Japanese-language newspaper, the *Takoma jiho*.[6] Kuniko Yamasaki, for her part, was one of only two women whose biography appears in the Otsuka and Fukui history of Japanese Tacoma (the other woman so distinguished was the owner of a clothing shop) (Otsuka and Fukui [1940] 1986, 68).

Ryo Munekata described the selection of Mr. Yamasaki as a "man of distinction":

> The company where this was researched . . . their office was somewhere up here on Jefferson Avenue, and in that book . . . they tried

to select ten outstanding Japanese citizens of the community, and lo and behold, the one that came out on top by the selection of the staff of the publishing company was Mr. Masato Yamasaki, our principal. And so, when I read those things, Mr. and Mrs. Yamasaki become that much more meaning[ful] for me in my life . . . I think many of us can relate our personal life with the Japanese school.

The other nine men in the poll are praised for their various contributions to the community and are extolled as "good-natured" and "modest" (Kenkichi Honda), "well-known and prosperous" (Hyogo Nakashima), or "knowledgeable" (Heiichi Anbo). One was even recognized as a person who could "drink all night and not have it affect him" (Magoichi Yamane). About another individual, Shuhei Oda, it was noted: "He is known as a hard drinker but lately he has moderated his habits as he is in the process of calling over his wife" (Otsuka and Fukui [1940] 1986, 99–102).

Amid these laudatory (and sometimes unintentionally humorous) profiles, Masato Yamasaki's indeed stands out:

He was a gentle and modest man, but he could mete out severe punishment if a principle was at stake. His favorite subject was philosophy and he successfully lectured to the students on this subject. He also excelled in debate and composition.

He is a man of integrity and his bornds [*sic*] are quite modest. He values friendship. He is compassionate. He has the confidence of the parents; and respect and affection of the students. At present he is not only the principal of the language school but also a fine teacher. . . . It is only fitting that he be selected number one in the *Tacoma Jiho* poll of men of distinction. (in Otsuka and Fukui [1940] 1986, 99)

A further mark of Mr. Yamasaki's prominence in the Japanese American community was the commendation he received in November 1940 from the Japanese Foreign Ministry, along with twelve other men from the Seattle area, as part of a ceremony held by the Seattle consulate to commemorate the 2,600th anniversary of the founding of the Japanese nation—alluding to the mythical date of the ascension to the throne of the first Japanese emperor in 660 BCE (Ito 1969, 1061).

Harue Kawano Ozaki, whose mother, Teruko Kawano, was a longtime teacher at the Tacoma Japanese Language School, believed the values emphasized by Masato Yamasaki were crucial to the shaping of TJLS and Tacoma's Japanese community: "It was values that I think made our community cohesive, because they had control over the children that way . . . [This came from] our leader . . . Yamasaki-*sensei*." Sister and brother Michie Taira Hori and Junichi Taira also gave credit to Mr. Yamasaki for Tacoma's strong Japanese community, though they wondered where the real influence lay—in Mr. Yamasaki himself or in already-existing community cohesion.

> JUNICHI: Well, you wonder if that's—which came first, the chicken or the egg. I mean, that could have solidified the community. Or . . . well, I don't know, it's hard to say. Yeah, I can't really relate which . . . mattered more . . . The community was pretty solid already, I think—
>
> MICHIE: Right.
>
> JUNICHI: Well, by the time *we* grew up.
>
> MICHIE: Well, I'm sure it was a desire of the parents for us to learn the language, too, you know that. Because it was almost mandatory . . . almost—I don't know if it was *mandatory*, but we felt that was the thing to do. There was no question asked.
>
> JUNICHI: Because we were looking forward to recess! (*laughs*)

Many former students depicted Mr. Yamasaki as strict. As Takao Jerry Kikuchi put it, "The only thing I remember is that he was very disciplined. Strict. Kind of hard to approach him . . . he was very disciplined. I don't know. Most Japanese parents are very disciplined. When you meet strangers you always bow your head, that sort of thing, you know." Sister and brother Michie and Junichi concurred:

> JUNICHI: I think it was just his position that we more or less honored, as I could recall. We sure didn't show much respect for the teachers, but for him, somehow . . . I don't know.
>
> MICHIE: That's amazing. He didn't say a word, he didn't yell, it was just his look . . . When the boys got too rowdy and noisy, then the principal would step out of *his* class and come to the window [of

the misbehaving classroom] and with a *stern* look, all he had to
do was look in the window, and we were all quiet. (*laughs*)

JUNICHI: Of course we were afraid of Mr. Yamasaki. (*laughs*)

MICHIE: Yes. All he'd have to do was—I'll never forget that face!
When he came to that window because we were too rowdy, boy,
I tell you, he didn't have to say a word.

JUNICHI: Well, you know, he must have been a great organizer or
a great administrator, because to get those teachers to handle us,
that's amazing. After six hours in an American school, and you
know, you go to the second school, you're not too . . .

MICHIE: Yeah, another two hours . . .

JUNICHI: But those teachers were so dedicated. . . So all the focus
seems to be on the principal, Mr. and Mrs. Yamasaki, but I give
a lot of credit to the teachers, too.

Anon Female A also remembered the effect of Mr. Yamasaki's face
peering through the classroom window, as well as the respect they had for
him: "If our class was giving the teacher a bad time . . . We used to call
him *kocho sensei*—*kocho* means "principal" . . . And he would periodically
leave his class and make, just, a check around. All the classroom doors
had a window, and all he had to do—all the boys in our class needed was
to see the principal standing there and they would all go back to their
desks and all act like little angels. (*laughs*) . . . He had an impact on us, for
sure."

Perry Yoshiaki Yano described Mr. Yamasaki's strict and imposing
demeanor:

I just have a picture of what they looked like. He was a—by that, by
that time he was, he's a lot older than he looks in this photo here, and
his wife, you know, of course is older too. She was, by that time she
was pretty stout, and he, he was a pretty stern-looking guy. You know
he, to me he looked very imposing, you know, pretty tall and pretty
scary guy. (*laughs*) I think he was very strict. But he never, I never saw
him . . . I don't think I remember him hollering at anybody, yelling at
anybody, or anything like that. Or his wife, either. And his daughters
are very, very, very nice. As far as I know. No, I never heard any bad
words said about them.

Masato Yamasaki's stern style was tempered with kindness, however. Taeko Hoshiwara Taniguchi recalled that "just by looking at him, I know he was a very educated person. You know, he was all—in a way he was [a] strict teacher, but he would also be very kind and . . . I have nothing but good memories of him."

In a handwritten (in Japanese), unsigned document titled "Research on Training Students in the Lower Primary Grades" and dated November 1931, school staff were reminded:

> Teachers should not yell at or intimidate students. Yelling at or intimidating students harms their dignity. We should treat and teach children as children. We should not force children to be too well-mannered or over-correct them or expect them to behave as adults. [On the other hand,] there are certain rules that are important for children, such as exchanging greetings when they arrive at and leave school, or taking off their hats in school, so we should not allow children to always behave as they please.[7]

A sense of the Yamasakis' character as a couple can be found in a story Tadaye Fujimoto Kawasaki told about a serious accident involving students on a field trip to [army base] Fort Lewis, the state capital in Olympia, and the Tacoma municipal power plant at Cushman Dam.[8] According to *History of Japanese in Tacoma* (1941, n.p. [55–56]), a group of thirty students invited to access the lower section of the power plant by tram were aboard when the tram's cable broke:

> The car [was] increasing speed . . . [when it] crashed into a concrete wall. All 30 passengers were thrown from the car and the accident caused injuries and wounds. A Caucasian medical doctor, Mr. Chard[,] with his nurses rushed to the site of the accident and immediately provided medical aid. The older ones and graduates among the students made stretchers with the help of power plant workers. They were made from lumber which was nearby. They carried the injured with the stretchers from the bottom of the valley, up the steep 45 degree slope of sand and small rocks. . . . All 30 injured and wounded were taken to the Tacoma General Hospital by 10 ambulances which were called in from various areas of Tacoma, Shelton, Olympia and Bremerton. . . .

The news of the accident was already known before all the patients were transferred to the hospital. About 100 parents, who were shocked to hear of the accident, hurried to the hospital one after another to find out the condition of their children. The scene of worried parents who waited for the ambulances to arrive could not be expressed in words.

Tadaye also remembered Mrs. Yamasaki's concern for other children and families, and mentioned that she had never before seen Mr. Yamasaki cry.

A RIGOROUS CURRICULUM

Mr. and Mrs. Yamasaki created a rigorous academic experience for the TJLS students. The school met each weekday afternoon from 4 to 6 p.m., and also organized activities on Saturdays and during the summertime. Learning at the TJLS was taken seriously: teachers kept attendance records and issued grade reports, which were sent home to parents. During her interview, Yuriko Lily Korin Harada perused one of her report cards from the TJLS and reminisced, "Okay, this is Japanese School naturally, so they don't have math. It says 'writing, speaking, and reading.' And 'understanding what you read' is here. I didn't write too well, but I was able to read. And 'comprehend' was very good—95. That's good." Jack Kazuo Hata reported, "Well, basically the language school was to learn the language, so that was the primary objective, I think, plus learning calligraphy and a little bit of history," while Katsuko Aochi Harano remembered, "Depending on the subject, we would be taught reading, *shuji* [penmanship], yes . . . and then history, and *shushin*." Michie Taira Hori and Junichi Taira outlined some of the curricular content:

> MICHIE: Well, we were supposed to learn how to read, so [the teacher] would assign us the chapter that we were supposed to read, and basically how to write. You know, she would go on the blackboard and show us how—especially the *kanji* [Chinese characters used in writing Japanese], you know . . .
>
> JUNICHI: Just the basic Japanese reading and writing. The calligraphy was also pretty important. I remember they emphasized where the pressure should be and stuff like that. We did learn history through the reading.

Chizu Tomita Takaoka recalled learning the somewhat esoteric subject of *kambun*, a Japanese form of classical Chinese writing developed in Japan's eleventh-century Heian period:

> When I went there, [Principal Yamasaki] asked us what we wanted to learn—anything in particular? And nobody spoke up, so I said (*laughs*) that I wanted to learn *kambun*, which is a Chinese form, it's a Japanese history written in Chinese form. So he started. He was such a scholar.
>
> And then I remember in the school, right on top of the blackboard, there was a scroll—not a scroll, it's a map, actually, starting from the era of gods . . . the history of Japan, and he would point to that and he would explain what was happening in the United States or in the world. It was just fascinating.

MR. YAMASAKI AND THE TARGETING OF LANGUAGE SCHOOLS

The resurfacing of anti-Japanese agitation after World War I was focused largely on the Nisei rather than the Issei, as had been the case earlier in the 1900s. Not surprisingly, this shift resulted in the targeting of Japanese language schools. The retired publisher of the *Sacramento Bee,* Valentine S. McClatchy, for example, singled out language schools as places where children "imbibe Japanese principles and ideas," thereby presenting a threat of Japanese encroachment on American sovereignty (Asato 2003b, 141). Exclusionists looked at the Japanese language school curriculum as "evidence" that they were promoting a pernicious "Mikado worship," in McClatchy's words (Asato 2006 53). While some scholars, such as Ken Adachi (1979, 129), have argued that Japanese language schools did not promote Japanese nationalism, others have maintained that the schools' curriculum was "definitely not apolitical" (Lemire 2016–17, 81). Nevertheless, attacks on the curriculum led the Nikkei in California, for one, to replace textbooks approved by the Mombusho (Japan's Ministry of Education) with their own compilations (Asato 2006, 63).

Archival records from the TJLS indicate that the school did not stop using textbooks from Japan, unlike in California. Most (but not all) of the textbooks used were published by Mombusho, and included texts for both reading and writing.[9] Other textbooks used at the TJLS included hand-copied versions of *Nihon gaishi*, a well-known history of Japan written by nineteenth-century historian and Confucianist Rai Sanyo, and "textbooks for female students from 12 to 16 years old."[10] These purchase records demonstrate that TJLS curriculum aligned with content officially sanctioned by the Japanese government.

Exclusionist suspicion surrounded teachers in the Japanese language schools as agents of "Japanization" (Asato 2006, 89), and the Japanese community itself debated the purpose of and need for Japanese language schools. *History of Japanese in Tacoma* (1941, n.p. [44]) records that "even among the Japanese people, there appeared those who advocated the discontinuation of Japanese language school as a neutralizing measure [i.e., to 'neutralize . . . anti-Japanese feelings']." Ohashi Chuichi, the Japanese consul in Seattle, advocated that Japanese language schools be abolished so that Nisei children could become "complete American citizens" (Ichioka 2006, 75).

In Pierce County, Superintendent of Public Schools Minnie Bean sought ways to legally shutter the Japanese language schools. Just prior to taking office in fall 1919, she announced in a letter to the staunchly anti-Japanese newspaper *Seattle Star* that her "first priority as superintendent was to close the Japanese Schools." The letter appeared under the headline "Plan to Oust Japs' Schools" (Asato 2003b, 143). In late July and early August 1920, the House Immigration and Naturalization Committee held hearings in both Seattle and Tacoma focusing on Japanese immigration, and specifically looked into the Seattle Japanese Language School (Asato 2003b, 145; *History of Japanese in Tacoma* 1941, n.p. [48]).

In 1920, amid a virulent uptick in anti-Japanese sentiment on the West Coast, Tacoma central school principal George A. Stanley met with Masato Yamasaki to complain that the Japanese Language School was deflecting attention away from English-language study, resulting in Nisei students who were ill-equipped for the public schools. Stanley threatened to force the closure of the TJLS if the Japanese students' English did not improve. In response, Principal Yamasaki asked for six months to rectify the situation.

In point of fact, however, of the more than sixty Japanese students at Tacoma Central School at that time (the elementary school attended by the majority of the Nisei), most were earning above-average marks in their public school classrooms, and "teachers noted in class register margins the exemplary behavior and excellent attendance record of the Nisei" (Magden 1998, 81). Only a handful of first-graders were having difficulty with reading. If there was a problem, the Yamasakis attributed it to the fact that most of the "failing pupils" had just arrived in the US from Japan. Between 1915 and 1919 the number of picture brides coming to Washington, Montana, Idaho, and the Alaska Territory had steadily increased (from 150 in 1915 to 267 in 1919), suggesting more pupils who had their earliest years in a Japanese-speaking home (Asato 2003b, 149n47). Magden (1998, 81) also records a big jump in the Nisei population of Central School between 1920 and 1930, from 66 to 249.

The Yamasakis addressed the language issue by enlisting Nisei high-schoolers to tutor grade-schoolers in English skills on Saturdays, with a focus on reading, writing, and vocabulary. Some 70–80 percent of TJLS students attended these sessions. Chizu Takaoka remembered: "In Japanese school, we had what's called the Saturday school. From nine to twelve, I think. And all the high school students had lower classes to teach English, more or less. And we [tutors] were paid twenty-five cents." Principal Yamasaki ultimately decided to provide English language instruction on an ongoing basis, targeting the youngest Nisei in particular but also offering instruction for Issei adults. In 1925, he engaged Baptist Mission teacher Electa Snyder to teach English to kindergarteners; in 1934, at the request of the parents, the TJLS added evening English classes (*History of Japanese in Tacoma* 1941, n.p. [58]). As the *History* notes, "Among the many Japanese language schools on the Pacific Ocean coast, very few schools set up a preschool and a language school where both English and Japanese were taught. The Tacoma Japanese Language School was one such school" (1941, n.p. [48]). Eileen Tamura has written of the important role American teachers played in exposing Nisei to "American ways" (1994, 171).

Electa Snyder was one of the three Caucasian "allies" who assisted with the purchase of land for the permanent TJLS in 1920 (see chapter 1). She taught English at the language school until her retirement in May 1940, when she was given an "appreciation party." Anonymous Female E remembered the impact of Mrs. Snyder and her English lessons: "I could see her, picture her face yet, I remember. Oh, we spoke nothing but Japanese at home right now, at that time . . . and I must have been about five, and I remember, I think that's how I learned English because I didn't have any problem going to Central School."

Nearly all of Tacoma's Nisei remember speaking Japanese at home, a practice that seems to have continued at least until incarceration. Masatoshi Fujii: "Japanese was our first language." Kunio Shibata even recalled his father punishing the children for speaking English in the home. Ryo Munekata remembered that during "our preschool years, our language was Japanese, because our parents didn't know that much English. And so, before we entered the first grade in the public school, we had very little knowledge of the English language." That Japanese was our interviewees' first language (and that they continued their Japanese language studies at the TJLS) was evident in their habit of interspersing the conversation with Japanese interjections—*ano ne, so, yo*—and the frequent use of Japanese vocabulary. In conversation among themselves, they frequently switched back and forth between English and Japanese.

Chizu Takaoka recalled that Mrs. Snyder "was *kocho-sensei's* idea. To help along with English. I remember learning 'Twinkle, Twinkle, Little Star' and 'My Country, 'Tis of Thee.' You know, that's just about all I remember. But I remember 'Twinkle, Twinkle, Little Star.'" Siblings Masatoshi Fujii and Fusae Fujii remembered:

MASATOSHI: Everything was Japanese. Because Japanese was our first language. We never acquired any English until we went to Mrs. Snyder's kindergarten class.

FUSAE: We used to wait at the corner for her [Mrs. Snyder's] streetcar to come, and when she got off the streetcar people would all wait for her to come and walk back to school with her. But that much I remember. Do you?

MASATOSHI: No, I don't remember that. But she also taught ESL to the Issei, the older immigrant parents.

In addition to focusing on the Nisei children, Mr. Yamasaki provided ongoing guidance to their Issei parents. He met with the parents, discussing not only their children's progress but also the standards of behavior he thought worthy of the Japanese community at large. Kimiko Fujimoto Tanbara spoke of Mr. Yamasaki's efforts specifically to help bridge the language and cultural gap by "teaching" the parents how to behave in their interactions at the public schools:

> KIMIKO: A lot of that I think we owe to our principal, Japanese school principal [Mr. Yamasaki], because he really steered us all into the right direction . . . The whole family.
> [*You mean not just the students?*]
> KIMIKO: Oh, ya. Because they use to have PTA [meetings] all the time, and I think the parents were equally told how to behave and you know, all that, so . . .

Riyeko Fujimoto discussed family involvement with the TJLS and the public schools: "Stadium [High School] was nice, . . . but you didn't get really involved in everything. Your parents didn't get involved very much. They had PTAs and everything, but they didn't go, because the main reason was they probably couldn't speak the language." Junichi Taira, too, wrote about the language school's role in equipping Issei parents with skills to better oversee their children's education: "Besides the respective churches, the JLS was a focal point for the Japanese community in Tacoma. The JLS served to help most of the first generation Japanese without English language skills to take an active part in their children's education and not just see report cards from English school to measure their constant emphasis on studying." Mr. Yamasaki also worked to ensure that people at the public schools understood the Japanese community. As Yoshiko Fujimoto Sugiyama remembered, "For school activities, Mr. Yamasaki always invited our public school principal and the superintendent. They're all in the picture. Ya, really. We had a good relationship with the school system."

Mr. Yamasaki was skillful at building relationships with the schools and other leaders in Tacoma. This acceptance of the TJLS shows that not all whites were exclusionists or part of some "monolithic racial group" (Kurashige 2016, 230). In Seattle, there were other such supporters. Ulysses Grant Murphy, a Seattle Methodist minister who for fourteen years had served as a missionary in Japan, for example, stated that school superintendents in both Seattle and San Francisco were of the opinion that "Nisei who attended the Japanese schools 'made better students' than Nisei who did not, because the schools taught etiquette as well as language" (Asato 2003b, 141). Even within these pockets of white "egalitarian" support for

Japanese language schools, however, there was concern that they might hamper the ability of Nisei children to assimilate—the expected trajectory for immigrants at that time. Some, such as Reverend Sidney L. Gulick of California, who championed Nikkei rights and advocated that Asian immigrants be granted the right of citizenship, for example, believed that Japanese language schools should be supervised by the government.

NISEI IDENTITY, EDUCATION, AND BRIDGING

Mr. Yamasaki's initiative in offering English classes at the TJLS reflected the dominant approach to Nisei identity in the early twentieth century, which emphasized two main elements: that the Nisei were "American first," and that they had a mission and duty to serve as a "bridge" between the US and Japan. As David Yoo wrote in *Growing Up Nisei*, "The bridge concept moved beyond the mere status of interpreter and required the Nisei to be contributors to American life and take up the responsibilities of US citizenship" (2000, 32). At the TJLS, the Yamasakis emphasized this dual ideal of Nisei as firmly rooted citizens of the US, who also possessed a strong understanding of and connection to their Japanese heritage. While Eiichiro Azuma (2006, 507) suggests this approach may have been an "adaptive strategy," designed to provide protection in an environment of exclusion, Mr. Yamasaki was explicit about the role of Japanese schools in "raising Nikkei to be productive American citizens" (Asato 2006, 93).

Such ideas emerged in TJLS student essays written in Japanese. For example, in an undated piece titled "Nihon" (Japan), Chiyoko Tamaki writes:

> Our teachers always say we should read many books, journals, newspapers, and magazines, and also we should often ask our parents about Japan so that we can gain much knowledge about Japan. Then, even though we have not visited Japan yet, if white people ask us about Japan we can talk to them without feeling shy. Therefore, since we are Japanese, don't you think it's good if we study hard about Japan?[11]

And in another undated essay, "Watashi-tachi no [gi]mu" (Our duty), Tokiko Okazaki writes:

As we are Japanese and have inherited our bloodlines from our mothers and fathers, we are born as second-generation Japanese Americans. With this lineage, we must be respectable people and work for peace between Japan and America . . . Because we were born as Japanese Americans . . . we should keep peaceful relations between Japan and America. That is our, second-generation Japanese Americans', task.

In particular, the concept of the Nisei as a bridge or link emphasized the need for the Nisei to "be Americans" (Nitobe 1933, 1) or be "good Americans" (Debuchi 1931, 1) without forgetting their parents' heritage. Teiko Kawano Peterson commented:

Well, I think Mr. and Mrs. Yamasaki . . . established all the fundamentals and ideas that we have. And I remember he said that we live—we're a minority people living in the United States and we can't change our background, but we should be very proud of our background, and he instilled upon us about our background.

Yoshie Jinguji, sister of interviewee Masaye Jinguji Fujita, expressed this as a high school freshman in a TJLS essay titled "Nihonjin to nihongo" (Japanese people and Japanese language): "I believe because we are living in this [Japanese American] society, we should have a Japanese soul and study both Japanese and English enough so that we will be people who are not ashamed to be Japanese American."

Cultivation of both Japanese and American elements, it was believed, would mold the Nisei into "good citizens." Indeed, the bridge metaphor stressed that they should rely on their Japanese-ness in their quest to be good American citizens. Jere Takahashi writes that this was not a political strategy; rather, "largely a personal and cultural approach, this perspective attempted to make Japanese American racial marginality a positive attribute. Marginality was not seen as exclusion from American society but as a means for Japanese Americans to preserve both their ethnic and American heritages" (1982, 49).

The Japanese government continued to emphasize these messages in their ongoing involvement with Japanese communities in the US (see chapter 1). The Issei, and even some older Nisei, followed along. For example, Jimmie Sakamoto (1903–55), founder and editor of the Seattle-based

English-language newspaper *Japanese American Courier,* which targeted a Nisei audience, "urged good citizenship and loyalty to America" while also arguing that the Nisei should acknowledge and embrace "Japan as the source of their cultural heritage" (Fiset 2009, 22). The *Japanese American Courier* played a key role in advocating the view of the Nisei as a "bridge" of understanding (Ichioka 2006, 100). Many of its articles were devoted to Japanese culture, and Sakamoto himself "embodied a strict moral code and conveyed respect for the emperor and his ancestors" (Fiset 2009, 22). In its inaugural issue, on New Year's Day 1928, the paper printed a message from Japanese ambassador to the US, Katsuji Debuchi, who advised: "The second generation in their good fortune . . . must not give up the good qualities that are ever-present in the culture of their parents; for there is good in all cultures" (Debuchi 1928, 1). The ambassador reiterated this theme three years later in another New Year's Day message titled "Become Good Americans," instructing the Nisei: "Be Filial . . . [because] . . . no one who flies in the face of their parents can be a good citizen in any country" (Debuchi 1931, 1).

Most importantly, these ideas formed the core of the Yamasakis' educational message at the TJLS. As Seiichi Konzo put it, "The Yamasakis had an enduring impact on hundreds of students. Every school assembly ended with the two teachers stressing that the Nisei should never forget their unique mission–to transmit Japanese culture to Americans" (in Magden 1998, 72).

According to Harue Kawano Ozaki, Mr. Yamasaki believed "that we [the Tacoma Japanese community] had the best of both worlds . . . We never doubted it for a moment, that we were part of America's bridge." Tadaye Fujimoto Kawasaki also noted Yamasaki's emphasis on the students being "like ambassadors of the two countries." The TJLS school song, written by Principal Yamasaki, played on these intertwined themes as well:

> Children of the pure blood
> From the Land of the Rising Sun
> And born in America
> Where the Star-Spangled Banner flies
> We have a special Mission
> A sense of Special Purpose.

Uniting both of the ways
and not neglecting to train ourselves
For the sake of the world
let us go forth, everyday
To cultivate our true minds.

(*History of Japanese in Tacoma* 1941, n.p.
[60]; see also Ito 1973, 601)

The student essays quoted above, though mostly undated, appear primarily to span the 1930s,[12] by which time the main post-1924 debate over Japanese language schools had died down, leaving in its wake a "greater consensus . . . among all parties that the Nisei needed to learn the ways of the home country to avoid further racial humiliation" (Yoo 2000, 29; see also Takahashi 1997; Kurashige 2002). For some, having to return to Japan was an underlying concern. In an essay titled simply "Nihon," TJLS student Yasumi Kubo wrote: "I do not like to ask my mother about Japan because she keeps saying she wants to go back to Japan."

In "Doshite nihongo wa taisetsu ka?" (Why is Japanese important?; figure 5.2), TJLS student and interviewee Yoneko Aochi also worried about the possibility of having to go back to Japan, as well as the idea that in order to find work in a discriminatory employment environment the Nisei would need to know Japanese (see also chapter 2).

We were born as Japanese people and therefore Japanese language is one of the most necessary tools for our lives. In our daily conversation [with one another] we use Japanese. Moreover, I think that since we were born as Japanese, we must be able to use Japanese language, and [yet] there are some people who can't understand Japanese at all, and those who can't understand what is being said even though they are listening to the conversation . . . Some people say that since these people are living in the United States, there is no need for them to speak Japanese. Moreover, if for some reason we have to return to the country of our parents, and at that time we cannot speak and take what others say seriously, it may lead to hatred and misunderstanding and people no longer talking to one another. Even those who graduate from university, if they don't know Japanese, have a hard time finding jobs. Therefore, they may have to become a farmer in order to eat.

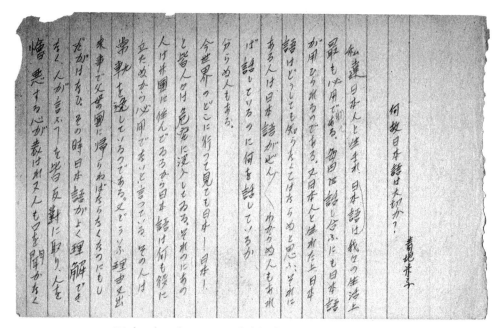

FIGURE 5.2. Undated student essay titled "Why Is Japanese Important" by interviewee Yoneko Aochi. Courtesy of University of Washington Libraries, Special Collections.

The Chinese people who have hated the Japanese now say, "Don't say, 'Japan! Japan!' and talk about Japan if you do not study Japanese," and even they have started to learn about Japan . . . I think we must study Japanese because we all have different situations.

DEMOCRACY AND EQUALITY AT THE TACOMA JAPANESE LANGUAGE SCHOOL

By emphasizing the importance of democracy, equality, and citizenship and at the same time promoting Japanese values and identity, the Yamasakis, and by extension the TJLS, provided a space that allowed the Nisei children to explore their identities as second-generation immigrants. Inculcating the traditional Japanese heritage and ethical principles—of filial piety, for example—was viewed not simply as a way to keep the young Nisei in touch with the values and behaviors of their Issei parents, but also as a way to shape them into, as Harue Kawano Ozaki expressed it, "democratic citizens of the United States." Yet retaining cultural practices and language among Japanese Americans did not mean they "reject[ed] American institutions and ideals of democracy, patriotism, economic opportunity, and cultural adaptation." Nor, however, did it mean that "Japanese Americans got beyond race by forging color-blind affinities and perceptions of social reality" (Kurashige 2002, 5).

A number of the interviewees referred specifically to equality and democracy as important parts of the curriculum at the TJLS. Support for these values reflected "Americanization efforts [that] received a boost from World War I," including "a staunch support for democracy, representative government, law and order, capitalism, general health (diet, hygiene, and sanitation), and command of the English language" (Yoo 2000, 22). The Yamasakis believed in equality and inclusion, both within the Japanese American community and relative to the larger, dominant white American society. They emphasized inclusion among Japanese, for example, by finding ways to cover tuition for families that might not otherwise be able to send their children to the TJLS. They also expressly rejected antiegalitarian impulses within the Japanese community, as Anon Male A observed:

He [Mr. Yamasaki] was very broad-minded . . . You know, in Japan [there is] a class system . . . [Mr. Yamasaki] emphasized none of those things . . . Some people made a big deal of those class systems . . . They had fights . . . The daughter wants to get married to the . . . [and] they said, "No, no. Their classification is lower than our classification, so they can't get married." Stuff like that.

Harue Kawano Ozaki concurred:

Yamasaki-sensei believed in equality. He really was someone who . . . never, never discriminated . . . but believed in equality. And because we all harbor that within ourselves, even to this day. And that would be part of the reason why the nondenominational language school was established from the onset. So everyone was welcome. I know that. But some parents did choose not to send their children to a Japanese language school . . .
[*Where did you get that message of equality?*]

Well, this is part of our indoctrination by Yamasaki-sensei . . .
to champion for equality, and to make it part of our life to be involved.
And luckily, he had teachers that just were as strongly influenced
as the students, because . . . you know, my mom being a, one of
the teachers, I don't think she ever doubted Yamasaki-*sensei*'s leadership. And so, of course, if your mother was like that, we never
doubted it for a moment, that we were part of America's bridge. I
never called it that, but it's true. So you do have family and institution
influences.

Harue Kawano Ozaki believed Mr. Yamasaki's emphasis on democracy
and equality was shared in the community, giving as an example her
mother's experience in the US:

I think that's the basis of what our leader believed in—a democratic
society. I think he liked that idea coming from, *ano*, Japanese emper-
or's nationalistic country and to come to this so-called land of opportunity. I think he really—he and his wife really embraced that concept.
It must have been very exciting.
[*Exciting?*]
Yes. Yes, and challenging. And I know my mother felt the same
way. Because I'd say, "Mama, don't you want to go back to Japan?" Or
you know, "Let's see how you stand right now." And she'd say, "Who
wants to live in Japan anymore?" She'd say, "You're so constricted
[there] and you don't have a chance to be a free woman." So then that
answered my question.

Although exclusionists accused them of maintaining a primary loyalty
to Japan, the emphasis at the TJLS was on being "American first," a value
that according to sisters Kimiko and Tadaye emerged clearly in the Yama-
akis' lessons:

TADAYE: Yes, US first. [We were] American, he always stressed that so
much.
KIMIKO: Ya, he always emphasized that we are Americans. You know,
we owe allegiance to America, that's all he said.

[*How did he do that?*]

TADAYE: Well, he said we were supposed to be like ambassadors of the two countries. But I don't know—

KIMIKO: . . . So we shouldn't do anything to shame ourselves . . . (in Sonnier 1993, 15)

The Japanese government also encouraged the Nisei to be "true Americans" who could serve as a link between the US and Japan. "Born as American citizens with Japanese heritage, the Nisei became inadvertently saddled with the mission of facilitating this process as a bridge of understanding between the two nations and the two worlds" (Azuma 2003, 43). From the perspective of the Japanese government, however, this mission was not necessarily an "inadvertent" one. After the 1924 Exclusion Act brought an end to new Japanese immigration to the US, relations between the two countries deteriorated. In the ongoing debate about Nisei education, in 1928 the "consul general of San Francisco criticized the Nisei for turning into 'spiritual half-breeds' who could be neither full-fledged Japanese nor Americans" (Kumei 2002, 118).[13]

Ambassador Debuchi's 1931 New Year's Day message to the Nisei in the *Japanese American Courier* (see above) came in the wake of the September 1931 Manchurian Incident, which resulted in Japan's military occupation of Manchuria and further damaged Japan-US relations. In this message, Debuchi exhorted the Nisei to be "good Americans" but also stressed their responsibility to serve as a bridge:

Young American citizens of Japanese descent have a particular mission to fulfill and a particular duty to perform. Being of Japanese descent, you are naturally expected to know more about the native country of your parents than does the average American. I urge you to live up to that expectation. You should study about Japan, about things Japanese, about the national spirit and ideals which are back of the marvelous progress achieved by that island nation in the last half century.

You are expected to be the most effective of the connecting links between Japan and America. You can live up to this expectation only by knowing and understanding Japan as you know and understand America. (Debuchi 1931, 1)

Relations deteriorated still further, with a concomitant increase in local suspicion of the Japanese American community in the US, after the outbreak of the Second Sino-Japanese War in 1937. On September 11 of that year, again in the *Japanese American Courier,* Henry S. Tatsumi (1937, 3) reminded the Nisei to devote themselves to the "protection of American ideals." How? By enlisting the code of the samurai:

> The American-born Japanese would naturally show their sympathy
> for their parents' country, but they must keep in mind that they are
> American citizens and their primary concern should be the protection
> of American ideals. Besides, it must be remembered that BUSHIDO,
> the traditional moral code of Japan, forbids one to serve two masters.[14]

Other Issei leaders, such as California newspaper publisher Kyutaro Abiko, promoted similar ideas, embodying a "new biculturalism that reflected the changing international landscape" (Kurashige 2002, 25).

The Nisei's role as a link between Japan and the US was espoused not just by the Japanese government but in Japanese intellectual circles as well. In early 1933, the prominent educator, author, and diplomat Nitobe Inazo made a tour of the West Coast. It included a stop in Tacoma, where he delivered three addresses to three separate audiences (all in one day!), including one delivered in Japanese to "a packed auditorium at the Japanese Language School" (Uyeda 1933, 4). Nitobe's message to the Nisei was captured in the *Japanese American Courier:* "I have heard on occasions that the second generation feels that they are between two walls, floating in the breech, so to say, and that they feel handicapped. This I believe to be a foolish attitude. They must assume a proper pride in their citizenship as well as in the high heritages of their race and transform what they believe to be their handicap into an advantage." Because of their unique position, Nitobe continued, the Nisei showed "real promise of becoming a joining link of understanding between America and Japan" and could learn ways to "explain the Far Eastern situation to Caucasian friends" (Nitobe 1933, 1). Sixteen-year-old Masaye Jinguji responded to the talk in a TJLS essay titled "After Hearing a Lecture by Dr. Nitobe":

> Two days before Dr. Nitobe arrived in Tacoma, our school principal
> came to our classroom and told us that we were mature enough to go

to Dr. Nitobe's lecture. I was very excited. On January 16, 1933, at 4 pm, Dr. Nitobe arrived at the Tacoma Japanese Language School. Many people filled the room. My teacher and father told me that what Dr. Nitobe was talking about should not be too hard for me to understand. However, I could not understand some points. There is one important thing I remember from the lecture. Dr. Nitobe said that even if we attain a high level of success, we should not boast because we are not as great as we think we are. When I heard that, I thought, "Exactly, that's right!" People boasting about their success often happens in our society. I believe there were a lot of people whose eyes were opened by Dr. Nitobe's lecture.[15]

While many documents, editorials, and influential individuals used the "bridge" metaphor for the Nisei, we argue that their everyday experiences were more varied, contested, and contingent than many assimilation and acculturation narratives would lead us to believe. Interviews with the former students indeed suggest not merely an either/or, this/that, American/Japanese identity, but a layered, fluid, and complex Nisei identity, a more fluid and contingent identity for these Nisei children even than for their Issei parents. In part this was due to the fact that Nisei were US citizens, a status their parents could not attain. As children, the Nisei were both freer and yet more constrained in their identity negotiations than were their parents. On the one hand, they were less inhibited by social expectations as children, with fewer responsibilities, and they typically possessed a greater degree of bilingualism and had greater exposure to American society than their parents. At the same time, they bumped up against the behavioral expectations of their parents, teachers, and other adults—including Mr. and Mrs. Yamasaki, who seemed to have had an outsized influence on many of our interviewees. As the site where they heard many of these ideas, the TJLS was a significant physical and symbolic space for the children who spent their afternoons there. At the same time, it served as a focal point for the Japanese community, the nexus where the various cultural, economic, social, generational, and gender elements intersected. As such, it contributed strongly to a subject formation that was at once emergent and historically contingent. For these reasons, we suggest a conceptual shift from the notion of the Nisei as a static bridge to the processual idea of bridging.

The dominant narrative trope in the 1920s and '30s was of the Nisei as a "bridge." Mr. and Mrs. Yamasaki used it, integrating affection and respect for cultural heritage with American ideals of democracy and equality. Influential Issei and Nisei such as Jimmy Sakamoto used it, as did Japanese government officials, encouraging Nisei to be deliberate about their roles as ambassadors, links, friends, and cultural interpreters. It is not surprising that much of the literature on Japanese Americans has adopted this term as well, calling, for instance, for Nisei to act as a "bridge of understanding," with Japanese schools as the space where they would learn the skills necessary to fulfill this role (e.g., Takaki [1989] 1998; Yoo 2000; Pak 2002; Fugita and Fernandez 2004). Others have focused on debates about assimilation and adaptation of the second-generation Japanese (Hayashi 1995; Tamura 1994), highlighted the Nisei's biculturalism and cosmopolitanism (Kurashige 2002), or examined Nisei ambivalence around ethnic identity (Takahashi 1997; Yoo 2000; Kumei 2002).

Yet we argue that a bridge, as an item of infrastructure, suggests something fixed and static, that can be crossed, and that has two distinct endpoints. In terms of assimilation and acculturation, a bridge suggests that Nisei moved (or didn't) along a singular line, from one well-defined place to another. The concept of "bridging," however, pushes beyond conversations about "fit" (or lack of fit) in one category or another and instead emphasizes the contingent and processual aspects of subject formation. As Lon Kurashige argues, rather than approaching identity "as a thing to be discovered and measured," research questions should shift "to *how* they have been constructed" (2002, 4); only then may we account for "a far more complex and dynamic process of negotiation and adaptation to conditions in North America than the simple paradigms of heritage or assimilation that have framed so much of prior immigration history" (Geiger 2011, 14). We thus argue for a conceptual shift from the idea of traversing a bridge between two points (a Euclidean line) to a more topological, layered, and dynamic understanding of becoming Nisei. The term "bridging" denotes this shift and provides a more appropriate metaphor for the interactive, ongoing process of subject formation.

Processes of becoming Nisei were affected significantly by the outbreak of war between Japan and the US, making the idea of being "a bridge" seem irrelevant. In the days following the attack on Pearl Harbor, Masato Yamasaki and twenty-one others in Tacoma's Japanese community were arrested by the FBI and placed in "custodial detention" (Magden 1998, 114). Mr. Yamasaki was eventually sent to Fort Missoula in Montana, then on to the US Army Internment Camp at Lordsburg, New Mexico, where he died in March 1943—a story that will be taken up more fully in the final chapter. As a community leader and principal of the language school, Mr. Yamasaki's arrest and death in custody symbolize the depth of trauma and racism experienced by the Japanese community with the outbreak of war between the US and Japan, a very real reminder of its erasure.

Both Kuniko and Masato Yamasaki were foundational for the TJLS, shaping its curriculum and creating a space that functioned as a community nexus where the Nisei children engaged in the active process of becoming Nisei. As Chizu Tomita Takaoka noted, "That's the kind of people they were. And you learn by osmosis. I can't pinpoint it. It's just that something happens, and I think of them. I see a beautiful sunset, and I think of Tacoma. Or I think of a poem that I learned. Things like that. There's so much. And then I'm very grateful."

The Yamasakis embraced the then-current ideology of shaping students who as "Americans first" should learn the culture of their parents and act as a bridge between the US and Japan, even if the students' own experience of identity formation was much more complicated and nuanced than the "bridge" metaphor can represent. The stories recounted by many of the former students held a common thread: a genuine appreciation for what the Yamasakis attempted to transmit to them—Japanese language, lessons on ethics (*shushin*) and decorum, and pride in their Japanese heritage, as well as the values of equality and democracy. These messages were key elements in the Nisei's own processes of bridging, becoming embodied through their daily experiences in the TJLS as well as across the urban landscape.

CHAPTER SIX

Ethical Lessons of Meiji Japan Woven into Nisei Stories

So my experience of Japanese School was very good because I learned a lot of Japanese so-called . . . that word I use—*shushin*— I think that's the main thing . . . holding the Japanese Tacoma people getting together . . . that we learned the subject called *shushin* in Japanese School.

—ANONYMOUS MALE B (B. 1919)

I N A BRIEF 1940 ESSAY WRITTEN IN JAPANESE, "WHAT I DID OVER Summer Vacation," Tacoma Japanese Language School student Kiyoshi Kinoshita described his family's summertime cherry-picking endeavors, concluding that "when cherry-picking season was over, I had come to hate it." But, the young author conceded, "It is good work." The teacher's comment, in red ink, noted, "Any kind of work is good work."[1] This brief essay and its crimson comment convey the values of family, hard work, and self-discipline—all part of the core ethical message of the TJLS (see also chapter 2).

As we have seen, becoming Nisei was a complex and ongoing process: identity formation was not straightforward. While the Issei navigated financial survival, the Nisei navigated lives in which American school, Japanese school, family homes, and other children intersected. They were embedded in a multiethnic and segregated city, tied to their parents' heritage, and understood that they were US citizens. We have called this messy process of identity negotiation "bridging." The cultural practice of ethics—*shushin*—that constituted the core of the Yamasakis' approach to Nisei education at the TJLS was a key aspect of these processes. The pervasive influence of *shushin* at the school became embodied in the Nisei through lessons, physical activities, and community events, again underscoring the significance of both transnational and spatial aspects of their subject formation.

Although the arguments of this book extend beyond the impact of language schools and language learning, these spaces and practices are nonetheless critical sites for understanding immigrant experiences. Japanese immigrants to the Hawaiian Islands opened the first Japanese language school in 1892, and by the turn of the century ten additional schools were in operation there. Most language schools in Hawaii, and later on the West Coast, were founded by and attached to Buddhist temples or Methodist and Baptist churches. Tacoma's school, however, like Seattle's, was opened as a secular, nondenominational institution, leading it to become "the most important civic and cultural center" for the Japanese immigrants in the city, bringing people from all religious and class backgrounds together (Morrison 1994, 1; see also chapter 1). Even though there were tuition fees for attendance, some of the wealthier families covered the costs for their less well-off neighbors, a fact only understood when the children became adults.

While the name Japanese Language School suggests a primary focus on Japanese language, an equally important element was *shushin*, a code of moral behavior based on filial piety: the belief that if children learned how to respect, honor, and obey their parents, all other values and corresponding good practices would naturally follow. Instruction in *shushin* accorded with Meiji Japan's 1890 Imperial Rescript on Education, but at TJLS these beliefs, together with lessons that reinforced the young Nisei's pride in their Japanese heritage, were taught alongside "American" values of democracy and equality. All this was ostensibly done to enable the young Nisei to become, in the words of former student Junichi Taira, "outstanding citizens" of the United States.

The daily lessons on *shushin* were reinforced through a variety of activities, such as storytelling and skits, picnics, field trips, sporting events, and ceremonies, as well as chores on the school grounds such as cleaning the classrooms and maintaining the gardens. These micropractices, repeated and habitualized activities, reinforced community bonds, but they also served as modes of identity formation, reinforcing the lessons taught at the school by putting *shushin* into action. Communal activities also encouraged disciplinary practices as the young Nisei interacted with other community members who knew what the expected behaviors were, and whom the Nisei understood as knowing what those expected behaviors were. As such, these activities constituted critical elements of identity constitution for Tacoma's Nikkei community and the young Nisei.

The Japanese ethics the children learned at the TJLS served as the basis for the fundamental rule of their lives, that as Nisei that they must never bring shame to the family or the community. This was in keeping with traditional Japanese (and Confucian) values, but it also served the Nikkei as a way to protect themselves amid racial discrimination and segregation. As Fiset and Nomura (2005, 10) argue, "protective" measures, such as not speaking Japanese in public and not calling attention to one's self in other ways were "not mere responses in reaction to and conditioned by exclusionary initiatives, but . . . self-conscious strategies to achieve their goal of permanent settlement." Such strategies also allowed the Nikkei to demonstrate "agency while operating within the constraints of oppressive legalized racism and discrimination." Being "good Japanese" would help the Nisei become "good citizens."

Yet as we consider the impact of *shushin* on Nisei identity development, it is necessary to remember that underneath the complex processes of identity negotiation were the everyday, lived experiences of childhood. These youngsters sometimes did things they knew their parents didn't want them to do, or they might *not* do things they knew their parents *did* want them to do. We need to keep in mind that subject formation is never "complete," but rather is contested; an ongoing negotiation rather than the reification of some "essence." Like children and young people everywhere, Tacoma's young Nisei sometimes rebelled. At times they were oblivious to the multiple positionalities they were navigating daily; at others, they displayed flexibility in those navigations. As an institution organizing their daily lives, the TJLS was a critical space for becoming Nisei.

ETHICAL LESSONS AS CENTRAL TO NISEI IDENTITIES

As products of the Meiji era, Issei brought "certain traditional Japanese values and behavior patterns: *oyakoko* (filial piety), *gaman* (perseverance), *giri* (sense of obligation), *haji* (shame), obedience, honesty, and diligence"

(Takezawa 1995, 64). Former TJLS student Seiichi Konzo summarized the school's educational philosophy as revolving around ethics based on the centuries-old Japanese social code: "Gratitude to your parents . . . should be deeper than the ocean and higher than the sky. When Nisei followed the virtuous life, the family would never be shamed . . . The code was not one-sided. Parents toiled long hours so that sons and daughters could climb the educational ladder as far as possible. For many parents, existence amounted to creating better lives for their children" (in Magden 1998, 72).[2] Ryo Munekata emphasized the importance of these ideas: "The concept[s] of filial piety to our parents, honesty, endurance, perseverance—I think these were essentially taught to us." Kunio Shibata agreed: "More than the language and everything, I thought it [shushin] was very important"; while Harue Ozaki said: "As Tacoma Japanese Language students, we were indoctrinated with the traditions, and it was ingrained in us, because we repeated over and over the procedures of how our culture would have to remain alive."

Shushin lessons were explicit in classroom instruction. Yuriko Lily Korin Harada, displaying her report card, explained: "This is called—it's not 'study.' It's 'morals.' I think they taught you—there was a class just teaching us right from wrong, dos and don'ts. And that's when my parents were strict about that, too, so I guess I got it both ways. And so I think that's what got me going, and to this day I'm kind of strict with my kids too, I think. And so it must have helped." These values in turn manifested as particular kinds of behavior. As Mitsuo Takasugi noted, the young Nisei were expected to "live in a certain way," with "rules" that were understood even if not articulated. Jack Kazuo Hata said that his mother, a teacher at the school, emphasized that they should not do anything to bring shame on the family or her, "so I was pretty straight-laced or whatever." He continued:

[The message was] to be a good citizen—you know, stay out of trouble. I think that was basically the expectations of the parent, or the community. I think we were pretty well known through the city that we were pretty good citizens, stayed out of trouble. I don't recall kids being taken to the police station for any reason . . . I think that goes down to one's behavior, not to bring shame to the community, the

Japanese community, and to your parents. I think morals was part of that behavior, not to be immoral.

Young Nisei learned that they should self-manage their behavior, not cause trouble for their parents, and regulate their actions, especially in public. Historian Lon Kurashige described this as an insistence on "Herculean efforts of self-control, discipline, and community solidarity," while being told that "the failings of mere mortals put the entire race in jeopardy" (2002, 34). This internalization of norms and "rules" reinforced desired Nisei behaviors. As an instrument or technique of power, *shushin* worked to control the Nisei—and yet where there is power, there also is resistance, as we shall see below.[3]

FILIAL PIETY AS THE ESSENCE OF *SHUSHIN*

The Tacoma Japanese Language School, as a strictly secular institution, stressed values that were not associated with any particular sect or religion, Buddhist, Christian, or otherwise, but rather were based on traditional Japanese values. The 1890 Imperial Rescript on Education provided a concise summation of those Meiji-era values promoted by the Japanese state; its first instruction called upon imperial subjects to "be filial to your parents, affectionate to your brothers and sisters; as husbands and wives be harmonious; as friends true" (deBary, Gluck, and Tiedemann 2006, 108); as Teiko Kawano Peterson succinctly summed up the core of *shushin*, "Filial piety. The meaning of life" (see also chapter 1).

Filial piety was expressed in a wide variety of ways, and many behaviors, such as exhibiting respect for elders, were counted as important expressions of filial piety. Yuriko Lily Korin Harada explained:

Well, you know, like even at home, you disagree with your parents a lot, because you don't want to do certain things or you want to say things that you're not supposed to say, but then you hold back because you have respect for your parents. A lot of respect. But you know, all this helped, because when I went to Japan we lived with my grandparents, and I continued to do as I did before and so we got along beautifully. Yes.

Another aspect of filial piety was the parental expectation that children set an example for their younger siblings. As Yuriko Lily Korin Harada reminisced:

> Well I was always scolded for being the oldest, for not doing whatever I was supposed to do. I guess because if I were to do something, the two younger ones would be watching and so if I were to set an example, it would be a good example so they would learn from me ... I did get in a lot of trouble. (*laughs*)

Harue Kawano Ozaki understood the element of discipline in the emphasis on filial piety, remarking: "Yes, yes, we knew the filial piety, that's for sure ... It was values that I think made our community cohesive, because they had control over the children that way." Chizu Tomita Takaoka, though recognizing the importance of filial piety, also noted the propensity of children to rub up against the boundaries: "Parents were a, a breed apart. You don't communicate with them. You listen to them, you try to obey what they say, and it's 'mm-hmm, yes' (*nods head up and down with eyes closed*), and that's it. And you did, you did whatever you want-, darn well please."

Parents worked hard for their families, modeling through their own behavior the core values of *shushin* (see chapter 2). As Masatoshi Fujii observed, filial piety went both ways: "I think the majority of us came from intact families. We had a mother and a father, we didn't have single parents. So I would say most of our personality really comes from the family. Because there is an old Japanese saying: 'It's for the sake of the children.' And the parents sacrificed. So I would give most of the credit actually to the parents."

Kunio Shibata recalled that proper behavior included contributing to the family financially: "I was oldest in the family and my father [was] old-fashioned. If you're oldest, and if my folks are rich, I'll get everything, but if you're not, and I have to do, I have to bear all the kinda burden, and I think that was until [age] twenty-four I used to give my check to my mother 'cuz ... my younger sister and two sister and brother have to finish high school."

In conversation, several interviewees listed the expectations surrounding filial piety:

YONEKO AOCHI: Respect.

KUNIO: Yes.

ANON MALE D: Humility.

YONEKO: Respect. Any elders. Respect.

They needed to demonstrate these expectations in habituated behaviors like bowing and saying "mm-hmm, yes" to parents.

HAJI: "DON'T BRING SHAME"

The most important dictum of filial piety for the young Nisei, repeated nearly universally in the interviews, was that they not bring shame (*haji*) to the family or the community. Anthropologist Yasuko Takezawa writes, "*Haji* was an especially pertinent cultural concept . . . requir[ing] that the family's reputation be maintained in the community and the community's reputation maintained in the larger society" (1995, 65). At its core, this message also represented a strategy for self-protection, reflecting the Issei's constant awareness of their vulnerability not only as a racial minority but also as persons ineligible for US citizenship. Accordingly, proper decorum in all areas, public as well as private, was constantly stressed in the language school and at home—another example of the constant negotiation required of Nisei as they sought to integrate the values of being a "good Japanese" and a "good American." Joe Kosai:

> But when I reflect back on this time period of my growing up, I always think in terms of the reinforcement that maybe the school gave my parents in our behavior. Because I know our parents always stressed, "Don't bring shame to the family or don't bring shame to the community." So they didn't just leave it at the family. They included the community . . . But things that were stressed in the family were that we do not bring shame to our family and to our community. This was stressed very hard at home. Sometimes it was difficult to follow those precepts, but I think we all tried very hard . . .

Fumi Sato Hattori said, "You were brought up to think of what effect [your behavior] would have on your family." She recalled a particular episode when she had to apologize for not upholding these behavioral standards:

> Once the church group, on New Year's Eve, went someplace, and I must have been a teenager, and so I got to go . . . the Japanese have a custom of eating something at midnight, New Year's Eve. And then, uh, the assumption was that I would go home afterwards, but no, some kids said, "Oh, let's go . . . "—you know, wherever it was that we went. Anyway, my mother got worried, so she called—because I didn't get home, and I didn't tell her that I was going to be late—and so she called several people, and eventually I came home. The next day I had to go apologize to everybody that she had called. On New Year's Day I went around apologizing . . . Bowing. And that really impressed me, because, you know, I had brought shame, really. So, that was something that I learned.

Some former students recognized that the emphasis on not bringing shame was a strategy to maneuver within an environment of racial discrimination. Yoshiko Fujimoto Sugiyama, stating that "it was through the Japanese School that we learned how to respect our parents, our elders and how to behave in public," recalled:

> It was very, very important to our parents for us to always behave. Never do anything that would reflect upon our family or community. This was stressed at Japanese School also. The Japanese School teachers lectured to us almost every day to mind our manners and behave in public. We were not allowed to talk loudly in public in Japanese, so that people would [not] notice us. (in Sonnier 1993, 15)

Yoshiko's sister, Tadaye Fujimoto Kawasaki, made a similar observation: "We were supposed to dress appropriately, too, so people wouldn't notice us being different." The TJLS, however, provided a space where the Nikkei and the young Nisei *could* speak Japanese, and loudly if they wished, thus safely expressing their Japanese identities and their connections to Japanese culture and traditions.[4]

The emphasis on not shaming the family overlapped with not shaming the community, reflecting the general insularity of the Japanese. Kunio

Shibata, in an interview together with Ryo Munekata, recollected the message: "'Don't bring the shame to your family.' Because not only yourself, but all—everybody in the family is going to suffer." He noted, however, that the location of Tacoma's Nihonmachi posed particular challenges:

> That area in Tacoma, it's so easy to get in trouble in those days. The
> red light district was all over. Next door above us, [there] was a red
> light right there. Next door, two blocks down. You know, this was on
> Fawcett Avenue. Market Street was notorious. So . . . and Fort Lewis—
> the soldiers used to come into the bars. We (*indicating Ryo*) were two
> squares (*drawing a square in the air with his finger*). We don't dare get
> into trouble like that. Like the *kocho-sensei* [Principal Yamasaki] said,
> "Don't bring shame to the family."

Junichi Taira, too, recognized the conflation of family and community: "Yeah, I think it's both. For one thing, you know, I think they all impressed upon us about not bringing shame to the family name, and that was a thing I know that Mr. Yamasaki emphasized. Not bringing shame, not just the name, but the Japanese community."

Mitsuo Takasugi recalled an incident that was seen as a potential threat to the community, and Principal Yamasaki's response:

> I don't think we had any real "rules," but we were supposed to
> live a certain way so that, you know, you wouldn't bring any
> shame on the family, or anything like that . . . I remember once
> [Mr. Yamasaki] called a whole assembly of the school into the audi-
> torium there, and he lectured us, actually. Somebody had written
> some Japanese graffiti downtown, and he sent a group of kids down
> to erase it. He said it would bring shame upon the whole Japanese
> community, and things like that. So, you know he did . . . uh, he
> tried to teach us some of the things about not bringing shame on
> the Japanese.

At the same time, said Yoshiko Fujimoto Sugiyama, Mr. Yamasaki "tried to convey to us the culture of our heritage." Fumi Sato Hattori, too, spoke of the school's role in fostering a sense of pride in the students' Japanese heritage:

The Japanese Language School? (*pause*) It must have played a big part because almost everybody went. And, uh, whether one realizes it or not, we learned things that probably impacted our lives, like you should be proud to be Japanese. I've always been proud to be Japanese; I don't know why, but I've never been, I've never felt inferior to anybody because I'm Japanese. Because I've always thought that, well, the Japanese have a pretty big, you know, long history, and they've done a lot of amazing things. They've also done some terrible things, too, I guess, but we were taught to be proud to be Japanese. And I think, even now, I think that our generation had quite a place in history because we were there when the war broke out. We went to camp. We led a different life afterwards; we made new friends. I have friends in Hawaii that I met when I went to work in Chicago, and, you know, that was let's see, 1940-something. And I still keep in touch with them. So it's, it broadened our horizons quite a bit.

Exemplifying the nuances of negotiations over identity, especially across institutions in the Nisei's lives, Perry Yoshiaki Yano commented that the language school "made me feel that I was a Japanese, not an American . . . I think I always thought of myself as being Japanese, and not an American, that's all . . . I feel more comfortable being with Japanese . . . " Such feelings not only explain, perhaps, why Kuniko and Masato Yamasaki were given so much credit for shaping who the Nisei became as adults, but they also reveal how the received messages and behavioral expectations contributed to the constitution of Nisei identity.

BEHAVIOR AND THE EMBODIMENT OF *SHUSHIN*

Shushin was not merely a static set of ideas; rather, it was incorporated into all aspects of the TJSL curriculum and, in the end, was a part of everyday life. The Nisei children internalized the norms of expected behaviors and proper decorum. The lessons learned—in classes, through plays, in official ceremonies—may be understood as techniques of subject-making, whether experienced as discipline from an elder such as Mr. Yamasaki, compassion from a parent, or self-monitoring, such as the regulated counting of footsteps during a ceremony. The young Nisei learned how to conduct an "exercise of the self on the self" in order to achieve the desired subjectivity (Foucault 1997, 282), with the goal, as Mitsuo Takasugi put it, to "live a certain way."

The mimeographed document "Research on Training Students in the Lower Primary Grades," presumably by Mr. Yamasaki and part of which we quoted in chapter 5, outlined basic educational philosophy for the school. It discussed the need to help students internalize their lessons in *shushin:*

> The standard of past practice was to focus primarily on externals, that is to say, on students [displaying] attitudes of being obedient and adultlike. However, nowadays we should put more weight on the internal spirit, the individual child's attitude toward work, and their ability to work cooperatively with their schoolmates. Therefore, children should work diligently [on tasks] such as cleaning and reading and writing assignments. Children should also work with other students in a spirit of cooperation with their classmates.
>
> Therefore, we (teachers and parents) should think of the positive outcomes of the children's behaviors and also give serious consideration to their motivations. If children do something just for getting applause from others, it is not worthwhile [i.e., motives should come from within].[5]

The ethical principles of *shushin* were to be expressed via very specific behaviors and actions, "practices of the self" to use Foucault's term, thus infusing not only these values but what constituted "Japanese-ness" into the Nisei's young bodies. Tadaye Fujimoto Kawasaki remembered, for instance, that "no one leaned on the table or slept on it, or anything. They were all proper." When he visited the students' classrooms, Mr. Yamasaki often told stories involving lessons on proper behavior in the classroom and on the streets.

YONEKO AOCHI: We weren't even allowed to eat on the street walking. Remember that? *Tabenagara aruite ikenai!* [Do not eat while walking!] Remember that?

TEIKO KAWANO PETERSON: No, I don't.

YONEKO: Oh, ya, I remember that.

KUNIO SHIBATA: I never got spanked or hit by my father, but boy, when he looked at me, that was worse than getting spanked. I never got spanked. But I think it's [about] respect for your folks, too.

Paternal discipline was mentioned in other interviews as well, as when Takao Jerry Kikuchi remembered how strict his father was:

Well, one thing he was very disciplined. I don't know. Most Japanese parents are very disciplined. When you meet strangers you always bow your head, that sort of thing, you know.

[*To show respect?*]

Yes. Yes. [My parents were] very strict on that.

Daily practices reinforced the values of respect for and honoring of the older generation. Harue Kawano Ozaki discussed how these values and behavior overlapped:

Well, to be very practical, [Japanese values were demonstrated via] day-to-day mannerisms, meaning, to begin with, the proper way of bowing, showing respect, especially to your elders and to each other, and to be very graceful and grateful for all the . . . you know— whenever we have get-together for our meals, and then when we go to sleep, we would always acknowledge each other with mannerisms, Japanese phrases: *oyasuminasai* [good night], *ohayo gozaimasu* [good morning] . . . so, to begin with, the day to day clichés of speaking. This was throughout the whole community . . . And I'm sure it must have looked really ridiculous or funny to an outsider to see these little [Nisei children bowing] (*giggles*) . . . It was a very normal thing to do for us.

Discipline was exerted in other more subtle ways too. Fumi Sato Hattori recalled:

We were always late. And my girlfriend says, "Don't you remember teacher always used to make us stand at the door when we came in?" And until she acknowledged our presence we couldn't sit down.

(*laughs*) . . . I think a lot of our behavior just comes from being there [TJLS], because cert-, standards were expected, you know. You just behaved a certain way. I don't know whether it's Japanese following, you know, the rules. I think a lot of that . . . we do follow rules. We obey the laws, you know, and things like that. It's just accepted that you do. And, uh, you know, if you did anything out of the ordinary, everybody knew about it. (*laughs*)

Chizu Tomita Takaoka recollected the need to police her behavior at mealtime—an exercise of the self on the self, keeping watch over her physical demeanor including table manners:

Oh, we were supposed to be a lady . . . My father used to deplore our manners, our way of speech, he was a stickler for, you know, table manners . . . Oh I know that, when we were eating, um, *itadakimasu*-ing ["let's begin eating"], or it—it's just normal. It comes. We were taught that *gochisosama* ["thank you for the meal"], *osaki ni gomenna-sai* ["excuse me for going before you"], all these salutations, just, just since we were kids. I think at the beginning we didn't even know what it meant.

The young Nisei participated in self-monitoring and self-disciplining while under the watchful eyes of the older generation both at home and in public. These actions were micropractices of subject formation, the small daily activities that became "naturalized" within the body through repetition—meals that required specific phrases to be spoken, social interactions that required bowing and greeting: all these illustrate how these values came to be embodied in the young Nisei.

Because outer behavior reflected inner qualities, ceremonies served as occasions to cultivate proper behavior and performance, reinforcing community standards and expectations. A number of the interviewees recalled ceremonies held on the stage in the TJLS's "great hall," such as New Year's Day ceremonies, graduation ceremonies, commemorations of events such as the emperor's birthday, and recitations of the Imperial Rescript on Education (figure 6.1). The TJLS was thus a space that foregrounded the internalization of desired behaviors and the communication of Meiji modernity to the Nisei. Fusae Fujii Yoshida remembered being instructed on "the

FIGURE 6.1. The great hall of the Tacoma Japanese Language School, looking east at the stage. Author photo.

proper way of going up there and receiving your certificate of achievement and things like that . . . We all had to go and watch the proper way to bow and how to receive the certificate . . . [Mr. Yamasaki] even counted the number of steps we had to take."

Jack Kazuo Hata recalled the formality of the community events at the school as well: "Well, I think that Mr. Yamasaki had the emperor's birthday or something . . . other than that . . . Oh, graduation day, I think they had a program . . . [He was] kind of strict. There was no, what do you say, fooling around." Michie Taira Hori and Junichi Taira had similar memories:

MICHIE: Ya, but see the one thing that I vividly remember—I don't
know what occasion, I thought it was connected with the graduation ceremony—but the principal used to do this certain cultural
thing or something that they did in Japan, or maybe because we

were in this country, but it was some kind of ceremony. He had white gloves on, he was all dressed in black, and there was a certain temple-like thing in the background, maybe it was a Shinto temple-like thing, and it was kind of a ceremony that probably took place in Japan. And so to teach us this culture, he portrayed this thing. You don't remember that?

JUNICHI: You had to go up to the stage and do your bowing and all that.

Mitsuo Takasugi remembered having to demonstrate *shuji* (calligraphy) before an audience:

We would get up on the stage and sing or recite something. And I remember once I had to do a—what is it, those, uh, Japanese character writing. . . So you get up in front of everybody and you write something in Japanese with a brush, you know, which isn't always that easy. And uh, yeah, I did that once. . . I was pretty young then, and I did it. I was standing there—you know, you're supposed to stand up in front of everybody. They'd hang the whole paper of characters out on the wall, and everybody gives you a hand. (*claps*) And I remember the principal pushing my head down to bow. (*laughs*) That's about all I remember from something like that.

Chizu Tomita Takaoka especially remembered the ritual:

There was, uh, New Year's—first thing in the morning New Year's you go there [to TJLS]. And then there's graduation ceremony, there's emperor's birthday. . . gee, what else is there? But anyway, there was a ritual. And then especially at graduation ceremony— . . . I never got it, but you know there's a first prize, second prize, and third prize for scholastic endeavor and for attendance. And, um, you go, maybe about five steps to the stage. And *Kocho-sensei*'s there, and there's a . . . (*unfolds a brochure*) about like this, I guess, and then he hands it to you (*holds brochure out flat in both hands and raises it*). and you receive it and you bow, and you one, two, three, step (*demonstrates stepping backward*), and then you turn around and go down. We used to practice that all the time.

CARING FOR THE SCHOOL AS A LESSON
IN ETHICS AND RESPONSIBILITY

To maintain the proper atmosphere at the TJLS and teach group responsibility, students were assigned various tasks to help keep the school clean and tidy. More important than the work itself was the moral instruction that came from shouldering these duties, seen as an important element of the total education of the child. School cleaning by students has a long history in Japan, where "no work, not even the dirty work of cleaning, is too low for a student; all should share equally in common tasks; the maintenance of the school is everyone's responsibility" (Cummings 2014, 117). These activities would in turn help students understand "key normative beliefs about the nature of community and the relationship of the individual to the social order" (Le Tendre 1999, 283). The 1931 document "Research on Training Students in the Lower Primary Grades," mentioned above, set guidelines for creating a physical environment conducive to the school's educational goals:

> When children enter school for the first time, the environment is new and larger for them. Therefore, we need to teach the students about the school environment. We must teach them the school rules regarding classrooms, the schoolyard, the library, the teachers, the principal, other students, the bathroom, exercise equipment, the drinking fountain, and so forth.
>
> Also, schoolrooms should be kept clean and the school decorated with flower arrangements, pictures, and portraits of illustrious persons so as to improve the students' artistic and moral sensibilities. . . . We should have posters in the classrooms and hallways that show common manners. . . .
>
> Another point is that we must keep the drinking fountain, the washroom, the toilets, and other facilities in perfect condition so as to prevent unnecessary antagonism and competition from arising.

Fumi Sato Hattori remembered: "We used to have to sweep after [school]. We used to have to clean the rooms, and as I recall, there was a garden outside, too, on the hillside," that the students worked in. Others mentioned similar daily responsibilities:

ANON MALE A: We were better janitors . . . we had to clean the
rooms every—all the kids have to put the sawdust, sweep, and
everything.
ANON FEMALE A: That's right.
RYO MUNEKATA: Yeah.
ANON FEMALE A: Every day was—had to sweep the room.
RYO: The hallway . . .
ANON FEMALE A: And they had pot-bellied stoves, and we had to
start the stove so that the room would be warm when the classes
started.
[*Each classroom had its own stove?*]
RYO: Mm-hmm. You had to haul in all the wood for the fire.

The underlying goal of this work was to teach the students responsibility,
as the Fujimoto sisters (Yoshiko, Tadaye, Kimiko) recalled:

YOSHIKO: And then once a week we had cleanup of the classrooms.
We didn't have a janitor.
TADAYE: I thought it was every day.
YOSHIKO: Hm?
TADAYE: It wasn't every day?
KIMIKO: Every day we swept.
TADAYE: Ya, every day we swept.
YOSHIKO: Every day, was it? But that taught us, you know, responsi-
bility and all.

Yuriko Lily Korin Harada remembered when her "turn to do the
cleaning" at the TJLS impacted her responsibilities as an older sister:

My brother and I are four years apart, so when I was ten, he was
six. He couldn't find me one day after school; he was just crying
and crying. One of the teachers would go all through the school,
and can't find me. Because we took the bus, and without me he can't
go home. And where do you think he found me? Another girl and I
were cleaning the bathroom. And so naturally they couldn't see us
because we were inside the girls' bathroom. And so that was one experience we laugh about today. And so what I did was, after we finished

and we were walking down the hill, I stopped and got him a box of Cheez-Its. A little box of Cheez-Its. And that made him happy. I felt so bad—he was so upset . . .

Care for the school extended beyond cleaning the building and included maintaining a school garden as well. In Japanese culture, keeping a garden and taking care of animals were believed to contribute to well-rounded, responsible citizens with a sense of connection to the natural world. As the document "Research on Training Students in the Lower Primary Grades" put it, "In order to develop an intimacy with the natural world, we should maintain flower beds, and raise small creatures such as birds, chickens and rabbits so that students learn to love and protect plants and animals." Kimiko Fujimoto Tanbara explained:

> Each class had a little plot of garden outside the school. Each class was assigned to that garden. It was up to us to keep it growing. You know, a lot of the Japanese families, because of economic reasons, they lived either upstairs [from] or behind their business. A lot of them didn't have gardens, you know, that they could appreciate. And I think that was one of the reasons why our principal did that, so that all the students had a chance to grow something. That's a big—you don't realize those things until you're older, you know. But what went through his mind all the time—to try to make things easier for all of us, you know. We really owe him a lot of thanks.
>
> [*What did you grow?*]
>
> I think it was flowers mostly, and shrubs. But we'd be all out there, whether we'd be doing any good or not, just to be having fun, you know. But just to have the opportunity of touching the soil and all that must have meant a lot . . . So I think that was one way that our principal made sure that we knew what it was to have things grow.

SHUSHIN THROUGH STORIES, SKITS, AND SONGS

In Japan's late Meiji and early Showa periods, educational policy promoted the use of folk tales as an educational tool to reinforce national consciousness (Antoni 1991). Folk tales were incorporated into the TJLS curriculum as well, to underscore the moral lessons of *shushin*. "Research on Training Students in the Lower Primary Grades" discussed their value in education:

> Fairy tales are exceptionally valuable for improving students' emotional state. Good fairy tales can encourage a student's sincerity and purity and, at the same time, provide an opportunity for the student to contemplate what they would do if they were in the story. This is helpful, as students feel sympathy and it can improve morality very well. Moreover, it is the basis of morality. Therefore, students can learn much from fairy tales.

The interviewees cited a number of traditional Japanese folk tales and stories, including those of Bunbuku Chagama, the shapeshifting raccoon dog; the young fisherman Urashima Taro; Momotaro the peach boy; and Tange Sazen, the one-eyed, one-armed samurai who persevered against all odds. According to Masatoshi Fujii, "The principal used to be a master storyteller, so during the summer, on a—I think it was on a Friday after school—he would gather those who wanted to hear stories in a downstairs classroom. . . I used to go to all of them, because they were very good."

Some recalled the iconic story of the diligent student Ninomiya Kinjiro, a farmer's son depicted in statues throughout Japan as walking with a load of wood on his back and an open book in his hands, reading even as he went about his daily chores. For the former students, the story reinforced values like industriousness and diligence:

> KUNIO: There is a picture . . . of a young boy reading a book and there's a basket behind it . . .
>
> MASATOSHI: That's Ninomiya Kinjiro . . . He was a farmer's kid . . . and in order to get ahead in life, that's what he did: while he was carrying things to the market and places like that, he read. You see statues of him at railroad stations.

Yoriko Lily Korin Harada remembered:

> That's what we used to study about. Let's be like Kinjiro—you know, let's be . . . not waste a moment of our valuable time. (laughs) . . . Yes, yes, yes. I think that's what we were taught.

Plays and skits were another vehicle for reinforcing *shushin* lessons in the students, another micropractice of inculcating Nisei subjectivity. Chizu Takaoka specifically remembered performing in them:

See this? (*shows us a photo of the school's exterior*) We used to dress in this room (*points*) and come up the stair [the] back way, because the stage is right here . . . so he had to coordinate . . . But anyway, they [Principal Yamasaki and other teachers] would write the script, they would make, maybe take an episode of something we learned and make a dialogue. And *Kocho-sensei*'s idea was, whether it's a play or poetry, whatever it is, when you have a drama like that, in a play, you've got to memorize it. Each kid had to memorize. Well, if you memorize it, it's yours. That was his idea of having these plays every year.

Harue Kawano Ozaki remembered enacting these stories, recalling the building and the use of the fire escape in staging these skits and plays:

Well, first of all there was the setup of the [TJLS]—I don't know if you saw the school at all when it was standing—but there was, to begin with, there was the fire escape. That was an important structure . . . because you see, the classrooms were connected with the stairs going up, and then at the top of the stairs was the so-called all-purpose . . . we didn't call it all-purpose room, but we called it a . . . stage! That's what we called it. We called it the stage . . . We used the fire escape like cues for when you go up those stairs as you present yourself on the stage, and to retreat again. And it was all—I remember he [Mr. Yamasaki] used to cover it with sheets so that it gave it a little enclosure, so you felt like it was special and safe.

Taeko Hoshiwara Taniguchi similarly recalled:

Well before war, before we were interned, I remember we used to always have a play. The classes used to have a play and all have a part in it. And also, we were, we always had an oratorical contest, you know. And then Yamasaki-*sensei*'s the one who wrote oratorical contest, all the . . . What do you call that, he wrote for every ch-, you know, every children. I think we had that every year, but it was every different grade, I think. Yeah, he wrote all of that. There were about twenty or so, many people . . . And then we had to memorize it, and then we would go to Japanese school and practice, you know, and then he would tell us what not to do, or things like that. And then I was the lucky one, I got the first prize. Yeah, I was very lucky. I still remember how I went in front of the audience, and they told me to breathe, you know, deep just before, so that's what I did. And then I did it, and then I was lucky enough to get [first prize].

Shigeko Gay Tamaki Yoshiwara reminisced about the integration of performance into the school curriculum: "Instead of just [using] the textbook, the teacher put on these folk tales for stage presentation for the parents." Kunio Shibata shared a humorous memory of his "acting days" that illustrates Mr. Yamasaki's keen involvement in the performances, including his emphasis of proper oratory technique:

I was supposed to [play] a navy officer in the Russian-Amer- . . . Japanese war. Well, anyway, this officer got a letter from his mother, saying [his father had] passed away. So the mother wrote to him, and I was supposed to read that letter. Now, here I was just reciting. [Mr. Yamasaki] says, "That's not the way." He says, "His father died! He's got to have emotion—not just read like a zombie!" He didn't say zombie—but something. So I said, "Well, how?" He said, "Well, you're supposed to read like this and shake" (*holds a make-believe letter in front of him and makes his hands tremble—laughter ensues*). So I did that. And then when the final play came, my mother and dad, my friends . . . they see my shaking, and my mother was embarrassed, she said, "You were just shaking like that." And my friends say, "Man, you were nervous!" I say, "No, the coach *sensei* told me to do that!" (*laughs*) That's the only part I remember. I don't know the words, but that's the part I remember, because it's the shaking part . . .

IDENTITY AND COMMUNITY BUILDING: CEREMONIES, OUTINGS, AND SPORTING EVENTS

Activities ranging from formal ceremonies to informal picnics organized by the TJLS brought the Japanese community together, providing opportunities to socialize across generational and religious boundaries. Indeed, many of the ethical values of *shushin* could only be taught within the context of relationship and community (see Le Tendre 1999, 283–310). The document "Research on Training Students in the Lower Primary Grades" highlighted this idea as well:

> Morality is something that is born naturally out of social life with groups of people. Moreover, students will gain moral lessons naturally from communicating with each other. This means that students learn habits of working and playing happily, respecting other people's rights, obeying rules in a group, creating good rules, and any other moral habits, by interacting with groups of people. Therefore, we should guide students through these lessons in their schooling, and make these lessons meaningful. We need to observe children's individuality and correct and encourage them when necessary to respectfully foster them in [developing] their individual identities.

In addition to the various formal events held on the stage of the communal hall, the TJLS organized outdoor activities away from school grounds, including sports days called *undokai*. Taeko Hoshiwara Taniguchi said, "We used to have it every year, we used to have *undokai* at the, what was the name of that . . . Spanaway. That's where we had *undokai*. We were divided, the red and white, and then compete against each other. We had a, what did you call, *tsunahiki*, or the big rope, and then we would be divided . . . (*pantomimes a tug-of-war*) That's what I remember." Chizu Tomita Takaoka remembered how the events united the community and allowed parents to socialize while the children played games:

> Running, and I remember they had a basket and then you throw the red ball and the white ball, you know, small ones (*demonstrates softball size*), and *kocho-sensei* always had, we had a song. For the red team and the white team. See, he wrote all these songs. [We played] running

games, a race, uh, what do you call it when two people tie their feet together? And then throwing a basket. And I think we ended with pulling the rope—red side and white side were pulling. I can't remember. But anyway, it was an outing. The whole community, uh, particip-, it had to. You know, when I think about it now, I mean the parents had to go and dig the latrine, fence off the place, put up these things (*demonstrates vertical poles*) . . . Well, who did it? It was all these parents, and it was the whole community. So that kind of participation, too.

. . . Oh, we had jacks, we had hopscotch, jump rope. We would make little dolls with scraps, everybody used to make their own clothes, so there was always scraps. And, um, things like that.

These outings and group picnics took the community out of their usual environment, such as central Nihonmachi, to locales such as Steilacoom Beach, Owen Beach, and Dash Point (figure 6.2). Organized field trips took the students even further afield, for example to Seattle, Portland, Snoqualmie Falls, and Olympia (Ito 1969, 701). Perry Yoshiaki Yano reminisced:

We did get to meet other Japanese at Steilacoom Beach. And. . . that was when probably when I was the happiest, you know, when I was on, playing on the beach and playing, playing in the water,. . . and having things to, good things to eat, and staying late at night, and shooting off firecrackers, and—or fireworks. So, yeah, I have a lot of happy memories.

The three Fujimoto sisters also had good memories of the outings:

YOSHIKO: And I don't know if we told you or not, but during the summer, we had Japanese school, and we also had outings. And the first beach I remember was Dash Point. I don't know if you're familiar with Dash Point. We would—we didn't have a bus then.

TADAYE: No, it was private cars, wasn't it?

YOSHIKO: Private big truck. And the principal would line benches in there and we would go to the beach that way. And somehow we had to stop going to Dash Point and then we went to Point Defiance.

FIGURE 6.2. Beach outing, possibly Steilacoom beach. Courtesy of the Nakano Family.

TADAYE: Owens Park [Owen Beach at Point Defiance Park] . . . I understood they didn't want us there [Dash Point] anymore.

YOSHIKO: Something like that.

TADAYE: [We played games like] bean bags—throw it in the basket, to see who would get the most.

KIMIKO: And relays. You had to run through tires. The teacher just said, "You're white. You're red. You're white. You're red."

TADAYE: It might mean we got numbered, I don't know. I can't remember.

KIMIKO: But it was fun.

YOSHIKO: Do you know where Yen Ching Chinese Restaurant is on South Tacoma Way? It's behind there. That's where we used to go.[6]

Team sporting events provided additional opportunity for Issei and Nisei to socialize and meet Japanese from the South Puget Sound and beyond. Though more of an outlet for the young Nisei men, sports also attracted some young women. As discussed earlier, because they were expected to attend the TJLS, most sports-minded students did not participate in public school sports but instead joined teams organized by the Japanese Methodist church or the Buddhist temple, or engaged in league sports organized by Jimmie Sakamoto's newspaper, the *Japanese American Courier*—which, incidentally, provided excellent coverage of the local Nikkei sports scene. Teams traveled to other communities to take part in various tournaments. Baseball was king, but football and basketball were also played, and some students practiced kendo.

Although the Nikkei sports scene, like the TJLS, provided community-building opportunities, it also promoted insularity, as Masatoshi Fujii recounts:

> MASATOSHI: Yeah, Japanese had their own segregated teams, from Fife and Tacoma, Auburn, and they played against each other. In fact, in Tacoma, at first they wouldn't let us use the playground to play baseball, so the Japanese built their own baseball field out toward the Standard Oil Refinery. Then later, right before the war, they got to use Stadium High School's baseball field.
>
> KUNIO SHIBATA: We crossed the Fifteenth Bridge, huh? Fifteenth Bridge, then walked across.
>
> MASATOSHI: That's right.
>
> KUNIO: Yes. That's where we played baseball. Football, too.
>
> FUSAE FUJII YOSHIDA: Remember the baseball tournaments every year?
>
> KUNIO: Yes, father was always helping us.
>
> FUSAE: My father was involved in that. The Buddhist Church Young Men's Association always sponsored a baseball tournament on a, something like a Labor Day weekend or something like that, and teens came from as far away as Seattle and Portland. But they had a tournament, I remember.

Baseball in particular was a way for Nisei from the Northwest to meet each other, playing games and participating in the tournaments. Kazuo Horita remembered:

> Well, most of my life I was very much involved in sports. I spent a lot of time on sports, including baseball, basketball, football, did some

bowling. So that was my life. It wasn't girls, it was sports. (*laughs*).
But, but my baseball was pretty good, pretty good . . . It was Courier
League, for the Japanese Americans in Seattle, Tacoma, and the
whole valley area, was a major thing for us. I mean, lots of our boys
played. I was on the All-Star team fairly frequently, and an All-Star
team meant that you were at least considered pretty good in the
Seattle, the valley, the Tacoma, and the whole area there.

POWER AND RESISTANCE:
NAUGHTY CHILDREN HAVING FUN

The Nisei students were children and as such they were capable of rowdy,
mischievous acts. Such "naughtiness" was also an important part of constituting the self for the Nisei as they tested the boundaries of acceptable
behavior.

Anon Female D remembered learning calligraphy (*shuji*) and the way
the practice reinforced behavior and discipline:

> And so to do this, you know, we had to make our own ink with
> charcoal, and there's a little black . . . what do you call this thing
> (*showing an inkstick*) that you have to [use to grind] the *sumie* [ink]?
> (*makes a back-and-forth motion with her hand*) And you know, we
> had to make that first. And it must have taken over half an hour,
> I felt it was, but . . . and then they didn't just let us go like this (*leans
> forward and repeats the hand motion rapidly*). We had to (*straightens
> her back*) stand, you know, and nice posture and everything. And
> I guess that was part of the behavior and, you know, things like
> that—discipline yourself. . . But anyway, I don't know why I kept
> this. But I think we stored—had to store a lot of things at the [TJLS
> because we] couldn't take, you know, very many things [to camp].
> And I think that's where I kept it, in there. So after the war, and
> they were able to get their things back then, I think, it was in my
> little box. So I just kept it.

The image of young students dutifully completing their lessons or
standing at attention carefully grinding ink is compelling. However, not
all our interviewees reported such obedience, reminding us that where

there is power, there is resistance. Takao Jerry Kikuchi, for example, offered a recollection of calligraphy lessons quite at odds with Anon Female D's: "I took that brush and I squirted the teacher, and her dress was—she was wearing a white dress with black spots on there already, so she didn't notice it."

Ryo Munekata remembered: "Of course, being young kids, we used to bother them [teachers] and annoy them and make them angry. Isn't that right? (*chuckles*) And when we think back about those things, sometimes you feel ashamed that you had done that to your teachers (*laughs*)." But as Junichi Taira pointed out, "We *were* eleven years old . . . "

> JUNICHI: Of course, you know how mischievous we could get and so were pretty rowdy, and I really now think back and admire Mrs. Hata[7] for putting up with that. And somehow we learned something. It was unbelievable.
>
> MICHIE TAIRA HORI: Yes, we did. We did learn. And you know, we had to make our own ink, when we had to do with the brush—writing the calligraphy stuff—and all the girls would hesitate sitting in front of the boys for fear that their hair would get dunked in the ink! (*laughs*) I remember, (*whispers*) "No, you go sit there." "No, I don't want to sit there!" . . . Boys!
>
> JUNICHI: I can't think of it now. (*laughter*)
>
> MICHIE: I remember that so well.
>
> JUNICHI: No, we were pretty bad. . . After the war, let's see, after I was in the service and came back, we went to visit Mrs. Hata. She was amazed I grew up. (*laughs*)

Kimiko Fujimoto Tanbara also expressed retroactive sympathy toward the teachers, pointing out the heavy demands the youngsters faced having to continue at TJLS after a full day in public school:

> I think it's a wonder they [the teachers] didn't all get ulcers. We were so bad. (*laughs*) Because you know, coming from public school, you're contained, and then when you get out of school, of course you're supposed to release your energy. Then you come to Japanese School and you're supposed to be good again. The boys were bad. Our boys were bad anyway, in my class. But I just wondered how those teachers ever

stood us! (*laughs*) The girls were okay. …[Other] classes were okay, but our class—we were more liberated, I guess. But we were bad. But the teachers hung in there.

Chizu Tomita Takaoka also commented on the challenge of additional school hours and, like Kimiko, spoke of gender differences in the classroom, where the "girls were okay," but "boys were lousy students. And you can't blame them, after all we went to school, regular school, and then from two to six, uh, from four to six it was Japanese school every single day. And they're tired." Michie and Junichi recollected:

JUNICHI: You know, there was a teacher that—a man teacher that really took a beating from us too, but I can't remember his name.
MICHIE: Man teacher?
JUNICHI: Well, it could've been on a Saturday. God, I can remember him chasing us into the closet, so … (*laughs*)
[*How did that happen?*]
MICHIE: Well, if you knew these boys, you would know.
JUNICHI: We were really bad.
MICHIE: It was his group. There were three boys, wasn't it? You and Senya [?] and—
JUNICHI: There were a few of us … Well, no, we won't mention names. I wish I could remember his [the teacher's] name, but I can't.

Other teachers included Harue Kawano Ozaki and Teiko Kawano Peterson's mother, Mrs. Kawano. Harue remembered:

[My mother's] uncle and auntie raised her and her brothers and a sister, because the parents died shortly after Mama was about ten years old. So this uncle and aunt did not have any children, but they were ahead of their time, they wanted to have all the children develop on their own. She taught for eighteen years at [the] Japanese Language School. She taught reading, writing, and all the cultural affairs of how to maintain the Japanese way of honoring everything. But, fortunately, she had a musical mind, so she was always the accompanist for all the programs that we used to have … I did not understand that

Mama was someone who had all this insight into handling people and affairs of relationships, but she did.

Chizu Tomita Takaoka remembered Mrs. Kawano, and other teachers:

Well, I had Mrs. Kawano, Harue's mother, the longest—I was lucky. And *Kocho-sensei* [Mr. Yamasaki]. The rest of it was Mrs., let's see, (*pauses*) there was a Kato-*sensei,* he was a man that was working, I mean going to CPS [College of Puget Sound], and he came in, the exchange student, and he was making money teaching. Mrs., Ms. Niiyama . . . And then, you know, that's about all I had. . . Mrs. Kawano, we were downstairs and went upstairs; I had her for about maybe seven years. And then I went into *Kocho-sensei*'s room right away. . . and of course with him it's high school, three years.

Memories of teachers also included mundane details. Fumi Sato Hattori:

I only remember one, no two, teachers. I can't remember whether it was Mrs. Hata or Mrs. Asada. One of them. She always wore the same dress all season. (*laughs*) Isn't that awful? You remember things like that. [The dress] was brown and simple. It was belted. Just a sort of a shirtwaist type dress, but she wore it every day. We went to Japanese school every day, and she wore that same dress all—I remember, all winter she wore the same dress.

Memories of the teachers were often tied to memories of discipline. Joe Kosai remarked, "One year my teacher happened to be my cousin. I know that reinforced my behavior—or good behavior! The reason is that, I think, if I misbehaved, my father would have heard about it before I got home. So it was something that—you can weigh these things out, and sometimes it is better to get a scolding at school than to get scolded at home."

As we have seen, student memories of their TJLS teachers included sympathy for what they put their teachers through, as well as respect for what was generally perceived as the excellence of the TJLS teaching staff. Ryo Munekata commented, "The standard of education for a Japanese school system here in Tacoma was much greater and higher—much higher than many of the language schools. Both of the educators [Mr. and

Mrs. Yamasaki]—well, in fact, not both, but all the teachers we had were very highly motivated teachers. And they were very good."

While the TJLS was not the only site for becoming Nisei, it did hold a particularly important place in the memories of the Nisei we interviewed and was central to establishing the norms and practices that shaped these second-generation children. Through lessons, oratory contests, skits, ceremonies, sports days, and outings they learned how to be in the world, testing positionalities in prewar urban spaces that required constant bridging and negotiation. The micropractices of becoming Nisei—proper behavior such as showing respect to parents, bowing when necessary, and following specific protocols in formal ceremonies—were ingrained in the children. These practices were both spatial, with the school at the center of their lives, and transnational, drawing on values from the Issei generation's Meiji Japan. *Shushin* and the behaviors meant to display them were inculcated in the TJLS and reinforced in the Nisei's homes and on the streets of Nihonmachi. *Shushin* lessons constituted essential aspects of Nisei subject formation.

Incarceration, Dispersal, and Erasure

Destruction of a Community

All of the old landmarks are gone. Our old home and place of business—gone—are both empty lots . . . The highway markets where the Japanese Americans did well—it's all built up and I only located them due to the fine work of our tour guides . . . The tideflats where we played ball and where Tokyo Beach was located—it's all filled and industrialized. I felt a lump, a down-fallen feeling . . .

—KAZUO HORITA (B. 1921), "TACOMA REUNION—ONE MAN'S VIEW"

K AZUO HORITA'S REFLECTION ON HIS RETURN TO TACOMA FOR the first reunion of the Tacoma Japanese in 1977 poignantly captures the loss and erasure of Tacoma's prewar Japanese community. The story of that community after the outbreak of war between the US and Japan in December 1941 follows a familiar outline: arrests of prominent individuals in the Japanese community, the issuance of Executive Order 9066, liquidation and disposal of assets in Tacoma, incarceration, and, for some young Nisei, military service. After release from the camps starting in 1944, the vast majority of the Tacoma Japanese did not return to their hometown.[1] Instead, against the backdrop of pressure from the War Relocation Authority, which pursued a policy of dispersing the Nikkei across the US in order to prevent the reemergence of concentrated communities, most of the

Tacoma Nikkei moved to other parts of the US. Some sought locales where they hoped to find better employment or less discrimination; some looked for larger Japanese communities in California, hoping to find "safety in numbers," while others moved to the Midwest, believing they might be able to live quietly and unnoticed. This dispersal is evident in the multiple locations of the interviews: Los Angeles, Oakland, Chicago, and Tacoma. For families that did return to Tacoma, the TJLS "was often their first destination" (Morrison 1994, 23), serving as a hostel while they found housing and employment. Many had stored their belongings in the first floor of the school only to discover that in their absence their goods had been looted, damaged, and destroyed.

The traumatic destruction and postwar dispersal of Tacoma's Japanese community as told by the Nisei in the interviews highlights the blunt realization that "citizenship" was an unstable status. It also delineates the spatiality of the exercise of control and oppression. Enclosing Japanese Americans in concentration camps during the war constitutes the most obvious example of spatial control, but the roundups, arrests, registration for incarceration, and uprooting of people from their homes are spatially based expressions of power as well. Then too, there was the postwar physical dispersal of Japanese across the country, putting the final touch on community dismemberment.

This physical and spatial erasure of Tacoma's Nihonmachi has resulted in a collective amnesia regarding Japanese American contributions to the economic and urban fabric of prewar Tacoma, devaluing their contributions while valorizing other forms of economic expansion and capital production, expressed structurally in parking lots and glass-encased office buildings. These contemporary aspects of the built landscape suggest that some interests (e.g., real estate development) have benefited from these erasures. After the destruction of the TJLS building in 2004, only two community buildings built by the prewar Japanese remained standing in Tacoma, and only one of those, the Tacoma Buddhist Temple, is still used in its original capacity. The other, the Whitney Memorial Methodist Church, now functions as instructional space for UW Tacoma.

In a twisted recognition of its significance in the community, in 1942 the TJLS was chosen by the US government as a Civilian Control Center where all those of Japanese ancestry in Pierce County were required to register prior to incarceration. The Nisei rationalized their and their parents' ordeal using terms such as perseverance and obligation, thereby distorting the empowering lessons from Mr. Yamasaki into ones of potential shame in the face of this extreme, and sanctioned, racism. The interviewees told powerful stories of family members being arrested by the FBI in the days following Pearl Harbor. Among those arrested was TJLS Masato Yamasaki, who was subsequently incarcerated and who died while detained. These actions followed decades of anti-Asian policies, from the Exclusion Act of 1924 to Alien Land Laws in Washington State in 1921 and 1923. In addition, the key role of the TJLS at this juncture is also evident in the fact that a significant number of its former students were recruited into the US military for intelligence work, due to their proficiency in the Japanese language.

Certainly the crisis of World War II was a profound inflection point for the subject formation of Tacoma's Nisei, undercutting whatever belonging these young people had established in the city, and could be the topic of a book in its own right. Our purpose in this conclusion, however, is to consider wartime incarceration and postwar realities through transnational and spatial lenses, as a way of expanding our collective understanding of these destructive events.

WAR AND CRISIS: IMMEDIATE IMPACT OF PEARL HARBOR

In Tacoma, the FBI "watch list" resulted in arrests starting on December 7 and continuing over subsequent days. During this fraught period, twenty-two members of Tacoma's Japanese community were seized, including Masato Yamasaki; all were placed in "custodial detention" (Magden 1998, 114). Some of those Tacoma Japanese arrested at this time were Gisaburo Abe, Tokiichi Asada, journalist and author Shuichi Fukui, Issei Hata (Jack Kazuo Hata's father), Fukoso Ii, Manpei Imai, Sosuke Kawai, Giso Kosai (Joe Kosai's father), Takeshi Matsumoto, Shintaro Miyazaki, Jotaro Mori, Gikan Nishinaga (minister at the Tacoma Buddhist Church), Hideo Oikawa, Zenshiro Okubo, Hiroshi Semba, and Motozo Yanagizawa (Magden 1998, 221n14, based on a list compiled by Yoshiko Fujimoto Sugiyama).

Tacoma, of course, was not alone. In those same few days, more than one hundred Japanese in Seattle and some twenty in Portland were placed under arrest (Ito 1973, 928). The FBI had conducted surveillance on select

Issei and Nisei along the West Coast since 1932, dividing them into three categories: "known dangerous," "suspected dangerous," and "peripheral members of Japanese intelligence network" (Magden 1998, 114; see also *Tacoma News Tribune* 1941). The resulting so-called ABC list had amounted to over two thousand files by 1941. On December 7, FBI offices in California, Oregon, and Washington were instructed to "immediately take into custody all Japanese who have been classified in A, B, and C categories in material previously transmitted to you" (Fiset 2009, 26).

The attack on Pearl Harbor and the declaration of war between the US and Japan was obviously a crisis point for the Nikkei. As one interviewee stated, "That's when we learned the word 'discrimination'" (Anon Male A). While few former students, who were teens and younger at the time, had been aware of the events leading up to Pearl Harbor, they had indelible memories of the event itself and its immediate aftermath. Here is Jack Kazuo Hata:

> I was attending a bowling tournament downtown. It was a Nisei bowling tournament, and all of a sudden I think we heard that Japan had attacked Pearl Harbor . . . I just walked home.
>
> [*Did you sit and talk with your parents at all?*]
>
> No. Not at all. I think the FBI came and I think that's the night that Dad was taken away . . . I think he was taken to Immigration in Seattle. I think that's where he was taken . . . Well, he was taken to Seattle, then, I think, to Missoula, Montana. And from there he was transferred to Lordsburg, New Mexico, whereas we were evacuated separately.

Others remembered experiencing confusion, unable to understand just what was happening, and uncertainty about whether to go to school the next day, Monday. Most did, however, and a number remembered a kind, if muted, response to their presence. Yoshiko Fujimoto Sugiyama, for example, recollected that she and other Japanese students at Stadium High School were asked by the principal to lead the student body in the Pledge of Allegiance that day.

The arrest of Issei parents was naturally traumatic for their children. Junichi Taira and Michie Taira Hori's father was taken early by the FBI, without explanation, as was Jack Kazuo Hata's father. Jack remembered that they said his father was under arrest "because of his photography, that

they were afraid he would go near a military site and take photographs."
Anon Male B recalled:

> Since our house was up there higher—Tacoma used to be a nice har-
> bor—ships would always have to pass by the house . . . So, they said
> that we were spying!
>
> I happened to be at a meeting, because they had some city election
> and they had some candidates come over to speak to the Japanese . . .
> and when I came home the house was dark, and I said, "Oh, my God!"
> We knew that we were going to be picked up because of our family
> in Japan and all that. Sure enough. So I naturally contacted the police
> department, hospitals, different organizations, and nobody knew
> anything about [his family's whereabouts]. And just about after mid-
> night or later, [I] called the police department again, and they said,
> "Yes, they're here. They're well taken care of. Don't worry." Because
> I naturally thought that this was the start of the roundup of Japanese
> in Tacoma.

MASATO YAMASAKI'S ARREST,
INCARCERATION, AND DEATH

Masato Yamasaki's arrest and incarceration, which a number of the interviewees discussed, was likely rooted in various factors, including his role
as TJLS principal, his other community leadership roles, and perhaps most
significantly, a May 1938 relief mission to Japanese soldiers in Manchuria,
with a visit to Japan en route. The outbreak of the Second Sino-Japanese
War in 1937 had vastly worsened US-Japanese relations. It also provoked
much discussion and debate in the Japanese American community.
Although little about Mr. Yamasaki's mission to Manchuria remains in
the historical record, given the divisions in the Nikkei community broadly
about Japan's war with China, we assume his trip was not without con-
troversy, especially with ongoing fears of a Caucasian backlash against
the Japanese in the US. Yamasaki's trip to Japanese-controlled Manchukuo
as a member of a soldier relief mission was organized by the Japanese
government in conjunction with the Northwest Liaison Japanese Association in Seattle, its purpose being to deliver over 1,500 comfort bags
(*imonbukuro*) containing such items as soap, razors, candy, and tobacco to

Japanese troops stationed there (Ichioka 2006, 37). Accompanying Yamasaki on the relief mission to Manchuria were Yasutaro Miyazawa of Seattle (Ito 1969, 1060) and Shintaro Miyazaki (Magden 1998, 104).[2]

Other factors no doubt contributed to Yamasaki's arrest, given the particular suspicion with which members of Japanese associations, Japanese language school principals, and anyone who had participated in "ceremonial acts of reverence toward the emperor" or other nationalistic celebrations were viewed (Flewelling 2002, 192). On each of these counts, Masato Yamasaki's record must have been damning in the eyes of the FBI. He was a member and past president of the Tacoma Japanese Association. He was the principal of the Tacoma Japanese Language School, which occasionally conducted ceremonies honoring the Japanese emperor. In November 1940, at the Seattle consulate, he had been commended by the Japanese government in a ceremony marking the 2,600th anniversary of the founding of the Japanese empire, an anniversary steeped in nationalism and Shinto myth. Yamasaki's position as head of the local kendo club would have been another red flag. As Daniel Lemire notes, North American kendo clubs "maintained more or less strong links with such organizations as the *Dai Nippon Butoku Kai* [Greater Japan Martial Virtue Society], a martial arts society whose leadership . . . and relationship to the Imperial Household made it very easy to disseminate the ideas sustaining the discourse of Japanese imperialism" (2016–17, 99). Branches of this society had spread into many West Coast Japanese communities in the late 1930s, as a way to "inculcate the 'Japanese spirit'" in young Nisei (Ichioka 2006, 39). There seems little doubt as to why—from the perspective of the US government—Yamasaki was deemed suspicious.

Masato Yamasaki and other Puget Sound detainees were questioned at the Seattle Immigration Service building. Some were released, while others, including Yamasaki, were placed in holding cells before being transferred to Fort Missoula, in Montana's Bitterroot Mountains. Built in 1877 as a military fort to provide protection for settlers from local Native American tribes, Fort Missoula had been quickly converted for use as a detention camp for "enemy aliens." In 1941, the fort already housed nearly one thousand Italian sailors, captured from Italian ships in 1939 (Flewelling, 2002, 190).

These must have been bleak days indeed for the detainees from the Puget Sound, suddenly transported from a relatively balmy coastal climate to Missoula's high-altitude winter. Detainees were housed in dormitory-style barracks, each containing forty or so cots. One Issei detainee from White River, Washington, wrote home shortly after arriving at the facility, commenting on the recent New Year's Day celebrations: "A party from Tacoma sent Rice cake so we had a piece of each size of a nickel. Sure taste of New Year Spirit."[3]

The Issei detainees at Fort Missoula were each given a hearing supervised by the Department of Justice, facing a more or less standard set of questions that included whether the individual had ever left the US, and if so, why and for how long. The questions were aimed at discerning the detainee's loyalty to the US, as well as "potential loyalty to Japan and the Japanese Emperor" (Flewelling 2002, 192). On September 1, 1942, Yamasaki was transferred to the US Army Internment Camp at Lordsburg, New Mexico, which functioned more or less as an interim facility for the arrested Issei.[4] Unlike other army-run camps, the facility at Lordsburg was designated specifically for prisoners of Japanese descent, housing up to 1,500 detainees.[5] Most of those held at Lordsburg were transferred to other Department of Justice enemy alien camps after May 1943. Masato Yamasaki, who had apparently taken ill, perhaps while in Missoula, died in the Lordsburg camp in March 1943. Harue Kawano Ozaki related a haunting version of a report she heard about Masato Yamasaki's death.

> Oh, Lordsburg, New Mexico. And he was kept there, and he championed, truly, for, for us to be democratic citizens of the United States. That was also as important as valuing the Japanese nationalistic beliefs . . . Other inmates [from Tacoma] that were released . . . had come back with stories that they could hear Yamasaki-*sensei* crying out, I think, in, in, in the middle of being tortured. He would cry out, "Is this the meaning of democracy?" And that's very unsettling to me.[6]

Fusae Fujii Yoshida's grandfather was also arrested and sent to Missoula, and later on to Lordsburg, before being allowed to join his family at Tule Lake Relocation Center in California. She recalled:

> To this day I remember, when he got off the bus at Tule Lake, when we went to meet him, he had turned into an old man. It had aged him so

much. It affected me. And another note is that Yamasaki-*sensei,* the principal, died at Lordsburg. And so my grandfather brought his fingernail [clippings] and hair back to give to his widow as a—the only remains she had of him. But he did bring it back from Lordsburg to Mrs. Yamasaki. That much I knew.

A memorial service for Masato Yamasaki was announced in the (handwritten) Japanese section of the *Minidoka Irrigator,*[7] the weekly newspaper of the Minidoka Relocation Center in Idaho, where many of the Tacoma Japanese were detained. The announcement noted his graduation from Waseda, his position as principal of the Tacoma Japanese Language School, and his "high-minded" and "noble" character. Observing that he was "widely known among the Japanese," it paid tribute to his "enormous contributions to Japanese language education." The bereaved wife, the notice stated, resided at Tule Lake.[8]

EXECUTIVE ORDER 9066 AND THE TACOMA JAPANESE LANGUAGE SCHOOL

On December 8, the day after the Pearl Harbor attack, the *Tacoma Daily Ledger* ran an article headlined, "Japanese in County Shocked by News of Attack on US: Both Old and Young Generations Saddened by Declarations of War." The article quotes a comment by *Takoma shuho* (*Tacoma Weekly*) owner and editor Shuichi Fukui: "We Japanese living in the United States are Americans" (Nimura 2017b)—echoing decades of effort toward legitimacy and belonging. That same day, the leaders of the Tacoma-Puyallup JACL issued a statement in the *Tacoma Times* newspaper:

> In this great hour of crisis we American citizens of Japanese ancestry stand solidly behind President Roosevelt and our fellow Americans in denouncing the treacherous acts of the Japanese military clique. We stand ready to defend with our lives this democratic system of life, which has given to us and our parents privileges and opportunities enjoyed only in countries where human liberties still prevail. We offer our wholehearted cooperation with the FBI, police, and military authorities in whatever work they may undertake. (in Magden 1998, 115)

The following Sunday, December 14, Tacoma's Japanese community took out a full-page advertisement in the *Tacoma Daily Ledger* to clarify their position within the nation at large, sounding the theme of "American first": "I am proud I am an American citizen of Japanese ancestry," the statement began, "for my very background makes me appreciate more fully the wonderful advantages of this nation." As Harue Kawano Ozaki put it, "I was told that it was one of the principles that were taught in all the families, that this is our country."

Nevertheless, on February 19, 1942, two months after Pearl Harbor, President Roosevelt signed Executive Order 9066 authorizing the evacuation of all persons of Japanese ancestry from the West Coast of the US. In March, some members of Tacoma's Japanese community gathered at the language school and pledged to "forswear and repudiate any other allegiance which . . . [we] . . . knowingly or unknowingly may have held heretofore" (in Magden 1998, 133), echoing messaging to Nisei during the prewar years.

As plans for forced removal moved forward, the April 9, 1942, issue of the *Takoma shuho* published advice for the community under a headline that read, "Let's Hurry to Prepare for Evacuation":

> Although it is reported that once evacuation orders are issued,
> two weeks will be allowed to prepare, recently in California and
> Bainbridge Island no more than five days to one week was allowed.
> Accordingly, since once the order is issued there will be no time to
> pack up, and since it is not known exactly when the order will come—
> it is predicted to come soon—early preparations are recommended.[9]

This (presumably) last issue of the weekly paper, which had been in publication since 1922, also carried a Japanese-language ad that foreshadowed the impending destruction of the community: local merchant Fred Hofstetter solicited Tacoma's Japanese *"shokun"* ("ladies and gentlemen") to bring him their furniture and household items, for which he would pay "ready cash."

Ironically, the TJLS continued to play a central role in the Nisei's lives—but now in the dissolution of their community. On May 13, 1942, Tacoma's Japanese residents were ordered to report the following day to the school, which had remained closed since the Pearl Harbor attack. The building was now designated a Civilian Control Center where they were required to register for incarceration. The contradictions embedded in this place emerged in multiple ways and, as it had been since its founding in 1911, the TJLS was a critical space for experiences of urban belonging, but now played a role in the dissolution of that community. Michie Taira Hori remembered going with her mother to register, enacting the lessons of filial piety learned at home and in school:

> I think I went with Mom because, you know, she didn't know English too well . . . So it was, you know, in the Japanese school, but I guess that's where they—you know, at that age I thought, this is what you're supposed to do, so you don't think about the ramification of, "What am I doing? Why are they doing it here?" No. You know, I didn't have feelings like that. You know, when you're kind of up in the air about where we're going or what's going to happen and everything, I don't think—you just do what you're supposed to do, you know, especially, you know, when you're supposed to be obedient all the time.

At the time, Shigeko Tamaki Yoshiwara worked for the state of Washington. She recalled: "At the time of the evacuation, I was sitting on the other side of the desk [at the TJLS] trying to help the elderly. I had to put them on the buses to go to the internment center. It was kind of a double-edged job, because I could speak to the elderly."

Only fifty-six families from Pierce County would opt to move inland to avoid evacuation to the camps, among them Ryo Munekata's family, who moved to Nampa, Idaho. The rest of Tacoma's Japanese packed up what goods they could and, if able, put them in the safekeeping of Caucasian friends or stored them at the language school and at the Buddhist and Methodist churches. Chizu Tomita Takaoka, for instance, remembered, "Oh, we moved everything to *Nihongogakko*, all our worldly possessions, which was very, very small to begin with, and then left . . . The order was to put everything into suitcases, and we did." As Ron Magden points out, 153 merchants in Tacoma "simply walked away from their stores" (1998, 140).

By the end of May, the Japanese were instructed to go to Tacoma's Union Station. Masatoshi Fujii recalled the irony of the situation: "You had to find your own way to the station. You're getting incarcerated, and they don't pick you up. You report to the railroad station." For Jack Kazuo Hata, leaving Tacoma was "something I could never forget":

It was my twenty-first birthday. Sunday. And it was about 50 degrees around Tacoma at that time. Two days and two nights on the train. Ended up in Fresno [California]. It must have been near 100 degrees. Then we took a bus to Pinedale [also in California].[10] I don't know how far it was from the train station. But we got there about noontime. We all lined up to go to the mess hall, and people were passing out right and left because of the heat. We just weren't used to that kind of heat. I remember going into the mess hall and sitting down, and one of the first things that they served was raw spinach salad. And I had never eaten raw spinach. My mother always cooked the spinach. I looked at it and I said, "Boy, I think I'm going to die here!" And after lunch we got our rooms assigned, and I remember we had asphalt floors—some barracks had concrete, I think, and others had wooden floors, I think. But we had asphalt floors. And I touched the bedpost and I had to pull my hand away because it was so hot. And the bedpost would sink into the asphalt. That's my recollection. And then almost every day at around four o'clock the dust storm would start and all the dust would get blown into our room. Those are the recollections I have of being in Pinedale. Then in July we went to Tule Lake. [It] was pretty much the same. Hot at that time, and every day, you know, the dust would blow, sand would blow—blow into your barrack room.

Mitsuo Takasugi also remembered leaving Union Station:

We all had to take our things down, whatever we could carry, and walk down to the Union Station, and we got on a train. We didn't know where we were going at all. And a soldier was stationed on every train, and we all were put on the trains, and then they'd start to move. And it was becoming night, and we—the last I remember, we were going through Portland. I was looking out the, you know . . . Well, actually, they had pulled all the shades down because they didn't want the lights to show because of the war, but we could see out, and you could see it was Portland. So we were going south.

Harue Kawano Ozaki had similar memories:

> We all gathered at the Union Station and got on the train. And you
> know, I was thirteen; it was like an adventure. I didn't feel badly about
> anybody or anything, except that we were all together. We didn't know
> where we were going, but we rode these old rickety trains until we got to
> Pinedale, which is next to Fresno, and I understand that that's one of
> the hottest spots in America. And they had the barracks there, and
> some of the experiences there were very insensitive, you know, unnec-
> essary deaths from bad exposure to the sun. So then we stayed there
> for three months until the permanent camp was built in Newell, Cali-
> fornia, which is Tule Lake, on the border near Klamath Falls, Oregon.
> We all went there. We all went to Pinedale, and then when the camp
> was ready, we all rode to Tule Lake . . . We didn't live in the same block
> anymore, and we saw different kinds of people from all different parts
> of the states, no longer just Tacoma, but other Washington people—
> Oregon and California. And it was just a new different life all over.
>
> And so we stayed in Tule Lake for one year. So I spent my life
> going to classes and the barracks, and that was my daily life. And I
> would occasionally see the Tacoma people, and whenever we saw each
> other, nothing had changed too much. I mean, it was very acceptable
> to be together and just chat on.

For the Nisei who were seniors at Lincoln High School, evacuation
meant they had to leave Tacoma before graduation. Eleven Lincoln High
School seniors were denied their diplomas, and George Kurose was denied
recognition as valedictorian. This injustice was finally corrected in 2002
when, after a years-long campaign on the part of Ronald Magden and Joseph
Seto, the diplomas were mailed to the graduates of sixty years prior and, at
a ceremony at Lincoln High, George Kurose was presented with the Valedictorian Medallion (Seto and Magden 2001, 8; *Tacoma News Tribune* 2002).

When reflecting on these experiences, a number of interviewees refer-
enced the phrase *shikataganai* ("it cannot be helped") and the value of
perseverance, lessons articulated to them as part of the *shushin* education
at the TJLS. According to Ryo Munekata, "Our teachers at the Tacoma
School and our religion taught us to accept the order [EO 9066] as a matter
of fact and to look at the bright side of the tragedy."[11] Joe Kosai believed that

the Issei, having been raised in the authoritarian environment of Meiji Japan and taught that the government was "always right," were constitutionally unable to question the US government's order. While the older generation was too docile, according to Joe, the Nisei generation was too young to offer resistance. Recognizing the use of these terms and concepts is not meant to proffer a culturally essentializing explanation for the acceptance of incarceration; rather, it considers how transnational processes, experienced in part through lessons learned at the TJLS, shaped the Nisei's narratives and understanding of self.

Having internalized the dictum of not bringing shame to the family or community, many Nisei turned that precept inward and felt humiliated for having been incarcerated. June Miyeko Shirozu Hayashi said,

> The Japanese that were taken from their homes and went to camp, we felt so ashamed. It wasn't like [we] felt bad because, you know, because . . . but we felt ashamed that they didn't trust us, and I think that is a really strong—I never thought about it. My husband never thought about it. So, a lot of people choose not to talk about it, because it's a very shameful part of their history. Why—weren't we good enough to have stayed here? I mean, weren't we good enough? Why did they take us? We have to be better when we come back so that we can assimilate, so that we can become Americans and they would want us back again. And so, I think that's what we've been doing all of our lives.

June also engages with the complexities of bridging, rejecting the "either/or-ness" of Nisei identity: "We, you know, you have to throw away your Japanese-ness in order to become a good American. I mean, that's what they were telling us, that we must be too Japanese and too loyal to Japan, and that's why they were afraid of us. I mean, that's the message, I think, that was sent."

JAPANESE LANGUAGE SKILLS AND NISEI MILITARY SERVICE

Not only was the TJLS turned into a Civilian Control Center by the Western Defense Command, but it also became well known within the military intelligence community. As Nikkei along the West Coast were being incarcerated, many Nisei already serving in the armed forces were summarily discharged. Although they were US citizens of draft age, young Nisei men were categorized as 4-C, "enemy aliens not desired for the armed service." In a moving recollection of the night before he was forced to leave Tacoma in 1942, Clinton Butsuda wrote:

> I slept on the floor, for our beds were given away. As I tried to sleep, angry thoughts filter[ed] through my mind. Why? Why is this nightmare happening to me? I'm an American citizen! What did I do? . . . Our last night at home we again tried to sleep on the hard wooden floor, but the nagging question kept me awake. Why? Why? Didn't I try to prove my loyalty that first Saturday after Pearl Harbor by volunteering for the Army? You rejected me because I was of Japanese ancestry. You further demeaned me by reclassifying me 4-C—undesirable enemy alien! My self-esteem plummeted to zero minus. I hated everything and everybody . . . I hated my mother and father for being Japanese. I hated myself for being born Asian. I hated myself for even thinking these thoughts. I was so mad and frustrated that I cried under the thin blanket to muffle the sound. Twenty-year-old boys don't cry—especially a Japanese-American. (1999, 121–23)

In February 1943, the 4-C designation was changed to allow Nisei to volunteer for military service. Eventually more than 33,000 Nisei served in the US armed forces during World War II, the vast majority in the European theater (Uyeda and Sakai 1991, 13).

In fact, preparations for the possibility of using Japanese Americans for intelligence purposes had begun much earlier. As early as 1932, army captain Kai Rasmussen visited Tacoma, gathering names of bilingual Japanese Americans from the TJLS lists. In March 1941, nine months before the outbreak of war, the Fourth Army Intelligence School was opened in San Francisco. By November of that year, fifty-eight Nisei students had begun training to serve as linguists (Uyeda and Sakai 1991, 16). Over the course of their military careers they "translated captured documents and messages, analyzed features of downed enemy aircraft, interrogated prisoners, broadcast propaganda, encouraged Japanese soldiers and civilians to surrender, helped prepare the instruments of surrender, worked on various aspects of the War Crimes trials, and were an important element of the occupation forces" (O'Brien and Fugita 1982, 67). As linguists, the Nisei utilized their language skills in part to prove their loyalty and win acceptance for their community. The Military Intelligence Service (MIS) was "virtually secret" during the war (indeed, until quite recently) as the US did not want Japan to know that it possessed the ability to translate their communications.[12]

Taeko Hoshiwara Taniguchi reflected on the general Japanese language ability of Tacoma Nisei as compared to other Nisei she encountered in the camps:

> Well one thing is we spoke a lot of Japanese. When the Tacoma people got together, we were able to speak Japanese all the time. We spoke Japanese. I don't know whether they [people from other areas] attended Japanese school or not, but I think . . . the teachers in [the Tacoma] Japanese school are good, [so they] were, are able to speak Japanese, you know. [Principal Yamasaki] taught us Japanese so that among us we could all speak Japanese, even to now, we speak Japanese to each other, you know. After all these years, because of the way he taught us.

After the war broke out, the Military Intelligence Service Language School (MISLS), first headquartered in San Francisco, was relocated to Camp Savage, Minnesota, and later in August 1944 to larger quarters in Fort Snelling, Minnesota (Ano 1977). Kai Rasmussen, now commandant of the MISLS, was concerned that Caucasians with no prior exposure to the language would have trouble learning Japanese. Thus, the decision was made to focus on training Nisei. However, in "an initial survey of 3,700 Nisei, MISLS officials deemed only three percent as accomplished linguists" (Swift 2008, xiv). Disagreement existed over the effectiveness of the Japanese language schools. Seattle's, for example, was deemed "minimally successful in teaching the language" (Miyamoto 1984, xi). The Vancouver, BC, school, on the other hand, like Tacoma's, had a reputation for producing able speakers (Lemire 2016–17, 82, 83). Intelligence specialist Richard Sakakida, who was decorated for his wartime language work, had been a student at Hawaii's Hongwanji Japanese School (Williams 2019, 152–53).

On his scouting trips in the early 1930s, Rasmussen found the Tacoma Japanese Language School to be particularly strong in language teaching, and indeed, the MISLS recruited a number of young men from Tacoma. One, an army colonel who researched Japanese language schools in the 1930s, called it "the best language school in the West, no question" (Ted Tetsuo Tamaki at TJLS Commemorative Event, University of Washington, Tacoma, November 18, 2003). The TJLS, the secular institution that had brought a diverse Japanese community together and taught Nisei children language, *shushin*, Japanese heritage, and the need to be American first had become an important source of human capital for US military intelligence. Junichi Taira remembered:

> When I went into the service I was assigned to counterintelligence corps. And when I went overseas they would assign me to a field office, and I had to go take a language test, and the captain said, "Where did you learn your Japanese?" I said, "Tacoma Japanese [Language School]." He said, "You're okay." Just like that. I was amazed. I couldn't believe the reputation that the school had . . . He didn't even test me.

Of the 106 young Nisei men from Tacoma who served in the armed forces during World War II, 55—more than half—attended the MISLS and served as linguists.[13] One family, the Setos, had six sons, five of whom served in the military: Paul T. Seto (b. 1917) in the US Army, the other four—Hugh Y. Seto (b. 1920), Matthew M. Seto (b. 1921), Joseph P. Seto (b. 1924), David K. Seto (b. 1926)—in the Military Intelligence Service. The sixth brother Thomas A. Seto, was born in Japan in 1922 when the family returned for a visit. As a result, unlike his siblings, he was not a US citizen; he was classified as an "enemy alien," ineligible for military service ("Seto Family History," n.d.).

Nisei from Tacoma's neighboring communities of Fife and Sumner also worked in the MIS, but at lower rates—fewer than one-third of those who served in the former case, and about one-fifth in the latter. The high percentage of Tacomans in military intelligence suggests that their Japanese language was strong, likely thanks to the foundation provided by Tacoma's Japanese Language School. TJLS alumnus Ted Tetsuo Tamaki, who attended the MISLS and served in Japan as a translator in

1946, insisted that his proficiency was "all because of background provided by my parents making me attend the [Tacoma] Japanese Language School."[14] The contributions of the Nisei linguists were lauded by the military, their efforts credited with "shorten[ing] the war by two years," although "the Nisei's military ranks . . . did not reflect the soldiers' value" (L. Tamura 2012, 88).

SPATIAL DISPERSAL AND COMMUNITY DESTRUCTION

In the aftermath of the destruction of the community through wartime incarceration, the US government adopted policies of relocation and dispersal, encouraging "the former incarcerees to disperse and not reestablish the tight ethnic communities they lived in before the war" (Fugita and Fernandez 2004, 10). It was also a further attempt to force "assimilation" and the loss of connection with Japan and the world of the Issei. The newly released Nikkei were subject to the government War Relocation Agency's policies and pressure from "within their own communities to 'assimilate' in order to avoid being perceived as foreign or threatening" (Robinson 2012, 70). This dispersal after the war accentuates the spatiality of community destruction.

When the war ended, few of Tacoma's Japanese families returned to that city. Many relocated to California and Chicago, concluding that they would have more opportunities elsewhere. Takao Jerry Kikuchi said, "No, we had no intention to go back to Tacoma because when we lived in Tacoma jobs are hard to find and it is a poor place to live in. Financially it's not very good." Joe Seto concurred: "Very few people owned any property, so therefore they had nothing to go back to, and like he says, the employment opportunities were very poor . . . Well, we knew that all the university graduates could not find jobs." June Miyeko Shirozu Hayashi noted that

in Tacoma itself, I think that there would be not too much employment to come back to. And so, unless you had, like, a dry-cleaning business . . . All the people that had dry-cleaning businesses came back, because there are, like, three or four Japanese dry-cleaning businesses in Tacoma . . . But it is almost—you can almost count them on your hands, but they had something to come back for, or come back *to*. Maybe they had even a house, I don't know. But otherwise, the fishing industry was totally gone. The lumber mills in Longview were probably no longer. I don't know. They weren't hiring ... So everybody had to find a new profession and a new way of life, and they really had to start all over again. So, most people came probably to California, I would think.

Eventually, reunions built around the Tacoma Japanese Language School by the Nisei and their children reasserted belonging and legitimacy in Tacoma in important ways. Taeko Hoshiwara Taniguchi spoke of the reunions as a mode of reversal of community destruction and the dispersal policies. "Tacoma was small, you know compared to Seattle ... Not too many Japanese came back to Tacoma, you know, they spread out all over the United States. . . But every time they have a reunion, especially a Tacoma reunion, I never missed. I always went ... I feel with Tacoma, very much."

During reunions after the war, which for Tacomans began in 1977, remaining Issei, the Nisei, and their families temporarily reestablished a physical presence in the city—with, as Kazuo Horita put it so powerfully, lumps in their throats as they confronted the structural forgetting and erasure in the city. The narratives they offered in the interviews made claims on belonging with detailed memories of childhood walks, disciplinary Issei eyes on them in public spaces, and rowdiness in the TJLS classrooms. Reasserting their presence in these urban spaces that have become parking lots, high-rise offices, and hotels reminds us that the past does not have to remain silenced and invisible. On the Prairie Line Trail that runs through campus, UW Tacoma has memorialized the TJLS with a beautiful sculpture by Gerard Tsutakawa, *Maru*.

An echo of the TJLS was heard in Tacoma as well when Robert Mitsuhiro Takasugi, brother of interviewee Mitsuo Takasugi, spoke as a federal judge. In the words of Ryo Munekata:

He was the first Japanese American to be federal judge[15] ... He left Tacoma with the evacuation from the Union Station. He said he was just an infant, practically. And then when the Union Station was dedicated as a federal court, he returned to Tacoma to be the guest speaker, keynote speaker for the dedication. And I think he mentioned in his speech, "It's ironic that this is the very place I was forced to leave, and I'm back here to dedicate your court building." And he lives in the Los Angeles area today.

In many ways the stories told here are spatial stories and transnational tales. Wartime incarceration and dispersal from the camps resulted from deteriorating international relations and the onset of war, and from anti-Japanese discrimination targeted at those who were connected with practices of Meiji Japan. Families sold businesses and treasured belongings, got on trains and left for the unknown, then worked to establish security in new places after the war with "nothing to go back to" in Tacoma. Identity formation was a constant in these processes, such that becoming Nisei should be understood as emergent, conditional, and ongoing, bridging transnational expectations and shaping urban landscapes.

Spatiality was a key aspect of becoming Nisei, but so were the transnational worlds traversed and inhabited by the Issei and their children. These processes of subject and community formation were complex and contingent, what we have termed "bridging" in this book. Putting our focus on the pre–World War II years, not as an interlude between major international events, but as a critical time and space for Nisei subject formation, also alerts us to the dramatic structural forgetting that has taken place across the city's built landscape. Traditional practices of urban development have revamped many parts of the city's built form. *Becoming Nisei*, however, asks us to remember the past, for although it may be buried, it is not dead.

APPENDIX A

Interviewees and Family Backgrounds

INTERVIEWEES BY FAMILY/MARRIED NAME, PLACE AND DATE
OF INTERVIEW, AND AGE (IF KNOWN)

Anonymous Female A. Age 81.

Anonymous Female B. Age 72.

Anonymous Female C. Age 78.*

Anonymous Female D. Age 76.*

Anonymous Female E. Age 83.*

Anonymous Male A. Age 81.

Anonymous Male B. Age 84.*

Anonymous Male C.

Anonymous Male D. Age 72.*

Aochi, Yoneko. Oakland, CA, October 18, 2003. Age 85.*

Fujii, Masatoshi. Oakland, CA, October 18, 2003.*

Fujimoto, Riyeko. El Monte, CA, January 26, 2005. Age 79.

Fujita, Masaye Jinguji. Los Angeles, CA, January 26, 2005 Age 87.

Harada, Yuriko Lily Korin. Los Angeles, CA, January 29, 2005. Age 74.

Harano, Katsuko Aochi. Oakland, CA, October 18, 2003. Age 80.*

Hata, Jack Kazuo. Northridge, CA, January 30, 2005. Age 84.

Hattori, Fumi Sato. Los Angeles, CA, January 27, 2005. Age 84.

Hayashi, June Mieko Shirozu. Los Angeles, CA, January 27, 2005. Age 65.

Hori, Michie Taira. Los Angeles, CA, January 30, 2005. Age 78.

Horita, Kazuo. Chicago, IL, March 11, 2005. Age 84.

Kawasaki, Chiyeko Tadaye Fujimoto. Tacoma, WA, July 7, 2004. Age 83.

Kikuchi, Takao Jerry (with his grandson, Drew, and Joseph Seto).
　　Huntington Beach, CA, January 26, 2005. Age 83.
Kosai, Joseph. Tacoma, WA, February 23, 2004. Age 69.
Munekata, Ryo (with Kunio Shibata). Tacoma, WA, August 7, 2003. Age 82.
Munekata, Ryo (with Anonymous Male C and Anonymous Female A).
　　Los Angeles, CA, January 28, 2005. Age 83.
Osada, Takeshi. Tacoma, WA, October 2, 2006. Age 79.
Ozaki, Harue Kawano. Tacoma, WA, September 15, 2004; Chicago, IL,
　　March 12, 2005. Age 76.
Ozaki, Sam. Tacoma, WA, September 15, 2004. (Grew up in CA, did not
　　attend TJLS; husband of Harue Kawano Ozaki.)
Peterson, Teiko Kawano. Oakland, CA, October 18, 2003.*
Seto, Joseph (with Takao Jerry Kikuchi and Jerry's grandson, Drew).
　　Huntington Beach, CA, January 26,2005. Age 81.
Shibata, Kunio, Oakland, CA, October 18, 2003; and (with Ryo
　　Munekata), Tacoma, WA, August 7, 2003. Age 80.*
Shirasago, Sally Someko Kimura. Los Angeles, CA, January 28, 2005.
　　Age 81.
Sugiyama, Yoshiko Fujimoto. Tacoma, WA, July 7, 2004. Age 85.
Taira, Junichi. Los Angeles, CA, January 30, 2005. Age 76.
Takaoka, Chizu Tomita. Chicago, IL, March 12, 2005. Age 85.
Takasugi, Mitsuo. Los Angeles, CA, January 9, 2005. Age 77.
Tanbara, Kimiko Fujimoto. Tacoma, WA, July 7, 2004. Age 80.
Taniguchi, Taeko Hoshiwara. Seattle, WA, March 17, 2006. Age 82.
Torimaru, Hanna Kae Nakagawa. Chicago, IL, March 12, 2005. Age 83.
Yano, Perry Yoshiaki. Chicago, IL, March 10, 2005. Age 74.
Yoshida, Fusae Fujii. Oakland, CA, October 18, 2003. Age 76.*
Yoshioka, Hiroko Betty Fukuhara. Chicago, IL, March 10, 2005. Age 82.
Yoshiwara, Shigeko Gay Tamaki. Oakland, CA, October 18, 2003. Age 87.*

*Individuals with an asterisk participated in one large group conversation in
Oakland, October 18, 2003.

FAMILY HISTORIES

The following are brief family histories for all the interviewees, except nine
who wished to remain anonymous. The information is based on material in the
interviews and thus is not uniform across families. For example, some families
had clear records on when their parents came to the United States, while others
were less specific about dates and early occupations. Also included are the
places interviewees remember living, to highlight the spatial aspects of the

childhood experiences of the Nisei. The paragraphs are organized in alphabetical order by original family name (maiden name for women).

AOCHI

Yoneko Aochi (b. 1918) and Katsuko Aochi Harano (b. 1923). Yoneko Aochi was the eldest of five Aochi siblings. The family originally lived on what is now Ruston Way near the old Asarco smelter. Their father worked at the Point Defiance sawmill, later buying a hotel on Jefferson Street, while their mother worked in the home. After their father sold the hotel, the family moved into a house across the street from the hotel, until a home burglary prompted a move back to what was then 4618 Waterfront Street.

FUJII

Masatoshi Fujii (birth year unknown) and Fusae Fujii Yoshida (b. 1927). The Fujii siblings' maternal grandfather came to the US in 1900, arriving via San Francisco; according to Fusae he "had some kind of a business in Napa, California." Their grandmother came to the US in 1906, shortly after the San Francisco earthquake. Their mother was born in 1907, and soon thereafter the family moved to Tacoma, to join the grandmother's uncle, Mr. Yanagita, who had a "logging business." Their grandfather later had a laundry business. In 1914, the family returned to Japan, leaving their mother with relatives in Fukuoka. She returned to Tacoma at age seventeen. Their father came to the US in 1917, and the parents were married in 1926. Mrs. Fujii taught at the Japanese Language School briefly. Their father had a produce market for a short while, but lost it during the Depression, after which he did odd jobs, finally becoming foreman at the Maroush seafood company in Tacoma shucking oysters.

FUJIMOTO

Riyeko Fujimoto (b. 1924). Born in Tacoma, Riyeko had one younger brother, Tadashi, born in 1926. Her father came to the US and then returned to Japan to marry Sumie Kikuchi. Both were from Kagawa on the island of Shikoku. Riyeko's father worked for the St. Paul & Tacoma sawmill and later in her childhood also ran a hotel with her mother, the Vendome Hotel on Market Street, while continuing to work at the sawmill.

Yoshiko Fujimoto Sugiyama (b. 1919), Chiyeko Tadaye Fujimoto Kawasaki (b. 1921), and Kimiko Fujimoto Tanbara (b. 1924). The three sisters' father, Masakata Fujimoto (b. 1875), was expected by his father to go to the US, be successful, and return to Japan.[1] He first went to Hawaii, and later moved to California, where he had a large onion ranch. He finally moved to Tacoma at the invitation of a friend who needed help with bookkeeping. Their parents' marriage was arranged by a family friend, who knew their mother (b. 1894) in Fukuoka. In 1918, Masakata started the Capital Cleaners and Dye Works, a wholesale cleaner on Court C between Market and Broadway. Their mother arrived in the US in 1914 at age twenty. Their mother, primarily a housewife when the children were young, later worked at the cleaners. The three girls also helped out, and Tadaye and her husband eventually took over ownership and operation of the business. This is the family that purchased the TJLS building after the war and later sold it to the University of Washington Tacoma.

FUKUHARA

Hiroko Betty Fukuhara Yoshioka (b. 1922). Hiroko was the eldest of six girls. Both parents were from Shizuoka. Her father came first to the US and later returned to Japan to bring her mother. He worked first in a lumber mill in Tacoma and later became a salesman (of stocks). Her mother was a housewife. She also remembered that when her mother first arrived in the US, she did not know how to cook, so "all the lumbermen had to teach her how to cook!"

HATA

Jack Kazuo Hata (b. 1921). Jack's parents were both from Toyama City. His father came to the US in 1915 at about age twenty-five (first to California), and his mother in 1920. Unusual for their cohort, the two of them met and fell in love; theirs was not an arranged marriage. Jack's father worked in the photography industry and acted as the photographer for the Japanese community in Tacoma. His mother, too, was well known in the community as a teacher at the Japanese Language School.

HORITA

Kazuo Horita (b. 1921). Kazuo's father, the youngest in his family and well educated compared to others in his generation of Japanese immigrants, came to the US in 1906 with his older brother to help make money to send home to his family. Apparently the family had debt, and this was their strategy for meeting those obligations. Kazuo's mother did not come to the US until 1920. Both parents were from Fukui Prefecture. Kazuo's father worked for a few years in a sawmill and then transitioned to a small business—in his case, a produce market. He opened the market prior to 1910 and eventually had two separate enterprises, one on the corner of 11th and Market, the other one nearby.

HOSHIWARA

Taeko Hoshiwara Taniguchi (b. 1924). Taeko's father came to the US as a student, but lack of finances prevented him from continuing his education once he arrived. He returned to Japan to marry in an arranged marriage. Taeko's mother was seventeen years old when she came to the US with her new husband, in 1918. In Tacoma, Taeko's father worked for the Rose Brothers fish company. The family also ran a hotel, and her mother worked as an oyster shucker. Taeko had two brothers and one sister.

JINGUJI

Masaye Jinguji Fujita (b. 1917). Masaye's father worked for the railroad, and had been in Tacoma "quite a few years before" she was born. He returned to Japan to marry her mother in 1917. Both were from Yamanashi Prefecture. Her father was a produce worker, with a shop on K Street called Jim's Market, which also had a flower shop. Her mother was primarily a homemaker. Masaye had two younger brothers and two younger sisters, all of whom helped out at the market.

KAWANO

Harue Kawano Ozaki (b. 1928) and Teiko Kawano Peterson (birth year unknown). The two sisters grew up in a family of two boys and three girls; a fourth girl died as an infant. Their father was born in 1885 and came to the United States from Tokushima Prefecture on Shikoku Island in 1910 when he was twenty-five years old. He returned to Japan and got married in 1918 to a woman from his same area who also had gone to college and trained as a teacher, unlike many of her generation. When the parents first returned to the US they lived in Seattle, where the father worked as a banker at the Bank of Okamuro. After the bank went bankrupt, they moved to Tacoma in about 1919. The family had a grocery store on North I Street, and their mother was a beloved teacher at the TJLS. We also interviewed Harue's husband, **Sam Saburo Ozaki, born in Los Angeles in 1924.** During World War II Sam volunteered to serve in the 442nd Regimental Combat Team. After the war he taught in the Chicago public schools, becoming Chicago's first Asian American school principal.

KIKUCHI

Takao Jerry Kikuchi (b. 1922). Jerry was the eldest of four children, with one younger brother and two younger sisters. His parents married in Japan and emigrated together from Shikoku. His father worked in a restaurant; his mother worked at Tacoma's Japanese-language newspaper, *Takoma jiho* (1915–21)/*Takoma shuho* (1922–42), doing the kanji typesetting.

KIMURA[2]

Sally Someko Kimura Shirasago (b. 1923). Sally was the second youngest in a family of three boys and four girls. Her father arrived in the US in 1907 and farmed vegetables in Fife, selling truckloads at Fort Lewis and McChord Field (now Joint Base Lewis McChord). After several years he returned to Japan to marry; they returned to the US together in 1912. Both were from Fukuoka. Sally's mother worked on the farm "when she was able," and later the family had a market in South Tacoma. Sally remembered this as the Airway Market, which was registered to someone in the Kimura family.

KORIN

Yuriko Lily Korin Harada (b. 1931). Yuriko's father came with his parents from Hiroshima to Seattle in 1919 when he was eleven years old. Her mother was born in Hawaii in 1913. Her parents married in 1930 and then moved to Tacoma. Her father worked for a wholesale Japanese food merchant taking orders and making deliveries to farmers on the city's outskirts. Siblings were Shoji Korin, born April 11, 1935, and Edward Korin, born in September 1941, both in Tacoma.

KOSAI

Joseph Kosai (b. 1935). Born in Tacoma, Joe was one of seven siblings. His grandfather settled in Auburn "in a little community called Christopher" in 1900, and was soon followed by other relatives. Joe's father was six years old at that time, and did not move to Tacoma until 1923 when he was twenty-four. When Joe's grandfather passed away in 1919, Joe's father returned to Japan with the ashes. While there he was drafted into the Japanese army; however, having come to the US as a six-year-old, he couldn't read or write Japanese, so after several months he was discharged. He met and married his wife in Japan, and they returned to the United States, settling in Tacoma. Both were from Shiga Prefecture. Joe's father worked in a sawmill, and his mother worked at the hotel where they also lived. Other interviewees noted that Joe's father worked the night shift and also helped supply workers from Japan to the sawmills.

MUNEKATA

Ryo Munekata (b. 1921). Ryo was the eldest of three children. His father, Tadajiro Munekata, was born in Hiroshima prefecture in 1890. At age sixteen he emigrated to Hawaii; six months later he joined a brother in Seattle, before relocating to Tacoma in 1906. He returned to Japan in 1919 for his father's memorial service and while there met Kasumi Okuhara, born in 1901, in their home prefecture of Hiroshima. The two married in November and returned to the US in December 1919, arriving on the 25th, a fact that his father recalled to the family every Christmas Day. Ryo's father worked at the Union Laundry between Market and Broadway in an alley off South 15th Street and attended Central

School to learn English. The Munekatas ran the Broadway Hotel, the New Tacoma Hotel, and later the Superior Hotel, located at 1317½ Broadway.[3]

NAKAGAWA

Hanna Kae Nakagawa Torimaru (b. 1922). Hanna's parents were from Hiroshima Prefecture and ran the State Cafe. The restaurant was originally on Pacific Avenue across from City Hall, but later moved to 1512½ South Jefferson. Her father and mother were from merchant and imperial court families.

OSADA

Takeshi Osada (b. ca. 1927). Takeshi's parents were both from Yamanashi Prefecture; his mother's maiden name was Jinguji, a fairly unusual name. Takeshi's maternal grandparents had come to Tacoma first, and brought their daughter to the US ("called her over") from Japan when she was about sixteen. His father had a laundry business and his mother owned a barbershop. Because all of his mother's siblings were also in Tacoma, "we were very closely tied to them." Takeshi was the oldest of nine children and was about fifteen when the war started.

SATO

Fumi Sato Hattori (b. 1921). Fumi, the firstborn, was the only girl of four children. Her father was born in 1882 and came to the US from Ehime Prefecture on the southern island of Shikoku in 1905. Her mother came to the US in 1920 upon marrying at age nineteen. Although Fumi's father came to the US as a student, he was unable to afford university, so sought work in the St. Paul & Tacoma Lumber Company, working as a planer in the sawmill. Her mother ran the Superior Hotel at 17th and Market in Tacoma,[4] where the family eventually moved after initially residing on the tideflats.

SETO

Joseph T. Seto (b. 1924). Joe's father, Toraichi Seto, was born in Wakayama Prefecture in 1888. He arrived in Vancouver, BC, on April 2, 1907, and three days later entered the US. He worked for the Pacific Fruit Company and Hammond Produce. Toraichi returned to Japan in 1913 to find a wife. Joe's mother, Kiyo Morita, also of Wakayama, was born in 1895. The two married in 1913, and Kiyo joined her husband in the US in 1916. They had seven children: Paul Tokio (b. 1917), Hugh Yasuo (b. 1920), Matthew Masami (b. 1921), Thomas Akiyoshi (b. 1922), Joseph T. (b. 1924), David K. (1926), and Grace Y. Seto (b. 1934). Paul served in the US Army during World War II, and Hugh, Matthew, and Joseph served in the army's Military Intelligence Service.

SHIBATA (FORMERLY URUSHIBATA)

Kunio Shibata (b. 1923). Kunio had six siblings, one of whom was left in Japan with grandparents. The Shibata family's father worked as a busboy or a waiter, eventually taking over running a "ham and eggs and pancake" restaurant. The father returned to his native Shizuoka to marry. Returning to Tacoma, he went into business delivering vegetables. Kunio's mother was a homemaker. The original family name was Urushibata. According to Kunio, it was legally shortened to Shibata in the 1950s.

SHIROZU

June Miyeko Shirozu Hayashi (b. 1940). June was the middle child of three, with an older brother and a younger sister. Her father was born in Fukuoka in 1907 and came to the US "probably in the 1920s or so," where he worked as a foreman in the sawmill camps of Longview, Washington. Her mother, whose family came to the US in the 1890s, was born in the United States. She did not work outside the home. When the war broke out, June's grandfather, who was farming near Tacoma, "called all his family together" and they were incarcerated together.

TAIRA

Michie Taira Hori (b. 1926) and Junichi Taira (b. 1929). Michie and Junichi's father, Takayoshi Taira, worked on freighters and had traveled all over the world, coming permanently to the US around 1919. He returned to Japan to marry sometime before 1921; the couple, both from Nagasaki Prefecture, returned to the US, first settling in Seattle. Takayoshi first worked in lumber mills, and later in a tofu manufacturing plant in Seattle. The family eventually moved to Tacoma, where Takayoshi started his own tofu plant, with his wife helping out.

TAKASUGI

Mitsuo Takasugi (b. 1928). Mitsuo, together with older brother Terry (b. 1921), sister Misau (b. 1923), and younger brother Robert Mitsuhiro (b. 1930), was one of four children. (Robert Mitsuhiro Takasugi later became one of the first Japanese Americans to serve as a federal judge; see Conclusion.) Their father arrived in North America in 1905 with his brother and began working in sawmills in Nanaimo, BC. In Tacoma, the family opened a Japanese restaurant (Iroha) and later a Chinese restaurant (Nikoro) on Broadway. Their home was on Fawcett Avenue. The Depression brought hard times to the family and his father found various jobs, including as a parking attendant at a movie house on 9th near Broadway.

TAMAKI

Shigeko Gay Tamaki Yoshiwara (b. 1916). Shigeko, the eldest of six children, was born in Eatonville, where her father worked as a logger. When she was about four years old, after the birth of her younger brother, her father moved the family to Tacoma and opened the Standard Meat Market. He invested in a rooming house, which was supervised by Shigeko's mother. After her father became ill, the family invested in a grocery store that her mother ran. We also spoke briefly with Shigeko's brother, Ted Tetsuo Tamaki (b. ca. 1926).

TOMITA

Chizu Tomita Takaoka (b. 1920). Chizu was one of seven children: the eldest was born in 1916, the next in 1918, Chizu in 1920, brother Masaho in 1922, brother Hiroyuki in 1924, brother Nobuyuki in 1926, and sister Junko in 1930. Their father, Tainojo Tomita, was born in 1885 in Fukushima Prefecture, just north of Tokyo. The youngest child in his family, he attended fourteen years of school in Japan. In 1917, when his father passed away, Tainojo emigrated to the US, not wanting to be a burden to his eldest brother and family. An older brother had a greenhouse in Seattle, where Tainojo worked before returning to Japan in 1915 to marry Kinko Nihei, born in 1895 and also well educated. The couple later relocated to Tacoma, where Chizu's father worked in a garage.

YANO

Perry Yoshiaki Yano (b. 1931). Perry's father came to the US in 1906, arriving in Seattle. He went back to Japan to marry, returning with his new wife in 1924. Both parents were from Marugame City, Kagawa Prefecture, on the island of Shikoku. Perry's father worked on a farm before joining a friend to run a pool hall. After marriage, he started delivering fruits and vegetables, eventually renting a grocery store. Perry had one older sister, Masako Mae Yano Matsumori. The family lived on an alley between Fawcett and Market.

APPENDIX B

Tacoma Japanese Language School Faculty

AS LISTED IN DOCUMENT TITLED "FACULTY OF NIHON GO GAKKO" (N.D.)
Principal: Masato Yamasaki, 1912–42

HIGH SCHOOL TEACHERS

Kikuko Fujii
Shinzaburo Kato
Inko Kuroda
Torayo Miyoshi
Shigeru Sakamoto
Minoru Tagawa
Satoko Yamasaki

ELEMENTARY SCHOOL TEACHERS

Yoshino Asada
Kiyoko Haneda
Teruko Kono
Eiko Kosai
Kiniko Kumasaka
Chiyoki Nimori
Miyoko Okada
Fujie Shinyama
Kuniko Yamasaki, 1911–42

NURSERY SCHOOL TEACHERS

T. K. Enari
Kiyo Haneda
Hana Nakamura
Mura Otsuka
Fumie Oyanagi
Electa Snyder, 1925–40
Shigeyo Tsuchimochi
Kisa Wakabayashi
Mitsue Wakabayashi

SUBSTITUTES

Chiyoko Kawagoe
Aiko Konzo
Misue Morikawa
Matsue Yamane

MUSIC TEACHER

Shisue Miyashita, 1927–?

ADDITIONAL TEACHERS NOT MENTIONED IN THE RON MAGDEN COLLECTION

Mrs. Hata[1]
Teruko Kawano

NOTES

INTRODUCTION

1 At the time of the interview, the Sheraton Hotel, 1320 Broadway; it is now (2020) the Murano Hotel.

2 Dubrow notes that "internment camps constituted the largest group of landmarks listed in the National Register of Historic Places that are associated with Japanese Americans" (2002, 5). This recognition does not necessarily mean preservation, however.

3 We understand the forgetting of Japanese presence across the city as a structural process, related to wartime incarceration as well as to contemporary geopolitics and market processes. Yet we also want to note that by focusing on a particular time we may be at risk of giving a "place a false 'essence,' by abstracting it from the history of the place itself" (Connerton 2009, 50). We do not, for instance, want to ignore the erasure of sovereignty as has happened with the ancestral lands of the Puyallup. Our approach here is to focus on processes of silencing and forgetting within a historical context.

4 The term Nikkei refers to people of Japanese ancestry who have emigrated and live abroad (though there are various interpretations; as Densho says, the exact meaning is "still being worked out").

5 The erasure of indigenous histories cannot be ignored; see Miller n.d. Day's "triangulation" also helps move "beyond a binary theory of settler colonialism" (2016, 19) to understand it through Asian racialization as well, with "alien" status institutionalized in immigration policies and alien land laws.

6 Tacoma should be situated in the existing understanding of leading Japanese American communities prior to World War II. Roger Daniels argues that while in terms of numbers Los Angeles was the "chief city of Japanese Americans" (1992, 438), San Francisco, with five thousand Japanese Americans in 1940, was the cultural lead. Yet Seattle, with almost seven thousand Japanese Americans in 1940, was, according to Daniels, in fact "the real second city of Japanese America . . . with another 2,700 in surrounding King County and

another 2,000 in adjacent Pierce County. Only four other cities—Sacramento and Stockton in California, Portland in Oregon and New York City—had as many as 1,000 ethnic Japanese" (1992, 438–39). Tacoma was a part of this Northwest network and a significant community in terms of population, though clearly not as large as Seattle, San Francisco, or Los Angeles.

7 Related to its significance, the TJLS established its alumni association in 1934 (*History of Japanese in Tacoma* 1941, n.p. [84]), and the Tacoma Japanese community was one of the first to hold a reunion after the war, in 1977.

8 Issei were not allowed to be naturalized as US citizens until the passage of the McCarran-Walter Act in 1952.

9 This is a more topological understanding of the spatiality in which they lived, as opposed to more Euclidean ideas of space in terms of discrete points, lines, and areas. This understanding of spatiality is important to our concept of "bridging". See Hoffman and Thatcher 2017; Ettlinger 2011.

10 Our argument should, in other words, be seen in contrast to arguments that have tried to explain Japanese wartime incarceration through cultural characteristics such as *enryo* (self-effacement). See, e.g., Kitano 1993.

11 Especially Doreen Massey, Allan Pred, and Michel de Certeau.

12 Scholars have long noted the spatial aspects of subject formation, whether feminists critiquing distinctions between public and private spheres (Rosaldo, Lamphere, and Bamberger 1974; Massey 1994; Hayden 2002), social theorists examining the intersections of space, power, and architecture (de Certeau 1984; Foucault 1979, 1980, 2007; Bourdieu 1990), or geographers considering movement through space (Pred 1981; Hanson and Pratt 1995; Lefebvre 1992; Merrill and Hoffman 2015) and the "intertwined" nature of subjectivity and spatiality (Pred 1984, 1990; Gupta and Ferguson 1999; Hoffman 2003). We have also consulted the work of those who have focused primarily on the immigrant experience, such as Kay Anderson, who argues that Vancouver's Chinatown does not represent some essential Chineseness, but rather is understood through "the filter of European imagining": difference, belonging and exclusion, us and them (1991, 3).

13 The importance of place-based memories contrasts with a "lack of public appreciation for the [TJLS] property" and "sparse attention" to the Japanese district of Tacoma, what Susan Morrison called the result of a "misreading of the urban fabric within which the historic school is sited" (1994, 69).

14 Special thanks to our research assistant Sarah Pyle for her excellent work following leads and finding sources.

15 See also the work of Henri Lefebvre (1992) on the social production of space and the power relations inherent to those processes.

16 The former students we interviewed consistently used the term "Buddhist church," reflecting what others have noted as attempts by Buddhists to

harmonize with "the host culture" (Yoo 2000, 45). In 1983, the Tacoma sangha (Buddhist religious community) decided to officially change the name from Tacoma Buddhist Church to Tacoma Buddhist Temple. The building remains in its original location at 1717 South Fawcett and is still in use in its original capacity today (Nimura and Wadland 2018).

17 There are excellent studies of Nisei experiences that address questions of "twoness." See, for example, the work of John Okada (Okada [1957] 1978; Abe et al. 2018) as well as E. Tamura 1994, Hayashi 1995, Takahashi 1997, Yoo 2000, and Kurashige 2002.

18 See S. Pyle 2018; also Nimura 2018, Howey 2010, and Jones 2010.

19 In 2020, only two of these buildings remain, the former Whitney Memorial United Methodist Church and the Tacoma Buddhist Temple, both on South Fawcett Street. The Lorenz Building on South Market Street, which held a Japanese-run hotel as well as an early iteration of the Buddhist church, was demolished in 2016 to make way for an apartment building (Sullivan 2017). The Whitney church building now functions as an arts center for UWT; only the Tacoma Buddhist Temple continues to serve in its original, intended capacity.

20 The administration has also memorialized the building, the school's leaders, and the Japanese prewar presence in campus spaces. See www.tacoma.uw .edu/node/22287.

21 While we do not classify our interviews as oral histories in the strict sense, they may be seen as a part of the oral history movement to collect personal stories of Asian Americans more broadly. Paul Connerton notes that "since the 1970s the rehabilitation of ethnic memories has been perceived in North America to be a vital part of personal identity" (2009, 2). See also the extensive collection spearheaded by Michael K. Honey, the Tacoma Community History Project at UW Tacoma; and Honey 1999 for more on the importance of oral histories as a way to recover forgotten voices.

22 *The History of Japanese in Tacoma* notes that the birth rate was highest in 1925 (1941, n.p. [20]).

23 Please see appendix A for a complete list of interviews, dates, and locations. We also provide brief backgrounds on each family interviewed. We recognize that while we were able to interview a goodly number of people, there are limitations in the population sample. We interviewed those who came to reunions or had otherwise kept in touch with one another, and thus who had some connections with their childhood and Tacoma. Because we were studying this community through the lens of the language school, we also focused on those who were alumni of the school. Despite the limitations inherent in the project, we hope this book will contribute to a greater understanding of Nisei lives.

24 On the notion of age-specific cohorts for Nisei, see, e.g., Spickard 2009, 74; and Bonacich and Modell 1980. As in Tacoma, based on a sample study, over 80 percent of the Nisei population in Seattle were born between 1916 and 1940 (Yanagisako 1985, 65; see also Spickard 2009, 74; Bonacich and Modell 1980).

25 In an effort to provide space for the Nisei's own voices, we provide many quotes from the interviews. At times we found it most effective to extract especially relevant comments, which means they are not always presented in the order in which they were stated in the conversation.

26 See Japanese Association of Tacoma Records, 1904–1942, Tacoma Japanese Language School Boxes 18, 19, 20, 21, 26, 27, 28, University of Washington Libraries, Special Collections. We thank both of our excellent research assistants, Sarah Pyle and Misaki Seto, for their time spent with archival materials. Mariko Kawamoto of Keio University Libraries also contributed through her work reorganizing and cataloguing these materials.

27 Michael Sullivan notes that "Tacoma also supported a large floating population of Japanese American workers, timber and agriculture wage earners, seamen, travelers and foreign nationals that filled the hotels and boarding houses but didn't get counted in the census data. A reasonable estimate was 5% of the total population of Tacoma, which in 1920 was less than 97,000 people" (personal communication, April 22, 2020).

CHAPTER ONE: ESTABLISHING A NEW COMMUNITY IN TACOMA

1 The phrase "rich country, strong army"—in Japanese, *fukoku kyohei*—comes from the Chinese Warring States period (ca. 475–221 BCE) classic *Zhan guo ce* (Strategies of the warring states).

2 For a thorough discussion of liberalism and democracy in prewar Japan, see Hanneman 1995.

3 We have worked with two early histories of the Tacoma Japanese community. In 1940, Shuichi Fukui edited, expanded, and reorganized Shunichi Otsuka's *Takoma nihonjin hattenshi* (1916 or 1917); in 1986, Fukui's version was translated into English by Dr. James Watanabe as *History of the Japanese of Tacoma*—herein cited as Otsuka and Fukui [1940] 1986. Tamiko Nimura (2017b) writes that Fukui "served as a Tacoma correspondent for the *Hokubei Hochi*, a Seattle Japanese-language newspaper. Just before World War II, Fukui had become the last editor and owner of Tacoma's own Japanese-language newspaper, the *Takoma Shuho* (*Tacoma Japanese Weekly*)." Nimura also notes that "to this day, the volume [translated by Watanabe] remains one of the two major primary sources on the history of Tacoma's Japanese Americans."

The other early source we rely on is *History of Japanese in Tacoma* 1941. Although no author is listed, we suspect there is a close relationship between the two histories; indeed, *History of Japanese in Tacoma* may be the original English-language version of Otsuka's history, later updated by Fukui and translated by Watanabe (see above). We thank Tamiko Nimura and Michael Sullivan for sharing the *History of Japanese in Tacoma* manuscript with us.

4 For more background on Japan's Meiji Constitution, see Hanneman 2001, chapter 1 and passim.

5 For the full text of the Imperial Rescript on Education, see deBary, Gluck, and Tiedemann 2006, 108.

6 Teiko's older sister, Harue Kawano Ozaki, was born in 1928, but we do not have Teiko's birth year.

7 The original Shibata family name was Urushibata. According to Kunio Shibata, the name was legally shortened to Shibata in the 1950s. See Appendix A under Family Histories.

8 For example, Meiji Japan's leading intellectual and public figure Yukichi Fukuzawa advanced this idea in his book *Bunmei ron no gairyaku* (An outline of a theory of civilization, 1875). His book *Seiyo jijo* (Conditions in the West, published serially in Japan, 1866, 1868, 1870) was an overnight sensation, selling over 150,000 copies when first published and subsequently going through two additional printings.

9 For a discussion of what "civilization" meant to Japanese intellectuals and governmental leaders during this period, see Hanneman 1995.

10 Paul Spickard (2009) delineates the phases of Japanese immigration to the US as the "frontier phase" (prior to 1910), the "immigrant community phase" (1910–ca. 1935), the "early second generation" (1930–45), the "later second generation" (1945–65), and the "era of the third and fourth generations" (since 1965). For more on this, see chapter 2.

11 Magden (1998, 10) calls the "Tacoma Japanese Society"—founded, by his accounting, in 1892—"the first such organization on the West Coast," while Ichioka (1977, 411) identifies the Greater Japanese Association, created in 1891 in San Francisco, as the first. *History of Japanese in Tacoma* (1941, n.p. [123]) confusingly reports that "the Japanese founded Nihonjin-kai [Japanese Association] in the year of 1891. But no record is found. Later it was renamed 'Doshi-kai' [another term for association] October 1908: Nihonjin-kai is created." Adding to the confusion, the Japanese term *kai* is translated interchangeably as "association" or "society," thus Tacoma Japanese Society/Tacoma Japanese Association. Although the Japanese word is the same, here we refer to the organization started in Tacoma in 1891 (according to *History of Japanese in Tacoma*) or 1892 (according to Magden) as the Tacoma Japanese Society

(following Magden's terminology), and to the 1908 version as the Tacoma Japanese Association, denoting that group's official affiliation with the Japanese consulate. See also note 16 below.

12 According to Ichioka (1977, 433) the relationship was terminated by the Japanese Foreign Ministry in 1926. With the 1924 Exclusion Act effectively ending Japanese immigration, there was no longer a need for the Japanese associations to issue certificates associated with immigration.

13 Japanese Association of Tacoma Records, 1904–42, Visa applications and supporting documents, Boxes 13/7–14/19, Special Collections, University of Washington Libraries.

14 Japanese Association of Tacoma Records 1904–42, Special Collections, University of Washington Libraries: Meiji Shrine, Box 2, Folder 16; Taisho accession celebration, Box 2, Folders 12–15; Showa Emperor marriage Box 2, Folder 36; Kanto Earthquake relief, Box 11, Folders 7–13. .

15 Discrepancies in numbers exist: according to Daniels (1988), there were 50 Japanese in Tacoma in 1891. Magden (1998, 30) mentions "70 Japanese among 36,006 Tacomans" in 1890, citing W. D. C. Spike, *Spike's 1891 Illustrated Description of the City of Tacoma* (n.p.), 51. Flewelling's number of 90, citing Consul Chinda on his 1891 inspection tour of the Pacific Northwest, comes from Wilson and Hosokawa 1982, 18–19.

16 This letter, dated 1884, states that it is from the president of the "Tacoma Japanese Society." But see note 11 above. The TJS was supposedly founded in 1891, according to the *History of Japanese in Tacoma*, which is the same source as this letter. While these early primary sources are historical treasures, they also contain inconsistencies.

17 Daniels questions the validity of Fujita's assessment, writing that his report's "class bias is clear and its sources of information are sometimes suspect" (1988, 105). Nevertheless, Fujita's assessment accords with the Japanese government's preoccupation with Japanese migrants and Japan's international image.

18 The Fife Language School was overseen by the Fife Language School Support Association, led by Yokichi Nakanishi.

19 The additional ten members were Shinro Inomichi, Tokuhei Kawai, Hiroshi Kurimoto, Hidekichi Manya, Masaharu Matsuo, Hyogo Nakashima, Shinjiro Okada, Shizuo Okamoto, Yonetaro Okamura, and Waichiro Ukaji.

20 Japanese Association of Tacoma Records, 1904–42, Japanese Language School Construction Donation, Box 2, Folder 4 (translated by Misaki Seto and Mary Hanneman), Special Collections, University of Washington Libraries.

21 The thirteen inaugural students were Misao Kawasoe, Nuri Kawasoe, Tetsuo Kawasoe, Seiichi Konzo, Masae Matsumoto, Tsunekichi Nakahara, Chiyo Nakayama, Kenjiro Nomura, Shuji Nomura, Hito Okada, Norio Okada,

Tome Osugi, and Fusako Yoshioka, They were dispersed across the "primary first and second grades" and the "grade school" first, fourth, and sixth grades (Otsuka and Fukui [1940] 1986, 56).

22 Original members of the School Support Society were Shosaku Fujii, president; Shigetaro Morinaka, vice president; and Ihei Hiraki, Sakunoshin Matsumoto, Jotaro Mori, Shoshichi Moriyasu, and Shinjiro Okada, trustees. Shosaku Fujii soon left to pursue business interests in Alaska and was replaced by Hyogo Nakashima (Otsuka and Fukui [1940] 1986, 57).

23 Prefectural associations (*kenjinkai*) were organizations for people who came from the same prefectures in Japan; they functioned as mutual aid societies and also provided opportunities for socializing.

24 Joseph H. Gordon was a founding member of the Tacoma law firm Gordon, Thomas, Honeywell.

CHAPTER TWO: STRUGGLE AND HARD WORK

1 According to Ron Magden (1998, 37), immigrants to Tacoma were predominantly from Ehime, Hiroshima, and Kumamoto prefectures. In Washington as a whole, Nomura (1989, 135) cites Hiroshima, Okayama, Yamaguchi, and Kumamoto as the most common prefectures of origin, while Spickard (2009, 15) gives a longer list of Hiroshima, Wakayama, Kumamoto, Fukuoka, Yama-guchi, Okayama, Nagasaki, Saga, Kagoshima, and later, Okinawa.

2 Drawing on Frank Miyamoto's research in Seattle, Roger Daniels (1992, 439) argues that most of that city's 900 Japanese businesses in 1935 "were small operations catering to white as well as Japanese trade."

3 This mapping research was conducted by Sarah Pyle (see also chapter 4). The historical sources she consulted included Otsuka and Fukui [1940] 1986; Ito 1973; and Morrison 1994. See also Takeuchi 1929, which we discovered just prior to publication of this book.

4 O'Brien and Fugita (1982) suggest that the term "middleman minority" is not always applicable to Japanese, Chinese, and Jewish immigrants, using instead "petit bourgeois" for some of the farmers in the California case they studied. Bonacich and Modell, in contrast, note of middlemen minorities that they "depend on the use of ethnic and familial ties, not on impersonal con-tracts" (1980, 33).

5 Kurashige adopts the notion of "modern racism" from Stanford Lyman (1970).

6 Unlike California, where Japanese entered the fishing industry, Washington State prohibited them from obtaining the necessary licenses after 1915 (Nomura 1989, 122–23). Japanese laborers also went to smaller mill towns in Washington, including Port Blakely, Port Townsend, Enumclaw, Onalaska, Snoqualmie Falls, and Selleck (Fiset 2009, 2).

7   When Clinton Butsuda visited the tideflats in the late 1980s he saw "an empty stretch of sand and weeds. Gone are the houses, the sounds of the lumber mill and the sweet smell of the wood I loved so much. Gone is our beautiful willow tree . . . everything is gone . . . except in my memories" (1992, 4).

8   At one point, the St. Paul & Tacoma Lumber Company was touted as "the world's greatest lumber producer" (Morgan 1982, 55–65). As competition in the industry increased in the early 1920s, the company sought to expand its markets, and Japan, which used wood primarily for construction, was "especially attractive" (Morgan 1982, 218). An effort to take advantage of the massive Kanto Earthquake of 1923, however, failed, as the Japanese ports were too hard hit to function (Morgan 1982, 219).

9   *Dan* indicates the level of proficiency of the practitioner.

10 We read this as meaning $30 per month.

11 See Ronald Olson's interviews with white mill workers. He summarized their attitudes: "Usually there is an expression of friendship for the Japanese in the local mill, then a hesitation, followed by a vigorous statement of the belief that the Japanese should not be employed with white workmen and that they should be excluded so that they could not compete with white labor" (1928, 15).

12 In addition, by 1932, during the Great Depression, many Tacoma mills had shuttered their doors, exacerbating the difficulties in the city, and the push-pull factors at work in gaining a livelihood (*History of Japanese in Tacoma* 1941, [n.p.] 5)).

13 See 1910 Tacoma and Pierce County Federal Census as reported in Magden 1998, 26.

14 See Japanese Association of Tacoma Records, 1904–42, "Business Record of Japanese within Tacoma, Occupation Business Record," Box 5, Folder 34. Special Collections, University of Washington Libraries. We estimate the year as 1920 based on population listed on this record and compared with "Census Result, October 20," Box 3, Folder 40. The "Occupation Business Record" also noted that the business community owned fifty-three cars; the association counted 1,697 men, 616 women, and 638 children (342 boys and 296 girls), for a total population of 2,951.

15 Morrison (1993, 57) documents the Sato family running the Superior Hotel at this location.

16 The Polk City Directory (1933, 821) lists the Vendome Hotel at 1327 Market Street.

17 The Polk City Directory (1933, 275) places the Grand Hotel, operated by S. Kosai, next to the Grand Cafe at 1514 Pacific Avenue.

18 See note 17.

19 His father also had a cousin in Tacoma who ran the Washington Hotel on 15th and Broadway.

20 Later in the interview Mitsuo indicated that the restaurant was named Iroha, which is mentioned both in Otsuka and Fukui ([1940] 1986, 17)—as Iroha Cafe—and in the Polk City Directory (1933, 344)—as the Iroha Tei Restaurant.

21 Mitsuo noted that the earlier restaurant was named Nikoro.

22 Ryo remembered his father's stories about the laundry truck: "It was horse-driven. And when he got up to K Street, that area [where the baseball field was], it was flat. And the horse always wanted to go in that direction. (*laughs*) Dad used to enjoy baseball. And he stopped the truck and watched the game, and that's where the horse wanted to go, so while Dad watched the game the horse gets to rest!"

23 Address was 1519½ Broadway (Polk City Directory 1933, 117).

24 "She was there for eighteen years," Harue remembered, "and I know she enjoyed her work very much. She was someone who enjoyed not only teaching the language, but she was also interested in music and dance, and so she was very prominently active in teaching the children for various shows and what we call *gakugeikai* [school arts festivals]. That went on until, of course, . . . we were taken away."

25 This account was both in their joint interview and in a written supplement they provided to us.

26 Takeshi's mother's maiden name was Jinguji, a somewhat unusual name that came up several times in our research. One Jinguji, perhaps an uncle of Takeshi's, worked at the St. Paul & Tacoma Lumber Company, and we also interviewed Masaye Jinguji Fujita. See also figure 3.1.

27 Fiset (2009, 18) reports that even with farms of 40 acres or less, Puyallup Valley Japanese farmers "contributed nearly one-third" of the produce in western Washington, "worth over $1 million," and, combined with other Japanese farmers across western Washington, contributed "produce valued in excess of $3 million (21.5 million in 2008 dollars)." John Nishinori, who did research for the Washington State History Museum's 2018 exhibit on Japanese Americans in Tacoma prior to World War II, noted that before the Alien Land Act Japanese farmers controlled 25,340 acres on 699 farms, but by 1925 they farmed less than 10,000 acres.

28 This included 226 acres of potatoes, 168 acres of hay, 140 acres of vegetables, and 24 acres of fruit, for a total of 558 acres. In addition, another 737 acres of pasture were maintained by Japanese farmers, with 316 cows, 184 hogs, 72 horses, and 346 chickens; 351,200 gallons of milk products were produced annually. Japanese Association of Tacoma Records, 1904–42, "Business

Record of Japanese within Tacoma, Occupation Business Record," Box 5, Folder 34, Special Collections, University of Washington Libraries.

29 Kazuo Ito quoted one farmer in the Yakima Valley who explained that "probably they were also suppressed by the whites as colored people, [so] the Indians were very friendly toward the Japanese and glad to lease their land" (in Spickard 2009, 43). Crops like berries were labor-intensive, harvested without machines, and thus similar to rice farming in Japan; this drew many into this industry, although as more families were started, the Japanese community became increasingly urban (Spickard 2009, 42, 45).

30 University of Puget Sound is in Tacoma. The name was changed from College of Puget Sound to University of Puget Sound in 1960.

31 Spickard (2009, 61) corroborates Kimiko's observation: The arrest rates for Japanese Americans between 1902 (when the first such survey was conducted) and the 1960s were lower than for any other major West Coast ethnic groups, despite the fact that during the frontier period the Issei constituted the kind of young, male, transient population that might be expected to have a high crime rate. In contrast to these comparatively low delinquency rates for Japanese immigrants, by 1940 LA's Little Tokyo had a higher crime rate and some Nisei felt the need to join gangs for protection (Kurashige 2002, 39).

CHAPTER THREE: JAPANESE AMERICAN URBAN LIVES

1 See also chapter 2. In 1920, 930 of 1,306 residents lived between 11th and 19th and Tacoma and Pacific (Morrison 1994, 28); ten years later, some 70 percent of Tacoma's Japanese community still lived in this neighborhood (HABS 1995, 5; Morrison 1994, 30). Morrison argues that this area "can be seen as a distinct and cohesive district" (1994, 36). In contrast, by 1930 Seattle's Japanese community had dispersed to different neighborhoods (Spickard 2009, 74).

2 Illustrating the larger and more fractured nature of Seattle's Japanese community compared with Tacoma's, in 1923 Seattle had a total of fifteen Japanese associations (Ichioka 1977, 411), compared to just one in Tacoma.

3 Kazuo Horita also recognized that some families used the reunion as an opportunity for family gatherings. The event, he noted in the article, drew "nearly 200 out-of-towners" and in total almost six hundred attended the banquet.

4 Japanese on the West Coast and those in Hawaii did have some notable differences. For instance, in Hawaii they tended to be in agriculture rather than small business and in general "were manual laborers longer than their West Coast cousins" (Spickard 2009, 51). Nevertheless, stereotypes did develop. For instance, "Californians derided Hawaiians as 'Buddhaheads.' The Hawaiians retorted that Californians were 'kotonks'—after the empty sound their heads were supposed to make as they hit the floor in fights" (Spickard 2009, 92).

Note, too, that the Japanese in Hawaii were not incarcerated on a massive scale during the war.

5 Kimiko may have been referring to the Konkokyo Shinto church (generally, "shrine") that was several blocks away from the TJLS.

6 Some children were lucky and had memories of someone driving them to school when it rained, such as the Fujimoto sisters, whose neighbor Mr. Abe had a car and would take them.

7 Japanese American newspapers in Los Angeles also used the term *clannish* in the mid-1930s as a critique of the Nisei generation for being too insular (Kurashige 2002, 36).

8 Kimiko Fujimoto Tanbara also remembered the *ken* (prefecture) associations: "They used to have those groups, you know—like, my father came from Kumamoto. They used to have a Kumamoto group, and you would have picnics together with other groups. Not just with the Kuma—but with the other . . . and then the parents would always hope that their children would marry from the same prefecture. (*laughs*) But all that's gone, now."

9 The notion that identity, including categories such as "race," is not fixed but is linked to historically specific social and power relations is key to our argument about the processual and emergent nature of becoming Nisei.

10 Allan Pred (1984, 1990, 1998) developed the highly dynamic notion of "space and society as produced through temporally specific practices, forms of knowledge, and individual biographies," captured in the idea of situated practices (Merrill and Hoffman 2015, 12).

11 For more on competition and conflict between Asian American populations in the constitution of citizenship, see Iwata 2005.

12 When asked if going to Japan and returning, the definition of Kibei, was common, Joe Seto responded, "Not among the Tacoma Japanese." Some use the terms Jun-Nisei (genuine Nisei) and Kibei-Nisei to distinguish between those who were educated in the US and those who received their schooling in Japan and then returned to the US (Takezawa 1995, 20).

13 As Uyeda puts it, "Time failed to erase the memory of this tragic event, and very few Chinese returned to settle in Tacoma" (2000, 10). See also Morgan 2003, Pfaelzer 2007.

14 Eleanor Roosevelt published "My Day" six days a week from December 1935 until September 1962.

15 The Nisei's narratives of flexibility seem to be in marked contrast with the scenario Duncan Ryuken Williams describes when he writes, "The appearance of Buddhists at a Christian gathering was rare in the prewar Japanese American communities on the west coast" (2019, 136).

16 Perry Yoshiaki Yano also mentioned having lessons with Mrs. Rye.

17 The Tacoma Buddhist Temple is part of the Jodo Shinshu Nishi (Western) Hongwanji tradition of Buddhism. Within Hongwanji, another strand is the Higashi (Eastern) temple tradition.

CHAPTER FOUR: EXPANDING THE MAPPING OF JAPANESE URBAN LIVES

1 Susan Morrison does list businesses and residences in South Tacoma, and in the description of the main commercial and residential core she recognizes that the area south of Pacific Avenue and into the tideflats had "a smattering of Japanese-American residences and businesses," including a boarding house for single men (1994, 42).

2 An online visualization of this and other research in this book was under construction at time of publication.

3 Boarders lived in rooms in the upper stories' shared facilities: "Each floor had two baths, two toilets, and a room for drying clothes" (Morgan 1982, 226). "Gink" was a derogatory term referring to itinerant workers and homeless men. The first "Hotel de Gink" was founded in Seattle in 1913; other such hotels were opened in other cities around the US over the course of the 1910s.

4 Asaka (2004) noted the Butsuda memoirs; others are held by Lynette Butsuda.

5 Asaka (2014, 125–26) argues that little attention has been paid to the bachelor life of Japanese immigrants; instead, researchers focus on "the normative family life before WWII." She argues this is in large part because of "the timing of oral history projects that started in the 1970s and 1980s," when many Issei had already passed away. Note, however, that "bachelor" was a misnomer, as many of the men "who lived as bachelors had wives and children back in Japan, but did not have the money to bring them to the U.S."

6 Mrs. Sato also cooked there. See Asaka 2014 for more on Japanese bachelors' hiring of cooks.

7 This should be Hupmobile.

8 See interview with Fumi Sato Hattori below and chapter 2.

9 Mrs. Asada was a teacher at the TJLS. Regarding the numbering of the houses on St. Paul Avenue, see note 10.

10 See Clinton Butsuda's list above, which placed Fumi's family in No. 11. Butsuda's memoir describes families living in houses numbered up to 21, but the maps only showed through fourteen houses. It is possible his numbering reflected common usage.

11 She recalled their Tacoma address as on the corner of 17th and G Street.

12 While we cannot confirm from the interview that Sally's maiden name was Kimura, based on this evidence we think that is the case.

13 In "Redefining Expectations" (1994) and *City Girls* (2014), Valerie Matsumoto documents the emerging worlds of Nisei women in 1920s–1940s Los Angeles as they moved into adulthood.

14 This empty field was noted in the Polk City Directory (1933, 854) at 8511 South Tacoma Way. Thanks to Sarah Pyle for confirming this.

CHAPTER FIVE: THE YAMASAKIS AND THE TACOMA JAPANESE LANGUAGE SCHOOL

1 Our understanding of power in micro, capillary practices comes from the work of Michel Foucault, esp. 1980, 1988, 1997.

2 At the group interview in Oakland, former students remembered Teruko Kawano fondly:

KUNIO: I'd like to let her [Teiko Kawano Peterson] speak, because her mother was a teacher.

YONEKO: Our teacher.

SHIGEKO: She was a wonderful teacher.

YONEKO: She was a wonderful teacher . . . *sensei.*

TEIKO: Did you all have her?

YONEKO: Yes.

TEIKO: She died five, eight years ago, I think. And she was ninety-eight when she died.

KUNIO: Wow.

TEIKO: She lived—had a long life, and a lot of the students remembered her, and wrote letters and things like that. And she was—her mind was clear until the end. And—but she had—her legs were amputated because of diabetes, so she couldn't get around, but my sister Harue took care of her at her home for all her life, I guess. So she remembers—I'm sure she will remember every one of you. (*smiles*) And she remembered a lot of people, and she knew most of the families that went to Japanese School. And so through that way I remember a lot of the names of the people, and so . . . but . . . so that was about all . . .

3 Other interviewees recalled that students *did* clean the bathrooms.

4 Mr. Yamasaki was two years younger than his wife. It was not uncommon for wives to be several years older than husbands in traditional Japan, on the premise that the wife must take care of the husband and so should be more mature and advanced in attending to household matters.

5 Greg Tanbara, son of Kimiko Fujimoto Tanbara, remembered that after the war, from 1955 to 1958, his family lived in these same quarters in the language school (personal communication, Feb. 7, 2020).

6 The *Takoma jiho* (literally, Tacoma News Report, but also translated as *Tacoma Japanese Times* or *Tacoma Weekly Journal*) ran from 1911/1912? to 1921. The University of Washington Library microfilm collection contains only the January 1, 1915, edition. The list of prominent men was later incorporated into Otsuka's book on the early Tacoma Japanese community (Otsuka and Fukui [1940] 1986, 99–102).

7 "Teigakunen shitsuke ho no kenkyu" (Research on Training Students in the Lower Primary Grades),translated by Misaki Seto and Mary Hanneman, University of Washington Libraries, Special Collections: Japanese Association of Tacoma Records, 1904–42, Box 18. Although the document is unsigned, the fact that it consists of instructions to teachers suggests that it came from Principal Yamasaki. It seems to be a summary of educational philosophy gathered from one or more books.

8 The harrowing event even received brief coverage in the September 30, 1935, issue of the *New York Times*, under the headline "29 Young Japanese Hurt in Coast Crash: Cage Runs Free Last 20 Feet of 470-Foot Tramway at Cushman Dam."

9 Purchase records for these textbooks are at University of Washington Libraries, Special Collections: Japanese Association of Tacoma Records, 1904–42. They include, for reading, *Koko shogako-dokuhon* (High school and elementary school readers) and Supplements (1928) (archival reference 18/43–45); and for writing, *Jinjo shogako kakikata tehon* (Common handbook of elementary school writing method) (1910, 1918–19, 1923) (18/46–51) and *Sogo kokugo gakushucho*(National language [Japanese] learning workbook (1934) (18/52).

10 Textbooks: *Nihon gaishi* (Japanese history), University of Washington Libraries, Special Collections: Japanese Association of Tacoma Records, 1904–42 (19/2–3); and *Kaitei joshi shinshohan* (Revised handbook for girls) (18/53).

11 Chiyoko Tamaki, "Nihon" (Japan), translated by Misaki Seto and Mary Hanneman, University of Washington Libraries, Special Collections: Japanese Association of Tacoma Records, 1904–42, Student Work: Writing and Kanji, 1936–41, Box 19, Folder 33. The documents cited in the following discussion were all translated by Seto and Hanneman, and are all found in the same folder.

12 Daniel Lachapelle Lemire makes use of essays by students of the Vancouver, BC, Japanese language school in his essay "Bittersweet Memories." These and other student essays written by the Nisei in the prewar period, including those in the University of Washington Libraries Special Collections, should prove to be a valuable and fruitful area for further research.

13 The term "spiritual half-breed" was also used in *History of Japanese in Tacoma* (1941, n.p. [43]) in discussing the need for Nisei to study the Japanese language. (See chapter 1.)

14 Capitals in original. *Bushido,* meaning the "way of the warrior," was a code that embraced such ideals as loyalty, duty, self-discipline, sincerity, and other martial values.

15 Masaye Jinguji, "Nitobe hakase no kogi o kiite" (After hearing a lecture by Dr. Nitobe), translated by Misaki Seto and Mary Hanneman, University of Washington Libraries, Special Collections: Japanese Association of Tacoma Records, 1904–42, Student Work: Writing and Kanji, 1936–41, Box 20, Folder 38. Masaye Jinguji Fujita was an interviewee too.

CHAPTER SIX: ETHICAL LESSONS OF
MEIJI JAPAN WOVEN INTO NISEI STORIES

1 Kiyoshi Kinoshita, "What I Did over Summer Vacation," translated by Mary Hanneman, University of Washington Libraries, Special Collections: Japanese Association of Tacoma Records, 1904–42, Student Work: Writing and Kanji, 1936–41, Box 19, Folder 31.

2 Sylvia Yanagisako in *Transforming the Past* illuminates the various ways that "family" functioned as a normative and yet amorphous domain, but always as a "constant referent" in Nikkei lives (1985, 241).

3 As noted, our approach to subject formation builds on the work of Michel Foucault. See, for instance, Foucault 1979, 1980, 1988, 1997, 2007.

4 For groups considered "on the margins" of mainstream society, "language is a critical issue" for making sense of their marginalization (Chen 2002, 243).

5 "Teigakunen shitsuke ho no kenkyu" (Research on training students in the lower primary grades"), translated by Misaki Seto and Mary Hanneman, "How to Educate Booklets," University of Washington Libraries Special Collections, Japanese Association of Tacoma Records, Box 21, Folder 16. Further quotations from this document refer to this source.

6 Sarah Pyle's mapping shows that this vacant lot play area was about one block from the Japanese-run Airway Market at 8224 South Tacoma Way. See map 4.2.

7 Jack Kazuo Hata's mother was a teacher at the TJLS.

CONCLUSION

1 When the war started, the Japanese in Tacoma numbered 900; by 1950 their population had dwindled to 264 (Morrison, 1994, 80).

2 Yamasaki's return from this mission was mentioned in a brief article in the *Japanese American Courier,* "Educator of Tacoma Returned after Tour of Points in Orient," by Yoshiteru Kawano (the older brother of Harue Kawano Ozaki and Teiko Kawano Peterson): "In Japan he [Yamasaki] was the guest of the

Japanese government, which enabled him to visit many of Japan's institutions of learning. He proceeded to the North China war front, where he received a first-hand account of the actual battles and war conditions. Upon his return to Japan he made a special trans-Pacific radio address" (Kawano 1938, 4).

3   Mat Iseri, quoted in Flewelling 2002, 190. Because letters from the facility were censored, and there were few Japanese-speaking staff, letters for the most part had to be written in English.

4   The date of his transfer is specified in "Prisoner Rosters for Confinement Sites in the Land of Enchantment: Japanese Americans in New Mexico," www.cabq. gov/culturalservices/albuquerque-museum/documents/prisoner-rosters-for-confinement-sites-in-nm.pdf.

5   Lordsburg was the site of the infamous "Lordsburg Killing," a July 1942 incident in which two elderly Japanese detainees were shot and killed by a guard while in transit to the camp. The guard was charged with murder but later acquitted.

6   Another Tacoman interned at Lordsburg was Buddhist priest Gikan Nishinaga; see document cited in note 4.

7   The *Minidoka Irrigator*, in English and Japanese, was published from September 10, 1942, until July 28, 1945. It was one of only three camp newspapers that was typeset and printed, although the Japanese portion was handwritten and mimeographed. See http://encyclopedia.densho.org/Minidoka Irrigator (newspaper)/.

8   *Minidoka Irrigator*, Hunt, ID, March 13, 1943, translation by Mary Hanneman, accessed at www.loc.gov/resource/sn84024049/1943-03-13/ed-1/?sp=8).

9   "Tachinoki o junbi isogimasho" (Let's hurry to prepare for evacuation), *Takoma shuho*, April 9, 1942, translated by Mary Hanneman and Kazuaki Suhama, University of Washington Libraries, Microforms and Newspapers Microfilm. The *Takoma shuho* was published between May 1922 and April 1942. An unpublished manuscript, "Pacific Northwest Japanese American Newspapers on Microform; Japanese Newspapers Held in the University of Washington Libraries," contains this explanatory note about the *Takoma shuho*: "One of the great tragedies for the Japanese language press in the Pacific Northwest, there are, so far, almost no surviving copies of this key paper but rumors continually circulate about hidden backfiles. The last editor, Shuichi Fukui, continued working as a journalist (and grocer) after World War II, and was a contributor to the *Hokubei Hochi* [Seattle's *North American Post*]." Indeed, the UW microfilm collection has only the April 9, 1942, edition of the *Takoma shuho*. The other newspaper of the Tacoma Japanese community, which predated the *Takoma shuho*, was the *Takoma jiho* (translated as *Tacoma Japanese Times* or *Tacoma Weekly Journal*), 1911/12?–1921. Here again, the UW microfilm collection has only the January 1, 1915, edition.

10 Although termed "assembly centers," places like Pinedale were among seventeen temporary detention centers run by the Wartime Civil Control Administration that held Japanese Americans until the permanent incarceration locations, administered by the War Relocation Authority, were finished.

11 Ryo Munekata, *Tacoma News Tribune*, August 15, 1977, quoted in Sonnier 1993, 31.

12 Dr. Louis Fiset, personal communication to Mary Hanneman, February 28, 2006.

13 Joe Seto, "List of Nisei Veterans from Pierce County," obtained from the "Go For Broke" Educational Foundation, Gardena, CA, Joe Seto Collection, Pacific Northwest Room/Special Collections, Tacoma Public Library.

14 Ted Tamaki, personal communication, November 18, 2003.

15 The *New York Times* (August 8, 2009) reported that Robert Takasugi was "one of the first Japanese-Americans to serve as a federal judge."

APPENDIX A

1 Greg Tanbara, son of Kimiko Fujimoto Tanbara, personal communication, February 2020.

2 While Sally Shirasago did not mention her maiden name in the interview, corroborating evidence (see below and chapter 4) leads us to surmise that it was Kimura.

3 Fumi Sato's mother also ran a "Superior Hotel" (noted in Morrison 1994), but the address was 17th and Market.

4 Ryo remembered that the Munekata family also ran a Superior Hotel, but the address was 1317½ Broadway.

APPENDIX B: TACOMA JAPANESE LANGUAGE SCHOOL FACULTY

1 Interview with Jack Kazuo Hata, January 30, 2005, Northridge, California.

BIBLIOGRAPHY

Abe, Frank, Greg Robinson, and Floyd Cheung, eds. 2018. *John Okada: The Life and Rediscovered Work of the Author of "No-No Boy."* Seattle: University of Washington Press.

Adachi, Ken. 1979. *The Enemy That Never Was: A History of the Japanese Canadians.* Toronto: McClelland and Stewart.

Anderson, Emily. N.d. "Japanese Associations." *Densho Encyclopedia.* https://encyclopedia.densho.org/Japanese_associations.

Anderson, Kay. 1991. *Vancouver's Chinatown: Racial Discourse in Canada, 1875–1980.* Montreal: McGill-Queen's University Press.

Ano, Masaharu. 1977. "Loyal Linguists: Nisei of World War II Learned Japanese in Minnesota." *Minnesota History* 45, no. 7 (Fall): 273–87.

Antoni, Klaus. 1991. "Momotarō (The Peach Boy) and the Spirit of Japan: Concerning the Function of a Fairy Tale in Japanese Nationalism of the Early Shōwa Age." *Asian Folklore Studies* 50, no. 1: 155–88.

Aochi, Yoneko. N.d. "Doshite nihongo wa taisetsu ka?" (Why is Japanese important?). Japanese Association of Tacoma Records, 1904–42, Student Work: Writing and Kanji, 1936–41, Box 19, Folder 32, Special Collections, University of Washington Libraries.

Asaka, Megan. 2014. "The Unsettled City: Migration, Race, and the Making of Seattle's Urban Landscape." PhD diss., Yale University.

Asato, Noriko. 2003a. "Mandating Americanization: Japanese Language Schools and the Federal Survey of Education in Hawaii, 1916–1920." *History of Education Quarterly* 43: 10–38.

———. 2003b. "Ousting Japanese Language Schools: Americanization and Cultural Maintenance in Washington State, 1919–1927." *Pacific Northwest Quarterly* 94, no. 3: 140–50.

———. 2006. *Teaching Mikadoism: The Attack on Japanese Language Schools in Hawaii, California, and Washington, 1919–1927*. Honolulu: University of Hawaii Press.

Azuma, Eiichiro. 2003. "'The Pacific Century Has Arrived.'" *History of Education Quarterly* 43, no. 1 (Spring): 39–73.

———. 2006. Review of Louis Fiset and Gail M. Nomura, eds., *Nikkei in the Pacific Northwest: Japanese Americans and Japanese Canadians in the Twentieth Century, Pacific Historical Review* 75, no. 3 (August): 506–8.

———. 2008 "'Pioneers of Overseas Japanese Development': Japanese American History and the Making of Expansionist Orthodoxy in Imperial Japan." *Journal of Asian Studies* 67, no. 4: 1187–1226.

———. 2009. "Dancing with the Rising Sun: Strategic Alliances between Japanese and Their 'Home' Government." In *Transnational Politics of Asian Americans*, ed. Christian Collet and Pei-te Lien, 25–37. Philadelphia: Temple University Press.

Baelz, Erwin von. 1932. *Awakening Japan: The Diary of a German Doctor, Erwin Baelz*. Bloomington: Indiana University Press.

Bonacich, Edna, and John Modell. 1980. *The Economic Basis of Ethnic Solidarity: Small Business in the Japanese American Community*. Berkeley: University of California Press.

Bourdieu, Pierre. 1984. *Distinction: A Social Critique of the Judgement of Taste*. Translated by Richard Nice. London: Routledge & Kegan Paul.

———. 1990. *The Logic of Practice*. Translated by Richard Nice. Stanford, CA: Stanford University Press.

Butsuda, Clinton. 1992. "Memories of St. Paul Avenue." Unpublished manuscript, 9/24/92, Box 2, Research Materials (Folder 7), Acc. 5185-003, Ronald Magden Papers, Special Collections, University of Washington Libraries.

———. 1999. "Leaving Home." In *Tacoma: Voices of the Past*, vol. 2. Tacoma: Private printing.

Chan, Sucheng. 1990. "European and Asian Immigration to the United States in Comparative Perspective, 1820–1920." In *Immigration Reconsidered: History, Sociology, and Politics*, ed. Virginia Yans-McLaughlin. New York: Oxford University Press.

———, ed. 2005. *Chinese American Transnationalism: The Flow of People, Resources, and Ideas between China and America during the Exclusion Era*. Philadelphia: Temple University Press.

Chen, Yong. 2002. "In Their Own Words: The Significance of Chinese Language Sources for Studying Chinese American History." *Journal of Asian American Studies* 5, no. 3: 243–65.

Connerton, Paul. 2009. *How Modernity Forgets*. Cambridge: Cambridge University Press.

Cornwall, G. 1938. "Fifty Years, 1888–1938: Three Generations; History of St. Paul & Tacoma Lumber Company [St. Paul, Minn.]." *Timberman*, 16–22.

Crenshaw, Kimberle Williams. 1991. "Mapping the Margins: Intersectionality, Identity Politics, and Violence against Women of Color." *Stanford Law Review* 43, no. 6: 1241–99.

Cummings, William K. 2014. *Education and Equality in Japan.* Princeton, NJ: Princeton University Press.

Daniels, Roger. [1962] 1977. *The Politics of Prejudice: The Anti-Japanese Movement in California and the Struggles for Japanese Exclusion.* 2nd ed. Berkeley: University of California Press.

———. 1988. *Asian America: Chinese and Japanese in the United States since 1850.* Seattle: University of Washington Press.

———. 1992. "Chinese and Japanese as Urban Americans, 1850–1940." *The History Teacher* 25, no. 4: 427–41.

Day, Iyko. 2016. *Alien Capital: Asian Racialization and the Logic of Settler Colonial Capitalism.* Durham, NC: Duke University Press.

deBary, William Theodore, Carol Gluck, and Arthur Tiedemann, eds. 2006. "Imperial Rescript on Education." In *Sources of Japanese Tradition: 1600–2000,* vol. 2. New York: Columbia University Press.

Debuchi, Katsuji. 1928. *Japanese American Courier,* January 1.

———. 1931. "Become Good Americans," *Japanese American Courier,* January 1.

de Certeau, Michel. 1984. *The Practice of Everyday Life.* Translated by Steven Rendall. Berkeley: University of California Press.

DeHart, Monica. 2021. *Transpacific Developments: The Politics of China and Chineseness in Central America.* Ithaca, NY: Cornell University Press.

Dubrow, Gail Lee (with Donna Graves). 2002. *Sento at Sixth and Main: Preserving Landmarks of Japanese American Heritage.* Seattle: Seattle Arts Commission.

———. 2005. "'The Nail That Sticks Up Gets Hit': The Architecture of Japanese American Identity in the Urban Environment, 1885–1942." In *Nikkei in the Pacific Northwest,* ed. Louis Fiset and Gail M. Nomura. Seattle: University of Washington Press.

Dubrow, Gail Lee, Gail Nomura, et al. 1993. *The Historic Context for the Protection of Asian/Pacific American Resources in Washington State.* Olympia: Office of Archaeology and Historic Preservation.

Ettlinger, Nancy. 2011. "Governmentality as Epistemology." *Annals of the Association of American Geographers* 101, no. 3: 537–60.

"Faculty of Nihon Go Gakko." N.d. Box 2, Folder 4, Acc. 5185-003, Ronald Magden Papers, 1879–2003, Special Collections, University of Washington Libraries.

Fiset, Louis. 2009. *Camp Harmony: Seattle's Japanese Americans and the Puyallup Assembly Center.* Champaign: University of Illinois Press.

Fiset, Louis, and Gail M. Nomura, eds. 2005. *Nikkei in the Pacific Northwest: Japanese Americans and Japanese Canadians in the Twentieth Century.* Seattle: University of Washington Press.

Flewelling, Stan. 2002. *Shirakawa: Stories from a Pacific Northwest Japanese American Community.* Auburn, WA: White River Valley Museum, distributed by the University of Washington Press.

Foucault, Michel. 1979. *Discipline and Punish: The Birth of a Prison.* Translated by Alan Sheridan. New York: Vintage.

———. 1980. *Power/Knowledge: Selected Interviews and Other Writings, 1972–1977.* Edited by Colin Gordon. New York: Pantheon Books.

———. 1988. *Technologies of the Self: A Seminar with Michel Foucault.* Edited by Luther H. Martin, Huck Gutman, and Patrick H. Hutton. Amherst: University of Massachusetts Press.

———. 1997. "The Ethics of the Concern for Self as a Practice of Freedom." In *Michel Foucault: Ethics, Subjectivity, and Truth: Essential Works of Foucault, 1954–1984,* ed. Paul Rabinow, 281–301. New York: New Press.

———. 2007. *Security, Territory, Population: Lectures at the Collège de France, 1977–78.* Edited by Michel Senellart, François Ewald, and Alessandro Fontana. New York: Palgrave Macmillan.

Fugita, Stephen S., and Marilyn Fernandez. 2004. *Altered Lives, Enduring Community: Japanese Americans Remember Their World War II Incarceration.* Seattle: University of Washington Press.

Fukuzawa Yukichi. [1875] 2009. *An Outline of a Theory of Civilization.* Translated by David A. Dilworth and G. Cameron Hurst III. New York: Columbia University Press.

Fujimoto, T. 1975. "Social Class and Crime: The Case of the Japanese-Americans." *Issues in Criminology* 10, no. 1: 73–89.

Gallacci, Caroline, and Ron Karabaich. 2006. *Tacoma's Waterfront (Images of America).* Charleston, SC: Arcadia.

Geiger, Andrea. 2007–8. "Negotiating the Boundaries of Race and Class: Meiji Diplomatic Responses to North American Categories of Exclusion." *BC Studies,* no. 156 (Winter).

———. 2011. *Subverting Exclusion: Transpacific Encounters with Race, Caste, and Border, 1885–1928.* New Haven, CT: Yale University Press.

Glenn, Evelyn Nakano. 1986. *Issei, Nisei, Warbride: Three Generations of Japanese American Women in Domestic Service.* Philadelphia: Temple University Press.

Gupta, Akhil, and James Ferguson. 1999. "Culture, Power, Place: Ethnography at the End of an Era." In *Culture, Power, Place: Explorations in Critical Anthropology,* ed. Akhil Gupta and James Ferguson. Durham, NC: Duke University Press.

HABS (Historic American Buildings Survey). 1995. *Nihon go gakko* (Japanese language school). Report prepared by Susan D. Boyle and Peter Mattson,

Boyle Wagner Architects, Historic American Buildings Survey, no. WA-209. https://www.theatlantic.com/health/archive/2020/04/pandemic-confusing -uncertainty/610819/?utm_source=pocket-newtabSan Francisco: Department of the Interior, National Park Service, Western Region, HABS.

Hanneman, Mary L. 1995. "Liberalism in Modern Japan: Origins, Evolution, and Demise." *Reason Papers* 20 (Fall): 55–67.

———. 2001. *Japan Faces the World*. Abingdon, UK: Routledge.

Hanson, Susan, and Geraldine Pratt. 1995. *Gender, Work, and Space*. London: Routledge.

Harmon, Alexandra. 1998. *Indians in the Making: Indian Relations and Ethnic Identities around the Puget Sound*. Berkeley: University of California Press.

Harrison, Scott Edward. 2005. "The History of the Seattle Japanese Language School." *North American Post* 60, no. 55 (July 13).

Hata, Donald Teruo. 1978. *"Undesirables": Early Immigrants and the Anti-Japanese Movement in San Francisco, 1892–1893: Prelude to Exclusion*. New York: Arno Press.

Hayashi, Brian. 1995. *For the Sake of Our Japanese Brethren: Assimilation, Nationalism, and Protestantism among the Japanese of Los Angeles, 1895–1942*. Stanford, CA: Stanford University Press.

Hayashida, Akiyoshi. 1933. "Japanese Moral Instruction as a Factor in the Americanization of Citizens of Japanese Ancestry." Master's thesis, University of Hawaii, Honolulu.

Hayden, Dolores. 2002. "From Ideal City to Dream House." In *Redesigning the American Dream: Gender, Housing, and Family Life*, 33–73. New York: W. W. Norton.

Hebbert, Michael. 2005. "The Street as Locus of Collective Memory." *Environment and Planning D: Society and Space* 23, no. 4: 581–96.

Hillier, Alfred J. 1945. "Albert Johnson, Congressman." *Pacific Northwest Quarterly* 36, no. 3 (July): 193–211.

History of Japanese in Tacoma. 1941. Author unknown. Translated by T. Imai, Hisato Miko, Norio Okada, George Yamane, and George Nakashima. Unpublished manuscript.

Hoelscher, Steven, and Derek K. Alderman. 2004. "Memory and Place: Geographies of a Critical Relationship." *Social and Critical Geography* 5, no. 3: 347–55.

Hoffman, Lisa M. 2003. "Enterprising Cities and Citizens: The Re-figuring of Urban Spaces and the Making of Post-Mao Professionals." *Provincial China* 8, no. 1: 5–26.

Hoffman, Lisa, Mary Hanneman, and Sarah Pyle. 2018. "Re-mapping Tacoma's Pre-War Japantown: Living on the Tideflats." *Conflux* 10. https://digital commons.tacoma.uw.edu/conflux/10.

Hoffman, Lisa, and Jim Thatcher. 2017. "Urban Studies and Thinking Topologically." *Territory, Politics, Governance* 7, no. 2: 141–55.

Honey, Michael K. 1999. *Black Workers Remember: An Oral History of Segregation, Unionism, and the Freedom Struggle*. Berkeley: University of California Press.

Horita, Kazuo. 1977. "Tacoma Reunion—One Man's View." *Pacific Citizen*, September 30, pp. 3, 7.

Hosokawa, Bill. 1969. *Nisei: The Quiet Americans*. New York: Morrow.

Howey, Meghan C. 2010. "Making the Invisible Visible: A Geospatial History of the Pre–World War II Japanese Community in Tacoma, Washington." GIS Certificate project, University of Washington, Tacoma. https://digitalcommons.tacoma.uw.edu/gis_projects/23.

Ichioka, Yuji. 1977. "Japanese Associations and the Japanese Government: A Special Relationship, 1909–1926." *Pacific Historical Review* 46, no. 3: 409–37.

———. 1980. "Japanese Immigrant Labor Contractors and the Northern Pacific and the Great Northern Railroad Companies, 1898–1907." *Labor History* 21, no. 3: 325–50.

———. 1988. *The Issei: The World of the First-Generation Japanese Immigrants, 1885–1924*. New York: Collier Macmillan.

———. 2006. *Before Internment: Essays in Prewar Japanese American History*. Stanford, CA: Stanford University Press.

Ito, Kazuo. 1973. *Issei: A History of Japanese Immigrants in North America*. Seattle: Japanese Community Service.

———. 1969. *Hokubei hyakunenzakura* (One hundred years of Japanese immigration in North America). Tokyo: Jikko Iinkai.

Iwata, Taro. 2005. "Rethinking Asian American Agency: Understanding the Complexity of Race and Citizenship in America." In *Asian American Studies after Critical Mass*, ed. Kent A. Ono, 177–194. Malden, MA: Blackwell.

James, Thomas. 1987. *Exile Within: The Schooling of Japanese Americans, 1942–1945*. Cambridge, MA: Harvard University Press.

Jansen, Marius B. 2000. *The Making of Modern Japan*. Cambridge, MA: Belknap Press.

Japanese Association of Tacoma Records. 1904–42. Attendance notification. Box 21, Folder 10, Special Collections, University of Washington Libraries.

———. Business record of Japanese within Tacoma, Occupation Business Record. Box 5, Folder 34, Special Collections, University of Washington Libraries.

———. 1904–42. Census result, October 20. Box 3, Folder 40, Special Collections, University of Washington Libraries.

———. 1904–42. Donation for celebration of Emperor Taisho accession, part 1. Box 2, Folders 12–15, Special Collections, University of Washington Libraries.

———. 1904–42. Donation for Meiji *jingu gaien*. Box 2, Folder 16, Special Collections, University of Washington Libraries.

———. 1904–42. Donation for Sesshomiya wedding celebration. Box 2, Folder 36, Special Collections, University of Washington Libraries.

———. 1904–42. Japanese Language School construction donation. Box 2, Folder 4, Special Collections, University of Washington Libraries.

———. 1904–42. Receipts for donation. Box 11, Folders 7–13, Special Collections, University of Washington Libraries.

———. 1904–42. Student Work (Writing and kanji: Junior high 2nd). Box 19, Folder 36; Special Collections, University of Washington Libraries.

———. 1904–42. Visa applications and supporting documents. Boxes 13/7–14/19, Special Collections, University of Washington Libraries.

Jinguji, Masaye. N.d. "Nitobe hakase no kogi o kiite" (After hearing a lecture by Dr. Nitobe). Translated by Misaki Seto and Mary Hanneman. Japanese Association of Tacoma Records, 1904–42, Student Work: Writing and Kanji, 1936–41, Box 20, Folder 38, Special Collections, University of Washington Libraries.

Jinguji, Yoshie. N.d. "Nihonjin to nihongo" (Japanese people and Japanese language). Translated by Misaki Seto and Mary Hanneman. Japanese Association of Tacoma Records, 1904–42, Student Work: Writing and Kanji, 1936–41, Box 20, Folder 33, Special Collections, University of Washington Libraries.

Jones, Judith A. 2010. "Making the Invisible Visible: A Geospatial History of the Japanese-American Community in Tacoma, Washington, 1888 to 1942." GIS Certificate project, University of Washington, Tacoma. https://digitalcommons .tacoma.uw.edu/ gis_projects/25.

Kawano, Yoshiteru. 1938. "Educator of Tacoma Returned after Tour of Points in Orient." *Japanese American Courier,* Dec. 3, p. 4.

Keene, Donald. 2002. *Emperor of Japan: Meiji and His World, 1852–1912.* New York: Columbia University Press.

Kinoshita Kiyoshi. N.d. "Natsu yasumi" (Summer vacation). Translated by Mary Hanneman. Japanese Association of Tacoma Records, 1904–42, Box 19, Folder 13, Special Collections, University of Washington Libraries.

Kitano, Harry H. L. 1969. *Japanese Americans: Evolution of a Subculture.* Englewood Cliffs, NJ: Prentice Hall.

———. 1981. "Asian-Americans: The Chinese, Japanese, Koreans, Pilipinos, and Southeast Asians." *Annals of the American Academy of Political and Social Science* 454, no. 1: 125–18.

———. 1993. *Generations and Identity: The Japanese American.* Needham Heights, MA: Ginn Press.

Kubo, Yasumi. N.d. "Nihon" (Japan). Translated by Misaki Seto and Mary Hanneman. Japanese Association of Tacoma Records, 1904–42, Student Work: Writing and Kanji, 1936–41, Box 19, Folder 33, Special Collections, University of Washington Libraries.

Kumei, Teruko. 2002. "'The Twain Shall Meet' in the Nisei? Japanese Language Education and U.S.-Japan Relations, 1900–1940." In *New Worlds, New Lives; Globalization and People of Japanese Descent in the Americas and from Latin*

America in Japan, ed. Lane Ryo Hirabayashi, Akemi Kikumura-Yano, and James A. Hirabayashi, 108–25. Stanford, CA: Stanford University Press.

Kurashige, Lon. 2002. *Japanese American Celebration and Conflict: A History of Ethnic Identity and Festival, 1934–1990*. Berkeley: University of California Press.

———. 2016. *Two Faces of Exclusion: The Untold History of Anti-Asian Racism in the United States*. Chapel Hill: University of North Carolina Press.

Lee, Shelley Sang-Hee. 2011. *Claiming the Oriental Gateway: Prewar Seattle and Japanese America*. Philadelphia: Temple University Press.

Lefebvre, Henri. 1992. *The Production of Space*. Translated by Donald Nicholson-Smith. Cambridge, MA: Blackwell.

Lemire, Daniel Lachapelle. 2016–17. "Bittersweet Memories: Narratives of Japanese Canadian Children's Experiences before the Second World War and the Politics of Redress." *BC Studies*, no. 192 (Winter).

Le Tendre, Gerald K. 1999. "Community-Building Activities in Japanese Schools: Alternative Paradigms of the Democratic School." *Comparative Education Review* 43, no. 3: 283–310.

Lyman, Stanford M. 1970 "The Significance of Asians in American Society." In *The Asian in North America*, 25–37. Santa Barbara, CA: ABC-Clio.

MacFarlane, Key, and Katharyne Mitchell. 2019. "Hamburg's Spaces of Danger: Race, Violence and Memory in a Contemporary Global City." *International Journal of Urban Regional Research* 43, no. 5: 816–32.

Magden, Ronald E. 1998. *Furusato: Tacoma–Pierce County Japanese*. Tacoma: Nikkeijinkai, Tacoma Japanese Community Service.

———. 2008. "Port of Tacoma: Thumbnail History, Part 1." HistoryLink.org, April 17. www.historylink.org/File/8592.

Massey, Doreen. 1994. *Space, Place, and Gender*. Minneapolis: University of Minnesota Press.

Matsumoto, Valerie. 1994. "Redefining Expectations: Nisei Women in the 1930s." *California History* 73, no. 1 (Spring): 44–53. (Special issue titled "Japanese Americans in California.")

———. 2014. *City Girls: The Nisei Social World in Los Angeles, 1920–1950*. Oxford: Oxford University Press.

Metsker, Chas. F. 1926 *Metsker's Complete Atlas of Tacoma, Washington*. Tacoma, WA: [C. F. Metsker].

Miller, Danica. N.d. "Puyallup Sovereignties." Unpublished book manuscript.

Merrill, Heather, and Lisa M. Hoffman. 2015. "Introduction: Making Sense of Our Contemporary Moment of Danger." In *Spaces of Danger: Culture and Power in the Everyday,* ed. Heather Merrill and Lisa M. Hoffman. Athens: University of Georgia Press.

Minidoka Irrigator (Hunt, ID). 1943. Memorial announcement for Masato Yama-saki. Translated by Mary Hanneman. March 13. Available at the Library of Congress, www.loc.gov/item/sn84024049/1943-03-13/ed-1.

Miyamoto, Frank. 1981. *Social Solidarity among the Japanese in Seattle*. Seattle: University of Washington Press.

Modell, John. 1968. "The Japanese American Family: A Perspective for Future Investigations." *Pacific Historical Review* 37, no. 1 (February): 67–81.

———. 1977. *The Economics and Politics of Racial Accommodation: The Japanese of Los Angeles, 1900–1942*. Champaign: University of Illinois Press.

Morgan, Murray. 1982. *The Mill on the Boot: The Story of the St. Paul & Tacoma Lumber Company*. Seattle: Washington State Historical Society and University of Washington Press.

———. 2003. *Puget's Sound: A Narrative of Early Tacoma and the Southern Sound*. Seattle: University of Washington Press.

Morgan, Murray, and Rosa Morgan. 1984. *South on the Sound: An Illustrated History of Tacoma and Pierce County*. Woodland Hills, CA: Windsor Publications.

Morris, Rosalind, ed.. 2010. *Can the Subaltern Speak? Reflections on the History of an Idea*. New York: Columbia University Press.

Morrison, Susan. 1994. "Tacoma's Nihongo Gakko: The Center of a Once Vibrant Community." Master's thesis, University of Washington, Seattle.

Nancy, Jean-Luc. 2000. "Eulogy for the Mêlée." In *Being Singular Plural*, translated by Robert D. Richardson and Anne E. O'Byrne, 145–58. Stanford, CA: Stanford University Press.

Neiwart, David. 2005. *Strawberry Days: How Internment Destroyed a Japanese American Community*. New York: Palgrave.

Neu, Charles E. 1966. "Theodore Roosevelt and American Involvement in the Far East, 1901–1909." *Pacific Historical Review* 35, no. 4: 433–49.

Nimura, Tamiko. 2016. "Tacoma Neighborhoods: Japantown (Nihonmachi)—Thumbnail History." HistoryLink.org. www.historylink.org/File/20177.

———. 2017a. "Taking Tacoma's Japantown Online." *Discover Nikkei*. www.discovernikkei.org/en/journal/2017/12/12/tacoma-japantown.

———. 2017b. "Japanese American Veteran and Journalist Shuichi Fukui of Tacoma Responds on December 8, 1941, to News of Japan's Attack on Pearl Harbor." HistoryLink.org. www.historylink.org/File/20448.

———. 2018. "Tacoma Japantown Then and Now." Exhibit at Washington State History Museum, Day of Remembrance, May 17.

Nimura, Tamiko, and Michael Sullivan. N.d. "Tacoma Japanese American History." https://tacomajapaneseamericanhistory.net.

Nimura, Tamiko, and Justin Wadland. 2018. "Tacoma Buddhist Temple." HistoryLink.org. www.historylink.org/File/20668.

Nitobe Inazo. 1933. *Japanese American Courier* 6, no. 263 (January 21).

Nomura, Gail. 1986. Foreword to Shunichi Otsuka and Shuichi Fukui, *History of the Japanese of Tacoma*. N.p.: Northwest District Council, Japanese American Citizens League, [1940] 1986.

———. 1989. "Washington's Asian/Pacific American Communities." In *Peoples of Washington: Perspectives on Cultural Diversity,* ed. Sid White and Sammy Edward Solberg, 115–55. Pullman: Washington State University Press.

Nunnaly, Derrick. 2016. "75 Years after Pearl Harbor, Its Tacoma Legacy Lingers." *News Tribune* (Tacoma), December 2. www.thenewstribune.com/news/local /article118714163.html.

O'Brien, David J., and Stephen S. Fugita. 1982. "Middleman Minority Concept: Its Explanatory Value in the Case of the Japanese in California Agriculture." *Pacific Sociological Review* 25: 185–204.

Okada, John. [1957] 1978. *No-No Boy*. Seattle: University of Washington Press.

Okazaki Tokiko. N.d. "Watashi-tachi no [gi]mu" (Our duty). Translated by Misaki Seto and Mary Hanneman. Japanese Association of Tacoma Records, 1904–42, Student Work: Writing and Kanji, 1936–41, Box 19, Folder 33, Special Collections, University of Washington Libraries.

Olson, Ronald L. 1928. *The Orientals in the Lumber Industry in the State of Washington*. No publisher identified. Special Collections, University of Washington Libraries.

Ong, Aihwa. 1996. "Cultural Citizenship as Subject-Making: Immigrants Negotiate Racial and Cultural Boundaries in the United States." *Current Anthropology* 37, no. 5: 737–62.

Onishi Katsumi. 1943. "A Study of the Attitudes of the Japanese in Hawaii toward the Japanese Language Schools." Master's thesis, University of Hawaii, Honolulu.

Ono, Kent A. 2005. "Asian American Studies in Its Second Phase." In *Asian American Studies after Critical Mass*, ed. Kent A. Ono, 1–16. Malden, MA: Blackwell.

Otsuka, Shunichi, and Shuichi Fukui. [1940] 1986. *History of the Japanese of Tacoma*. Translated by James Watanabe. N.p.: Northwest District Council, Japanese American Citizens League. (Originally published in 1916 or 1917 as *Takoma nihonjin hattenshi*.)

"Pacific Northwest Japanese American Newspapers on Microfilm: Japanese Newspapers Held in the University of Washington Libraries." N.d.https:// content.lib.washington.edu/otherprojects/nikkei/newspapersuw.pdf.

Pak, Yoon K. 2002. *Wherever I Go, I Will Always Be a Loyal American: Schooling Seattle's Japanese Americans during World War II*. New York: Routledge.

Polk, R. L., & Co. 1928. *Polk's Tacoma City Directory, Volume XLIII*. Tacoma: R. L. Polk & Co. Publishers.

———. 1933. *Polk's Tacoma City Directory, Volume XLVIII.* Tacoma: R. L. Polk & Co. Publishers.

Pred, Allan. 1981. "Social Reproduction and the Time-Geography of Everyday Life." *Geografiska Annaler, Series B, Human Geography* 63, no. 1: 5–22.

———. 1984. "Place as Historically Contingent Process: Structuration and the Time-Geography of Becoming Places." *Annals of the Association of American Geographers* 74, no. 2: 279–97.

———. 1990. *Making Histories and Constructing Human Geographies: The Local Transformation of Practice, Power Relations, and Consciousness.* Boulder, CO: Westview Press.

———. 1998. "Memory and the Cultural Reworking of Crisis: Racisms and the Current Moment of Danger in Sweden, or Wanting It Like Before." *Environment and Planning D: Society and Space* 16, no. 6: 635–64.

———. 2004. *The Past Is Not Dead: Facts, Fictions, and Enduring Racial Stereotypes.* Minneapolis: University of Minnesota Press.

———. 2007. "Situated Ignorance and State Terrorism." In *Violent Geographies: Fear, Terror, and Political Violence,* ed. Derek Gregory and Allan Pred, 363–84. New York: Routledge.

Pyle, Kenneth B. 1969. *The New Generation in Meiji Japan: Problems of Cultural Identity, 1885–1895.* Stanford, CA: Stanford University Press.

———. 1973. "The Technology of Japanese Nationalism: The Local Improvement Movement, 1900–1918." *Journal of Asian Studies* 33, no. 1: 51–65.

Pyle, Sarah. 2018. "A Forgotten Japanese Community: Tacoma in 1890–1942." GIS Certificate project, University of Washington, Tacoma.

———. 2019. "Remapping Tacoma's Japantown History." Master's thesis, University of Washington, Tacoma.

Robinson, Greg. 2012. *After Camp: Portraits in Midcentury Japanese American Life and Politics.* Berkeley: University of California Press.

Roosevelt, Eleanor. 1941. "My Day." December 16. https://tacomahistory.live/2016/11/21/my-day.

Rosaldo, Michelle Zimbalist, Louise Lamphere, and Joan Bamberger. 1974. *Woman, Culture, and Society.* Stanford, CA: Stanford University Press.

Said, Edward. 2000. "Invention, Memory, Place." *Critical Inquiry* 26, no. 2: 175–92.

Sanborn Fire Insurance Map from Tacoma, Pierce County, Washington. 1912. Sanborn Map Company. Vol. 1.

Sawada, Mitziko. 1991. "Culprits and Gentlemen: Meiji Japan's Restrictions of Emigrants to the United States, 1891–1909." *Pacific Historical Review* 60, no. 3: 339–59.

Seto, Joseph T. N.d. Joe Seto Collection. Pacific Northwest Room/Special Collections, Tacoma Public Library.

Seto, Joseph T., and Ronald E. Magden. 2001. "Redress of Nisei Graduates and Valedictorian George Kurose of Lincoln High School, Tacoma, Washington." Unpublished manuscript.

"Seto Family History." N.d. Unpublished manuscript, shared with the authors by Joseph P. Seto.

Smith, Michael P. 2001. *Transnational Urbanism: Locating Globalization.* Malden, MA: Blackwell.

———. 2005. "Transnational Urbanism Revisited." *Journal of Ethnic and Migration Studies* 31, no. 2: 235–44.

Sone, Monica Itoi. 2014. *Nisei Daughter.* Seattle: University of Washington Press.

Sonnier, Brenda. 1993. "Tacoma's Nihon Go Gakko: Japanese Language School." https://digitalcollections.lib.washington.edu/digital/collection/tacoma comm/id/119.

Spickard, Paul. 2009. *Japanese Americans: The Formation and Transformation of an Ethnic Group.* New Brunswick, NJ: Rutgers University Press.

Spivak, Gayatri Chakravorty. 1988. "Can the Subaltern Speak?" In *Marxism and the Interpretation of Culture*, ed. Lawrence Grossberg and Cary Belson. Urbana: University of Illinois Press.

St. Paul & Tacoma Lumber Company Records. 1903–18. Time books (Mills and Camps), 1903–18, Box 230, Night Shift, February 1915, Acc. no. 0315-001, Special Collections, University of Washington Libraries.

Sullivan, Michael. 2016. "Nihonmachi, ca. 1920." *Tacoma History.* https://tacoma history.live/2016/06/10/nihonmachi-ca-1920.

———. 2017. "Still Chasing the Story." *Tacoma History.* https://tacomahistory.live /2017/03/03/still-chasing-the-story.

Swift, David W., Jr. 2008. *First Class: Nisei Linguists in World War II; Origins of the Military Intelligence Service Language Program.* 2nd ed. San Francisco: National Japanese American Historical Society.

Tacoma News Tribune. 1941. Editorial, December 14. https://tacomahistory.live /2016/11/21/my-day.

———. 2002. Editorial, June 9.

Takahashi, Jere. 1982. "Japanese American Responses to Race Relations: The Formation of Nisei Perspectives." *Amerasia Journal* 9, no. 1: 29–57.

———. 1997. *Nisei/Sansei: Shifting Japanese American Identities and Politics.* Philadelphia: Temple University Press.

Takaki, Ronald. [1989] 1998. *A History of Asian Americans: Strangers from a Different Shore.* Updated and revised ed. Boston: Back Bay Books.

Takeuchi, Kojiro. 1929. *Beikoku seihokubu nihon imin minshi* (History of Japanese immigration in the Northwestern United States). Seattle: Taihoku Nipposha.

Takezawa, Yasuko I. 1995. *Breaking the Silence: Redress and Japanese American Ethnicity.* Ithaca, NY: Cornell University Press.

Takoma shuho (Tacoma Japanese weekly). 1942. "Tachinobi o junbi isogimasho" (Let's hurry to prepare for evacuation). April 9. Microforms and Newspapers Microfilm, University of Washington Libraries.

Tamaki, Chiyoko. N.d. "Nihon" (Japan). Translated by Misaki Seto and Mary Hanneman. Japanese Association of Tacoma Records, 1904–42, Student Work: Writing and Kanji, 1936–41, Box 19, Folder 33, Special Collections, University of Washington Libraries.

Tamura, Eileen H. 1994. *Americanization, Acculturation, and Ethnic Identity: The Nisei Generation in Hawaii*. Champaign: University of Illinois Press.

Tamura, Linda. 1993. *The Hood River Issei: An Oral History of Japanese Settlers in Oregon's Hood River Valley*. Champaign: University of Illinois Press.

———. 2012. *Nisei Soldiers Break Their Silence: Coming Home to Hood River*. Seattle: University of Washington Press.

Tatsumi, Henry S. 1937. "What Must American-Japanese Do in the Face of the Far-Eastern Crisis?" *Japanese American Courier*, September 11.

"Teigakunen shitsuke ho no kenkyu" (Research on training students in the lower primary grades). 1931. Translated by Misaki Seto and Mary Hanneman. University of Washington Libraries, Special Collections: Japanese Association of Tacoma Records, 1904–42, Box 18.

Uyeda, Clifford I. 2000. *Suspended: Growing Up Asian in America*. San Francisco: National Japanese American Historical Society.

Uyeda, Clifford, and Barry Sakai, eds. 1991 *The Pacific War and Peace: Americans of Japanese Ancestry in Military Intelligence Service, 1941 to 1952*. San Francisco: Military Intelligence Service Association of Northern California and the National Japanese American Historical Society.

Uyeda, Susie. 1933. "Out of Town." *Japanese American Courier* 6, no. 263 (January 21): 4.

Williams, Duncan Ryuken. 2019. *American Sutra: A Story of Faith and Freedom in the Second World War*. Cambridge, MA: Belknap Press.

Williams, Duncan Ryuken, and Tomoe Moriya. 2010. *Issei Buddhism in the Americas*. Urbana: University of Illinois Press.

Wilson, Robert A., and Bill Hosokawa. 1982. *East to America: A History of the Japanese in the United States*. New York: Quill.

Yanagisako, Sylvia Junko. 1985. *Transforming the Past: Tradition and Kinship among Japanese Americans*. Stanford, CA: Stanford University Press.

Yoo, David K. 2000. *Growing Up Nisei: Race, Generation, and Culture among Japanese Americans of California, 1924–49*. Champaign: University of Illinois Press.

INDEX

A

Abe, Gisaburo, 205

Abiko, Kyutaro, 169

Adachi, K. (employee at St. Paul & Tacoma, 1915), 69

agency, 14, 24–25, 44; Issei, 51, 56; of Nisei children, 97, 113, 175

agriculture, 31, 62, 91–92, 243nn27–28, 238n27, 244n29; cherry and berry picking, 92, 93, 173. *See also* farms

Airway Market, 129, 138, 139*map*, 140, 227, 249n6

Alaska, 77, 158, 241n22

Alien Land Laws, 12, 56, 75, 98, 126, 205, 243n27

American values, 26, 145, 174. *See also* democracy and equality

Americanization, 15, 26, 157, 166. *See also* assimilation; bridge metaphor; bridging

Anbo, Heiichi, 151

Anderson, Kay, 236n12

Anonymous Female A, 153, 189

Anonymous Female B, 76

Anonymous Female D, 198

Anonymous Female E, 158

Anonymous Male A, 137, 189, 206; on Mr. Yamasaki, 144, 166

Anonymous Male B: on the arrests of his parents, 207; on the sawmills, 69, 132; on TJLS teaching of traditional values, 37

Anonymous Male C, 72

anti–Japanese language school movement, 48, 50–51, 156

Aochi, Katsuko, 225

Aochi, Yoneko: family history, 225; on her parents' employment, 67–68; on the Japanese Hotel, 131; student essay "Why Japanese Is Important," 164–65, 165*fig.*; on TJLS teaching of traditional values, 37, 183

Arishima Takeo, 41

Asada, Mrs. (teacher), 201, 246n9

Asada, T. (employee at St. Paul & Tacoma Lumber Company, 1915), 70

Asada, Tokiichi, 133, 205

Asada family, 133

Asaka, Megan, 71, 246n5

Asato, Noriko, 48, 51

Asian American studies, 22; "second phase," 25

assembly centers, 251n10; Pinedale, 13, 213, 214, 251n10

assimilation: versus blending, 59; versus bridging, 10, 15, 170, 171; versus contested understanding of

assimilation (*continued*)
subjectivity, 10, 15, 170, 171; and dispersal after World War II, 219; and Japanese language schools, 161; and self-segregation, 112; and shame about incarceration, 215. *See also* Americanization; bridging; bridge metaphor, segregation and self-segregation

Association of Railroad Tie Producers, 129

Azuma, Eiichiro, 28, 161

B

bachelors, 130*map*, 131, 246n5

banks, 66, 227

Baptist church, 101, 121

barbershops, 72, 75–76, 85, 229

baseball, 70, 122, 136, 197–98, 243n22

bazaars, 109, 121

Bean, Minnie, 157

belonging, 11, 12–13, 14, 17, 22, 49, 205; discrimination and, 119; reunions and, 220; spatiality of, 98, 105, 126, 129, 142; TJLS and, 107–12; World War II and, 205, 210. *See also* Nisei

berries, 91, 92, 93, 244n29

Bonacich, Edna, and John Modell, 62, 65, 71, 72, 78, 238n24, 241n4. *See also* middlemen; Modell, John; *tano-moshi* (money pooling)

Bourdieu, Pierre: *habitus*, 144

bowing, 40, 52, 152, 184, 185, 202; when apologizing, 180; to elders, 27, 102, 105; to the emperor's portrait, 36; to parents, 179; at TJLS community events, 186–87. *See also* micro-practices; subject formation

boys, 13; and behavior, 99, 100, 152–53, 199–200; and education/schooling,

13, 73, 106, 146; from Hawaii, 100; and religious establishments, 123, 124–25; and sports, 112, 198. *See also* gender; girls

bridge metaphor (for Nisei), 145, 161–63, 167, 168–69, 170–72. *See also* bridging

bridging: and agency, 14, 97; as conceptual shift from bridge concept, 8, 10, 14–15, 145, 161–63, 168, 170–71; explanation of term, 14–15; and Nisei identity formation, 10, 15, 26, 145, 170, 172, 173–74, 202, 215, 221; and spatial approach, 14, 97, 236n9; and transnational perspective, 8–10; and Yamasakis, 145, 161, 170. *See also* bridge metaphor

Broadway (Tacoma): Japanese-run businesses and lodgings, 3, 63, 64*map*, 76, 79, 80, 96; in Nihon-machi ca. 1940, 5*fig.*; in overview map, 18*map*; present-day, 235n1; view looking down, in 2020, 5*fig.*

Broadway Hotel, 64*map*, 80, 229

Buddhism, 109, 145; Buddhist-Christian divide, 109; Jodo Shinshu (True Pure Land), 125, 246n17. *See also* Buddhist temple (Tacoma); Buddhist temples

Buddhist temple (Tacoma): activities at, 13, 113, 121–22, 124, 125; arrest of minister, 205; funerals, 122; as Jodo Shinshu Nishi Hongwanji, 246n17; as last remaining structure serving original function, 20, 204, 237n19; name changed from "church" to Tacoma Buddhist Temple, 237n16; sports teams, 70, 197; use of term, 236–37n16

Buddhist temples: community-building role, 53, 108; in Hawaii, 48, 53. *See also* Buddhist temple (Tacoma)

bushido, 169, 249n14

business associations, 66; Association
of Railroad Tie Producers, 129;
Japanese business associations in
Tacoma, Barbers' Association, 66;
Grocery Association, 66; Japanese
Bank, 66. *See also* Tacoma Japanese
Association

Butsuda, Clinton: descriptions of
St. Paul Avenue, 131, 132; family residence and gardens, 132; on father's
role in sawmill, 71; Lynette Butsuda
(daughter), 246n4; on rejection by
the military, 216; on the tideflats
in the 1980s, 242n7

C

Cain, Harry P., 117–19

California: discrimination in, 117;
immigration to, 66, 214n6; Japanese
language schools, 109, 156; relocation to, 220. *See also* Los Angeles;
San Francisco

calligraphy, 146, 155, 187, 198

canneries, 6, 77. *See also* fishing
industry

Capital Dry Cleaners, 83–84, 84*fig.*, 226

cars, 84, 98, 104, 142, 245n6; driven by
women, 84; of Kunio Shibata's father,
85, 86; Matsui family Hupmobile,
132, 246n7

Central School, 103, 106, 112, 142, 157–
59; Issei language instruction, 79,
228–29

ceremonies: Nisei subject formation
and behavioral protocols, 185–86,
202; at TJLS, 35, 52, 185–87, 208. *See
also* imperial birthday celebrations;
micropractices; New Year's Day;
subject formation

Chicago, 22, 107, 116, 182, 204, 219,
223–24

Chinatowns, 41, 236n12

Chinda Sutemi, 44, 46, 240n15

Chinese: Exclusion Act of 1882, 9;
expelled from Tacoma, 114, 117,
245n13; restaurant employees, 77

Christians, 49, 120, 125, 135, 245n15;
Buddhist-Christian divide, 109, 123.
See also Methodist church

citizenship: Issei ineligibility for, 8, 28,
45–46, 50, 56, 98, 179, 236n8; and
military service, 216, 218; of Nisei,
50, 62, 161, 163, 169, 175, 176; after
Pearl Harbor, 210, 211; taught at
TJLS, 165, 190, 209; as unstable
status, 204

Civilian Control Centers, 13; Tacoma
Japanese Language School as, 204,
211–12, 215

"civilization," 38, 239nn8–9

class, 13, 14, 33, 57, 87–89, 127, 166, 174;
class differences, 13, 58, 87–89, 95

College of Puget Sound, 111*fig.*, 201

community, Japanese of Tacoma, 6, 17–
20, 26; closeness of, 6, 17, 25, 26, 44,
53, 98–101, 105, 106–7, 122, 126, 127,
152, 178, 244n1; decline of, 119; erasure of, 203–4; families who moved
to avoid incarceration, 212; leaders
of, 143; lobbying for consulate, 46–47;
location of, 17, 26; map of, ca. 1920s,
15–17, 16*fig.*; overview, ca. 1900–1942,
18*map*; after Pearl Harbor, 210–11,
211; postwar dispersal and relocation of, 26, 203–4, 205, 211, 219, 220;
religious affiliations of, 120; and
religious establishments, 121–24,
160; resource pooling, 57, 62, 63, 65,
71, 94; size of, 46, 47, 240n15, 249n1;
survey of children, 52–53; walking

community, Japanese of Tacoma (*continued*)
  scale of, 107; written histories of, 238–39n3. *See also* Civilian Control Centers; erasure; ethics (*shushin*); Executive Order 9066; *History of Japanese in Tacoma* (1941); Nihon-machi (Tacoma); South Tacoma; Tacoma: *tanomoshi* (money pooling); tideflats; TJLS (Tacoma Japanese Language School): and community closeness; TJLS (Tacoma Japanese Language School): and community events; Yamasaki, Masato: as community leader
Confucian values, 36. *See also* ethics (*shushin*); filial piety (*oyakoko*)
Connerton, Paul, 4, 12, 235n3, 237n21. *See also* erasure; structural and systemic forgetting
Cushman Dam, 154–55, 248n8

D

Dai Nippon Butoku Kai (Greater Japan Martial Virtue Society), 208
Daniels, Roger, 24, 80, 235–36n6, 240n17
Dash Point, 195–96
Debuchi, Katsuji, 163, 168
de Certeau, Michel, 12, 101
dekasegi (going out to work) versus *teiju* (emigration), 62. *See also* Issei
delinquency rates, 94, 244n31
democracy and equality, 26, 145, 165–67, 172, 174. *See also* American values
discipline, 93, 182, 184–85, 198, 201; and Nisei subject-making, 144; self-discipline, 36, 173, 178, 198, 249n14. *See also* subject formation
discrimination, 12, 26, 53, 221; in California, 117; and employment, 61,

63, 65, 72; Nisei children's awareness of, 119–20; and Nisei subject-making, 144; after Pearl Harbor, 206; and self-segregation, 96, 98, 112–13, 115, 125; strategies for coping with, 49, 113, 175. *See also* Issei: and discrimination/racism
Doi, R. (employee at St. Paul & Tacoma Lumber Company), 70
domestic workers, 73
dual identity paradigm, 14, 15, 237n17. *See also* bridge metaphor; Nisei
Dubrow, Gail L., 4, 59, 234n2

E

Elder, Jane (Caucasian classmate), 116
emperor (Meiji Emperor), 8, 30, 33, 34–37, 45, 151; birthday celebrations, 35, 37, 52, 110, 185, 186, 208; and Meiji Japan, 30–31, 33, 34–37, 45; as symbol of modernization, 8–9, 28; Taisho Emperor, 45; and transnationalism, 8, 9, 28, 30, 35, 37, 52; Showa Emperor, 45. *See also* Imperial Rescript on Education; Yamasaki, Masato
Enari, T. K., 234
enryo (self-effacement), 236n10. *See also* ethics (*shushin*)
erasure, 8, 11–12, 17, 19–20, 127, 128, 138, 142, 172, 203–4, 220; indigenous, 6, 235n3; and reconstituting the self, 12, 102. *See also* Connerton, Paul; spatial approach and spatiality; structural and systemic forgetting
ethics (*shushin*), 175; behaviors associated with, 27, 102, 105, 172, 183; and community, 177–81, 184; curriculum at TJLS, 9, 37, 145, 165, 172, 174–77, 214; as means of control, 177, 178;

and Nisei subject formation, 4, 202; spatiality and, 97; taught through folk tales and plays, 190–93; and transnationalism, 8, 10. *See also enryo* (self-effacement); filial piety (*oyakoko*); *gaman* (perseverance); *giri* (sense of obligation); Imperial Rescript on Education; shame (*haji*); micropractices; *oyakoko* (filial piety); respect for elders; *shikataganai* (it cannot be helped); TJLS (Tacoma Japanese Language School): ethics curriculum

ethnic economy, 62, 71, 72, 78, 87, 91, 94, 128. *See also* Japanese-run business

evacuation. *See* wartime incarceration

Exclusion Act (1924), 22, 24, 29, 32, 43, 51, 85, 168, 240n12

exclusion movement, 48, 50, 156

Executive Order 9066, 13, 117, 203, 211, 214. *See also* Civilian Control Centers; wartime incarceration

F

family histories, 26, 74–78, 224–31

farms, 71, 72, 73, 75, 91, 123. *See also* agriculture

FBI arrests, 172, 205–8

Federal Survey of Education in Hawaii, 51

Fife: agricultural production, 91, 123, 138; Japanese language school, 48, 51, 240n18; Nisei in military intelligence, 218

filial piety (*oyakoko*), 9, 10, 36, 37, 87, 163, 174, 175; as core of *shushin*, 177–79. *See also* ethics (*shushin*)

financial strain, 91–92, 93, 123. *See also* Great Depression

Fiset, Louis, 25, 108, 114, 163, 175

fishing industry, 219–20, 241n6. *See also* canneries

Fort Lewis, 181; field trip to, 154–55, 248n8

Fort Missoula detention camp, 172, 208–9, 250n3

Foucault, Michel, 183, 236n12, 247n1, 249n3; power and resistance, 177; "practices of the self," 183. *See also* micropractices; subject formation

Fourth Army Intelligence School (San Francisco), 216

Fresno Japanese community, 109

Fugita, Stephen S. and Marilyn Fernandez, 65, 78, 171, 219

Fujii, Masatoshi: on after-school activities versus Japanese school, 111–12; on evacuation, 212–13; family history, 225; on Japanese as first language, 159; on Ninomiya Kinjiro, 191; on parental sacrifice, 178; on segregated sports teams, 197

Fujii, Shosaku, 241n22

Fujii family, 225. *See also* Fujii, Masatoshi; Yoshida, Fusae Fujii

Fujimoto, Masakata, 225–26

Fujimoto, Mitsu, 226; with daughters at Capital Cleaners, 84*fig.*

Fujimoto, Riyeko: family history, 225; on family involvement with schools, 160; on her parents' employment, 73; on religious affiliation, 125; on social class, 88; on TJLS and community closeness, 120; on walking home from school, 103

Fujimoto, Tadashi, 225

Fujimoto sisters, 20, 58, 93, 100–101, 135, 245n6; daily path to and from school, 102*map*; family history, 225–26. *See also* Kawasaki, Chiyeko Tadaye

Fujimoto sisters (*continued*)
Fujimoto; Sugiyama, Yoshiko Fujimoto; Tanbara, Kimiko Fujimoto
Fujita, Masaye Jinguji: daily path to
and from school, 102*map*; family his-
tory, 227; with friends at College of
Puget Sound, 111*fig.*; on the Methodist church, 120–21, 124–25; student essay on lecture by Nitobe,
169–70; on use of TJLS for special
events, 110–11
Fujita, Yoshiro, 46, 240n17
Fukuhara family, 226; Hiroko Betty
Fukuhara Yoshioka, 74, 116
Fukui, Shuichi: as editor of *Takoma
shuho*, 210, 238n3, 250n9; FBI arrest
of, 205; *History of the Japanese of
Tacoma*, 128, 150, 238–39n3, 248n6;
on role of TJLS, 54
Fukushima Prefectural School of
Literature, 147
Fukuzawa, Yukichi, 239n8
funerals, 90, 122

G

gaman (perseverance), 37, 145, 175, 176,
205, 214. *See also* ethics (*shushin*)
gamblers and prostitutes, 43, 46–47, 150
gardening, 90, 188, 190
gender, 13, 14, 74, 140; in the classroom,
200; demographics with immigration, 72; and employment and
strategic deployment, 61, 71, 72,
73–76, 75–76; and recognition of
women, 150; and religion, 124–25.
See also boys; girls; TJLS (Tacoma
Japanese Language School):
teachers
Gentlemen's Agreement of 1907–8, 9,
32, 41–43, 48, 50, 61

giri (sense of obligation), 62, 112, 175.
See also ethics (*shushin*)
girls: behavior, 200; and Buddhist
temple/Methodist church, 13, 120–
21, 123, 124; census of school-age
children in Tacoma, 242n14; education and schooling, 13, 24, 106, 146;
sports, 13, 120–21. *See also* boys;
gender
Gordon, Joseph H., 58, 241n24
Grand Hotel, 64*map*, 74, 242n17
Great Depression, 76, 77, 82, 92
grocery stores, 6, 56, 64*map*, 72, 75, 79,
93, 138, 139*map*, 141, 231; business
association, 66; Kawano family,
82, 227. *See also* Airway Market;
business associations; markets
Gulick, Rev. Sidney L., 161

H

haji (shame). *See* shame (*haji*). *See also*
ethics (*shushin*)
Haneda, Kiyo, 234
Harada, Yuriko Lily Korin: on being
the oldest sibling, 178; family
history, 228; on filial piety, 177; on
her father's employment, 141–42;
on Mrs. Yamasaki, 147, 148–49; residences of, 142; on school cleaning
tasks, 189–90; schools attended by,
142; on TJLS, 59, 155, 176; on walking to and from school, 103
Harano, Katsuko Aochi: on her
parents' employment, 67–68; on
taking the streetcar, 106; on tideflats Japanese hotel, 131–32; on
TJLS, 37, 155
Hata, Issei, 205, 206–7
Hata, Jack Kazuo: on arrests and evacuation, 206–7, 213; family history,

226; on his parents, 89–90, 206–7; memories of the tideflats, 136; on not bringing shame, 176–77; on religious affiliation, 120; on TJLS, 125, 155, 186

Hata, Mrs., 199, 201, 234, 249n7

Hattori, Fumi Sato: on being made to apologize, 179–80; on the death of her father, 133; on discrimination, 117; family history, 229; on funerals, 122; on her brothers, 133; on her movement to and from school and TJLS, 105; on her parents' employment, 61, 73, 133–34; religious affiliation, 120, 122, 135; on St. Paul Avenue, 133; on Tacoma's hotels, 80; on teachers, 201; on TJLS, 109, 181–82, 184–85, 188

Hawaii: Buddhist temples, 48, 53; Federal Survey of Education in Hawaii, 51; Japanese community, 100, 244n4; language schools, 48, 57, 174; migration to, 39; stereotypes of, 244n4

Hayashi, June Miyeko Shirozu: family history, 230; on her family, 123; incarceration with her family, 230; on religion, 123–24; on returning to Tacoma, 219–20; on shame at incarceration, 215

Hayashi Grocery, 138

Hayashida, Akiyoshi, 57

Heath, Frederick, 58

Heath & Gove, 58–59

Henry Horiuchi Fruit, 138

high schools, 13, 106, 110. *See also* Lincoln High School; Stadium High School

highway markets, 19, 96, 128, 138–42. *See also* Airway Market; Nishijima family

Hiraki, Ihei, 241n22

historic preservation, 4, 20–21, 235n2

History of Japanese in Tacoma (1941), 43, 238–39n3; Japanese consulate in Tacoma, 44; Japanese language schools, 51; Japanese language skills and instruction, 51–52, 157, 158, 248n13; Japanese in the lumber industry, 67; Japanese-owned businesses, 71, 72, 138; and mapping Tacoma, 128; Masato Yamasaki, 150–51; Tacoma Japanese community, 43, 46; TJLS, 56–58, 150, 154, 158; unions and Japanese employees, 77.

Hofstetter, Fred, 211

Honda, Harry, 99

Honda, Kenkichi, 69, 151

Honey, Michael K., 237n21

Hongwanji Japanese School (Hawaii), 217

Hongwanji tradition of Buddhism, 246n17

Horace Mann Elementary School, 142

Hori, Michie Taira: on discrimination, 119–20; family history, 230; father's arrest, 206; father's employment and family tofu business, 82; on friendships outside the community, 114–15; on misbehavior, 199; on Mr. Yamasaki, 152; on registering for incarceration, 212; on TJLS, 110, 112, 155, 186–87

Horita, Kazuo (Kaz): family history, 226; on highway markets, 141; on his father's employment, 76; on religious affiliation, 121–22; on the reunion, 203, 220; on sports, 197–98; on Tacoma's closeness, 98–99; on TJLS as secular, 109; on the Yamasakis, 145–56

Horita's market, 92

hotels, 3, 4, 237n19, 243n19; Aochi family, 68, 225; boarders, 74, 129, 238n27; as childhood residences of Nisei, 66, 80, 114; Fujimoto family, 73, 88, 225, 242n16; Hoshiwara family, 227; "Hotel de Gink," 129, 246n3; Japanese Hotel boarding house, 130, 131, 132; Kikuchi family, 75; Kosai family, 74, 75, 113, 228, 242n17; management of, 71; as meeting place, 108; Munekata family, 3, 76, 79–80, 80–82, 91, 229; Pacific Hotel, 81*fig.*; present-day, 235n1; residents of, 80, 113, 114; Sato family, 73, 90, 133–34, 229, 242n15; in Seattle run by Issei, 80; St. Paul and Tacoma, 129, 132; women's role in, 72, 73–74, 75

House Immigration and Naturalization Committee hearings (1920), 157

Hylen, N. H., 59

I

Ichioka, Yuji, 28, 45, 239n11, 240n12

identity formation, 10, 13, 14, 27, 28, 102, 128–29. *See also* Nisei; subject formation

Ii, Fukoso, 205

Ikeda, Sachio, 114

Imai, Manpei, 205

immigrant communities: Chinese, 28, 40; frontier and settler periods for Japanese, 42, 48, 61, 239n10, 244n31; Japanese American, 22, 24, 235–36n6, 237n22, 238n24; studies of, 24, 25. *See also* community, Japanese of Tacoma

immigration of Japanese to US: as *dekasegi* (going out to work with plan to return to Japan), 62; to Hawaii and California, 66, 241n6; House hearings of 1920, 157; labor-contracted, 39; phases of, 42, 48, 74, 239n10; to Tacoma, 46; US policies, 32, 42–43. *See also* Alien Land Laws; citizenship; Exclusion Act (1924); Gentlemen's Agreement of 1907–8; Issei

imperial birthday celebrations, 35, 37, 52, 110, 185, 186, 208. *See also* emperor (Meiji Emperor)

Imperial Rescript on Education (1890), 36, 239n5; and ethics education, 36, 145, 174; recitation of, 36–37, 52, 110, 185; as summation of traditional Japanese values, 9, 28, 30, 36, 177. *See also* ethics (*shushin*)

Inomichi, Shinro, 240n19

Inouye, Paul, 133

Inouye family, Tommy's Produce Stand, 65*fig.*

internment camps. *See* wartime incarceration

interviews: dates and locations, 237n23; interviewees by family name, place, and date, 223–24; methodology, 22–23, 238n25; prewar focus of, 4–6; relation to oral history, 237n21

Iroha Cafe, 230, 243n20

Iseri, Mat, 250n3

Issei: acceptance of evacuation order, 214–15; agency of, 51, 56, 57; behavioral expectations of Nisei, 26, 27, 93, 105, 165, 220; and creation of TJLS, 49–50, 57, 60; and discrimination/racism, 39, 50, 63, 65, 97, 113, 156, 179; employment of, 61, 62–63, 66–67, 70, 72–73, 78, 80, 83, 93, 94; English instruction, 79, 158, 228–29; FBI arrests of, 205–9; as foremen who provided workers, 66; generational identity of, 12, 22, 244n31; going to Tacoma, 6; guidance at TJLS, 158, 159–60; ineligible for citizenship, 8, 28, 45–46, 50, 56, 98, 179, 236n8; influenced by Meiji Japan, 9, 28, 29–31, 35, 37–38, 39, 175, 202, 215; and Japanese associations, 31, 56; as Japanese nationals, 28, 31, 44, 45–46; prefectural origins, 61, 241n1; sacrifice and hard work, 62, 92, 94; social lives of, 108, 113, 120, 125, 196; traditional values of, 175–76; and transnationalism, 37–38, 46, 60, 221. *See also* immigration of Japanese to US

Ito, Kazuo: *The Issei*, 17; map of Tacoma's prewar Nihonmachi, 15–17, 16*fig.*, 19, 127, 128

Ito Miyoji, 41

Iwakura Mission, 38

J

Japan: as colonial power in Asia, 32, 41; education in, 56; international image of, 38–39, 44, 240n17; possibility of return to, 164, 167; relations with US, 168–69; requirements for emigration, 38–39; travel to, 207, 245n12. *See also* emperor (Meiji Emperor); Japanese government; Meiji Japan

Japan Town. *See* Nihonmachi (Tacoma)

Japanese American Citizens League, 22, 99, 117, 118; statement after Pearl Harbor, 210

Japanese American Courier (Seattle), 163, 168, 169, 197, 249–50n2

Japanese American National Museum (Los Angeles), 22

Japanese associations: Fife, 43; Japanese government involvement, 9, 31, 43–45, 240n11; management of relations with consulates, 44; San Francisco, 44; Seattle, 44; Sumner, 43. *See also History of Japanese in Tacoma* (1941); Tacoma Japanese Association

Japanese Canadians, 24

Japanese consulates, 9, 56; oversight of Japanese associations, 31, 44, 240n11; relocation from Tacoma to Seattle, 47; San Francisco, 44; Seattle, 44, 151, 208; Tacoma, 6, 44, 46. *See also History of Japanese in Tacoma* (1941)

Japanese government: commendation of Yamasaki at consulate, 208; encouraged Nisei to be bridge, 168; involvement with local communities, 28, 29, 31, 162–63; and Yamasaki's trip to Manchuria, 207, 249–50n2. *See also* immigrant communities; Issei; Japanese associations; Tacoma Japanese Association

Japanese Hotel boarding house, 130, 131, 132

Japanese language, 51–52, 100, 157–59, 248n13; polite phrases, 184, 185, 214; TJLS student essays in Japanese, 23, 161, 162, 164. *See also* Japanese language schools; Military Intelligence Service; Nisei: spoke Japanese at home; TJLS (Tacoma Japanese Language School): language instruction; TJLS (Tacoma Japanese Language School): student essays in Japanese

Japanese language schools: and assimilation, 160; in California, 156; curriculum and textbooks, 156; effectiveness of, 217; Fife, 48, 51, 240n18; funding of, 57–58; Hawaii,

Japanese language schools (*continued*) 48, 57, 174, 217; Issei rationale for, 49–50; religious and prefectural affiliations, 6; San Francisco, 48; Seattle, 48, 49, 157, 217; sectarian, 48–49, 101, 174; Spokane, 49; student essays, 248n12; students' mixed feelings, 111–12; targeted by exclusionists, 50–51, 57, 156–58, 167; Vancouver, BC, 217; Washington State, 51. *See also* TJLS (Tacoma Japanese Language School)

Japanese-run business, 63–66, 71–73, 76–85, 94, 241n2; catering to white customers, 80–82; complementing sawmill employment, 71, 73–74; in downtown Tacoma, 64*map*; employment of Nisei children, 92, 93; in Los Angeles, 74–75; run by women, 72, 73, 75–76. *See also* ethnic economy; hotels; Issei: employment of.

Jinguji family name, 229, 243n26

Jinguji, M. (employee at St. Paul & Tacoma Lumber Company, 1915), 69

Jinguji, Masaji (Stogie), 121–22

Jinguji, Masaye. *See* Fujita, Masaye Jinguji

Jinguji, Mrs., barbershop of, 75

Jinguji, Yoshie, 162

Jodo Shinshu (True Pure Land) Buddhism, 125, 246n17

Johnson, Albert, 43

Johnson-Reed Act, 43. *See also* Exclusion Act (1924)

judo, 70, 131

K

Kadayama, H. (employee at St. Paul & Tacoma Lumber Company, 1915), 70

Kanai En, 31

Kanto Earthquake (1923), 45, 242n8

Kawagoe, Chiyoko, 234

Kawai, Sosuke, 205

Kawai, Tokuhei, 43, 240n19

Kawano, Harue. *See* Ozaki, Harue Kawano

Kawano, Teiko. *See* Peterson, Teiko Kawano

Kawano, Teruko (Mrs.): students' memories of, 247n2; as teacher at TJLS, 82, 147, 152, 200–201, 234, 243n24

Kawano, Yoshiteru, 249–50n2

Kawano family grocery store, 82, 227

Kawasaki, Chiyeko Tadaye Fujimoto: at Capital Dry Cleaners, 84*fig.*; on the closeness of Tacoma Japanese community, 100–101; on ethical behaviors, 180, 183; purchase of TJLS building, 20, 226; on TJLS, 58, 189, 195–96; took over Capital Cleaners, 226; on the Yamasakis, 148, 154–55, 163, 167, 168. *See also* Fujimoto sisters

Kawashima, K. (employee at St. Paul & Tacoma Lumber Company, 1915), 69

Kawasoe, Misao, 240–41n21

Kawasoe, Nuri, 240–41n21

Kawasoe, Tetsuo, 240–41n21

Kawasoe, Totaro, 53, 56

kendo, 131, 150, 197, 208

Kibei, 114, 245n12

Kido Koin, 38, 39

Kikuchi, Sumie, 225

Kikuchi, Takao Jerry: on calligraphy lessons, 199; on ethical behaviors, 184; family of, 75, 91–92, 227; on friendships outside the community, 114; on Mr. Yamasaki, 152; on returning to Tacoma, 219; on TJLS and community closeness, 108–9

Kimura family, 139, 227–28, 246n12. *See also* Airway Market; Shirasago, Sally Someko

Kinoshita, Kiyoshi, language school essay of, 173

Kitare nihonjin (Come, Japanese, 1886), 39–40

Kobayashi, Ichitaro, 81*fig.*

Kondo, Kiyoshi, 70

Konkokyo Shinto church, 245n5

Konzo, Aiko, 234

Konzo, Seiichi, 240–41n21; on TJLS and the Yamasakis, 146, 163, 176

Korin family, 141–42, 228. *See also* Harada, Yuriko Lily Korin

Kosai, Giso, 69, 205

Kosai, Joseph (Joe): on acceptance of evacuation order, 214–15; on discrimination and segregation, 113; family history, 228; on friendships outside the community, 115–16; on impact of Meiji Japan, 29–30; parents' employment and hotel, 74–75, 242n17; on roaming the streets, 103; on shame, 179; on teachers and discipline, 201; on TJLS, 53, 107–9

Kosai, S., 242n17

Kubo, Mrs., barbershop of, 75

Kubo, Yasumi, student essay, 164

Kubo and Son Fruits and Grocery, 138

Kumasaka, Mr., 141

Kumasaka, Shichiro, 70–71

Kurashige, Lon, 15, 65, 66, 171, 177, 241n5

Kurata, M. (employee at St. Paul & Tacoma Lumber Company, 1915), 70

Kurimoto, Hiroshi, 240n19

Kurose, George, 214

Kurose, Hatsuye, with friends at College of Puget Sound, 111*fig.*

L

labor unions, 63, 77–78

laborers, Japanese, 43, 63, 66–67, 131, 241n6; and contracting, 39, 66–67, 69; and labor boss system, 66, 69, 108. *See also* Issei; lumber industry; railroad industry

laundries and dry cleaners, 72, 76, 79, 83–85, 219, 225, 226, 228, 243n22

League of Nations Charter, racial equality clause, 32

Lefebvre, Henri, 236n15

Lemire, Daniel Lachapelle, 24, 208, 248n12

Liberty Florists and Market, 138, 141

Lincoln High School, 13, 106, 114, 214. *See also* boys; girls; Magden, Ronald E.; Seto, Joseph T. (Joe)

longshoremen, 78

Lordsburg Internment Camp, 206, 209, 250nn5–6; incarceration of Masato Yamasaki, 172, 209–10; "Lordsburg Killing," 250n5

Lorenz Building, 237n19

Los Angeles: Fumi Sato Hattori on, 117; interviews conducted in, 22, 204, 223–24; Japanese community of, 100, 101, 235–36n; Japanese-run businesses, 72, 74–75; Little Tokyo, 66, 191, 244n31; Nisei women in, 247n13; Ryo Munekata on, 100

lumber industry, 67–69, 238n27; employment in, 62, 63, 68–71, 74, 82, 128, 136, 225, 226, 228, 230, 231; foremen, 69, 71; labor unions, 77; shipping port, 132; shutting of mills during Depression, 242n12; transitional employment in, 71, 74, 76; white workers' view of Japanese,

lumber industry (*continued*)
242n11; after World War II, 220.
See also St. Paul & Tacoma Lumber
Company; tideflats

M

Magden, Ronald E., 91, 158, 212;
campaign for high school diplomas
of evacuees, 214; *Furusato*, 17, 25,
112, 130; papers of, 23, 129; on
Tacoma Japanese Society, 43, 46,
239n11; on TJLS, 143, 146
Magi, C. (employee at St. Paul &
Tacoma Lumber Company, 1915), 70
Manchuria, Masato Yamasaki's
mission to, 207–8
Manchurian Incident (1931), 168
Manya, Hidekichi, 240n19
mapping, 15–17, 26, 127–28, 129; and
daily paths, 7, 97, 102*map*, 113, 125,
128, 140; downtown businesses,
64*map*; remapping of Japanese community in Tacoma, 15–20, 127–42;
official mappings, 101; overview
of Tacoma Japanese community
ca. 1900–1942, 18*map*; paths to and
from school, 102*map*; South Tacoma
Way businesses, 139*map*; Tacoma's
Nihonmachi, 16*fig.*; tideflats,
130*map*. *See also* de Certeau, Michel;
Pyle, Sarah; spatial approach and
spatiality
markets, 76, 92, 96; highway markets
of South Tacoma, 19, 96, 128, 138–
42, 139*map*, 227; produce, 19, 65*fig.*,
82, 225, 226, 227. *See also* Airway
Market; grocery stores
Maroush seafood company, 225
Maruoka Grocery, 56
Mata, David, 115

Matsui, Tashiro, 70
Matsumori, Masako Mae Yano, 231
Matsumoto, Masae, 240–41n21
Matsumoto, Sakunoshin, 241n22
Matsumoto, Takeshi, 205
Matsumoto, Valerie, 247n13
Matsuo, Masaharu, 240n19
McCarran-Walter Act (1952), 236n8
McCarver School, 18*map*, 104
McClatchy, Valentine S., 156
Meiji Japan: female education, 34,
146; impact on Issei, 9, 26, 28, 29–31,
35, 37–38, 39, 175, 202, 215; influence
on Yamasakis, 144–45; Meiji Con-
stitution, 9, 28, 30, 35–36, 239n4;
Meiji Restoration of 1868, 8–9, 33;
military modernization, 40–41;
reforms and modernization, 9,
33–35, 38; values and customs, 7,
28, 185. *See also* emperor (Meiji
Emperor); Imperial Rescript on
Education; Issei
Methodist church, 13, 120–25, 135;
location and building, 20, 204,
237n19; offer to house language
school, 48; sports and activities,
13, 120–22, 197.
M. Furuya Company, 64*map*, 141
micropractices, 26, 144, 174, 185, 192,
202, 247n1. *See also* Foucault,
Michel
middlemen, 91; "middleman minority"
concept, 65–66, 241n4. *See also*
ethnic economy
Military Intelligence Service, 205, 215–
17, 229; Language School, 7, 217–18
Miller, Danica, "Puyallup
Sovereignties," 235n5
Minidoka Relocation Center, 210;
Minidoka Irrigator, 210, 250n7
missionaries, 135–36

Mitchell Lumber Company, 67

Miyamoto, S. Frank, 24, 241n2

Miyashita, Shisue, 234

Miyazaki, Shintaro, 205, 208

Miyazawa, Yasutaro, 208

Mochizuki, T. (employee at St. Paul & Tacoma Lumber Company, 1915), 70

Modell, John, 49, 56, 63, 74–75, 87. *See also* Bonacich, Edna, and John Modell; ethnic economy; middlemen

Mombusho, textbooks approved by, 156

Morgan, Murray, 130

Mori, Jotaro, 205, 241n22

Morikawa, Misue, 234

Morinaka, Shigetaro, 241n22

Moriyasu, Shoshichi, 241n22

Morrison, Susan, 119, 128, 236n13

Mostrom family, 132, 134

movies, 89, 103, 122

mukoyoshi (adopted sons-in-law), 149

Munekata, Ryo: on acceptance of evacuation order, 214; attended Methodist church, 123; on behavior and discipline, 104–5, 181, 199; on community closeness, 100; comparison with Kunio Shibata, 86–87; family history, 228; family move to Idaho to avoid incarceration, 212; father's advice on education, 49–50; on his family's businesses, 79–82; on Japanese as first language, 159; on Japanese-run businesses, 75–76; memories of Tacoma, 3–4, 79, 139; path to and from school, 102*map*; on the tideflats and Tokyo Beach, 137–38; on TJLS, 37, 176, 189, 201–2; work at Horita's market, 92–93; on the Yamasakis, 146, 147–48, 150–51

Munekata, Sachi, 103

Munekata, Tadajiro, 79, 228, 243n22

Munemitsu, Mutsu, 44, 46

Murano Hotel, 80

Murayama, Mrs., 89

Murphy, Ulysses Grant, 160

N

Nakagawa, Hanna Kae. *See* Torimaru, Hanna Kae Nakagawa

Nakagawa, I. (employee at St. Paul & Tacoma Lumber Company, 1915), 70

Nakahara, Tsunekichi, 240–41n21

Nakako, Yone, 105

Nakamura, Hana, 234

Nakamura, Ted, with Eleanor Roosevelt, December 1941, 118*fig.*

Nakanishi, Yokichi, 240n18

Nakashima, Hyogo, 151, 240n19, 241n22

Nakayama, Chiyo, 240–41n21

New Tacoma Hotel, 64*map*, 79, 80, 229

New Washington Hotel, 64*map*, 79

New Year's Day: celebrated at Fort Missoula, 209; ceremonies at TJLS, 35, 52, 185, 187; messages from the Japanese ambassador, 163, 168

New York Times, "29 Young Japanese Hurt in Coast Crash," 248n8

Nihei, Kinko, 231

Nihon gaishi (Japanese history text by Rai Sanyo), 157

Nihonjin (The Japanese, 1901), 49

Nihonmachi (Tacoma): ca. 1920s, 15–17, 16*fig.*; ca. 1940, 5*fig.*; development of, 47–48; lack of attention to, 25; location in red light district, 181; maps of, 129; in UW Tacoma master plan, 20; walking scale of, 17, 26, 98, 100, 101–2, 125. *See also* community, Japanese of Tacoma; Los Angeles;

Nihonmachi (Tacoma) (*continued*)
mapping; San Francisco; Seattle;
Spokane; Vancouver, BC
Niiyama, Ms., 201
Nikkei, meaning of term, 235n4
Nimura, Tamiko, 25, 238n3
Ninomiya Kinjiro, 191–92
Nippon Yusen Kaisha, 47
Nisei: age-specific cohorts, 22, 238n24;
described as Americans first, 161,
167, 169, 211; described through
"twoness" and dual identity, 14,
15, 237n17; dominant narrative as
bridge between US and Japan, 145,
161–63, 167, 168–69, 170–72; identity,
8, 14, 23, 29, 66, 96, 170, 182, 215, 221;
Issei behavioral expectations of,
26, 27, 93, 105, 165, 220; Jun-Nisei
and Kibei-Nisei, 245n12; military
service in World War II, 203, 216,
218; shaped by immigration policies,
43; as "spiritual half-breeds," 168,
248n13; spoke Japanese at home,
158–59; use of term, 22. *See also*
bridging; identity formation; subject formation
"Nisei Week," 66
Nishijima family: and Yakima Fruit
and Produce Company, 140*fig.*
Nishinaga, Gikan, 205, 250n6
Nishinori, John, 243n27
Nitobe Inazo, 169; essay by Masaye
Jinguji, 169, 70, 249n15; promotes
Nisei as "bridge" 162, 169
Nomura, Gail, 50, 175
Nomura, Kenjiro, 240–41n21
Nomura, Shuji, 240–41n21
North American Butoku Kendo
Association, 150
Northern Pacific Railroad, 6

Northwest American Japanese Associ-
ation, 44
Northwest Liaison Japanese
Association, 207

O

obligation (*giri*), 62, 112, 175. *See also*
ethics (*shushin*)
O'Brien, David and Stephen S. Fugita,
63, 78, 216–17
Oda, Shuhei, 151
Ohashi Chuichi, 157
Ohta, Setsuzo, 70
Oikawa, Hideo, 205
Okada, Hito, 240–41n21
Okada, Hitoshi, 70
Okada, Mrs., 131–32
Okada, Norio, 240–41n21
Okada, Shinjiro, 240n19, 241n22
Okamoto, K. (employee at St. Paul &
Tacoma Lumber Company, 1915), 70
Okamoto, Shizuo, 240n19
Okamoto, Yonezo, 53
Okamura, Yonetaro, 240n19
Okazaki, Tokiko, TJLS essay, 161–62
Okubo, Zenshiro, 205
Okuhara, Kasumi, 228
Olson, Ronald, 77, 242n11
Omori, George, 122
Omori, Yoshiye, with friends at Col-
lege of Puget Sound, 111*fig.*
Opium War (1842), 33
oral history, 237n21
Oriental Trading Company (Seattle),
66
Osada, Takeshi: family of, 85, 229,
243n26; on playing at "Tokyo
Beach," 136–37; on TJLS as secular,
109

Osaka Shosen Kaisha, 47, 57, 150
Osugi, Tome, 240–41n21
Otsuka, Mura, 234
Otsuka, Shunichi, 128, 150, 238–39n3, 248n6
Owen Beach, 129, 195, 196
oyakoko (filial piety), 10, 87, 175. *See also* ethics (*shushin*); filial piety (*oyakoko*)
Oyanagi, Fumie, 234
Oyanagi, Waichi, with Eleanor Roosevelt, December 1941, 118*fig.*
oyster shucking, 93, 225, 227
Ozaki, Harue Kawano: on being American, 211; birth year of, 239n6; cared for her mother, 247n2; on ceremonies at TJLS, 35, 52; on ethical behaviors, 178, 184; on evacuation, 214; family history, 227; on friendships outside the community, 116–17; on fundraising, 57; on her mother, 30, 200–201; on social class, 88; on TJLS, 176, 192; on the Yamasakis, 52, 147, 152, 163, 165–67, 209
Ozaki, Sam Saburo, 227

P

Pacific Citizen, "Tacoma Reunion— One Man's View" by Kaz Horita, 99, 244n3
Pacific Hotel, 64*map*, 81*fig.*
Pacific National Lumber Company, 67, 77
Pearl Harbor, 172, 206, 210, 216
perseverance (*gaman*), 37, 145, 175, 176, 205, 214. *See also* ethics (*shushin*)
Peterson, Teiko Kawano: birth year of, 239n6; family history, 227; on filial piety, 37, 177; on her mother, 247n2;

on taking the streetcar, 106; on the Yamasakis, 147, 162
photographers, 90, 206–7
picnics, 11, 108, 125, 174, 194, 195, 245n8
picture brides, 42, 61, 150, 158
Pinedale Assembly Center, 13, 213, 214, 251n10
plays and skits, 192–93. *See also* micropractices; subject formation
Point Defiance, 195; Owen Beach, 129, 195, 196; sawmill, 67, 68
Polk's Tacoma City Directory, 63, 128, 139, 141, 242n16, 242n17, 243n20, 243n23, 247n14. *See also* Pyle, Sarah
politics of memory and remembering, 11–12, 19; and reconstituting the self, 12, 102; collective/shared memories, 108. *See also* erasure
postwar dispersal, policy of, 13, 26, 203–4, 219. *See also* wartime incarceration
Port of Tacoma, 6, 40, 47, 132, 137, 150
Portland, 46, 83, 90, 141, 195, 197, 213, 236n6; FBI arrests, 205
Pred, Allan, 11–12, 19, 113, 126, 245n10. *See also* situated practices (Pred)
prefectural associations (*kenjinkai*), 6, 57, 63, 108, 120, 241n23, 245n8. *See also* Issei
prefectural identification, 13, 106, 108, 245n10. *See also* Issei
prostitution, 43, 46–47, 150
PTA, 160
public schools, 50, 53–54, 58, 102, 106; after-school activities and sports, 112, 124, 197; preparation for, 158–60; relations with TJLS, 160; segregation at, 112. *See also* Central School; high schools; Lincoln High School; Stadium High School

Puyallup Valley: agriculture, 91–92, 243n27; immigration to, 62; as tribal land, 6, 235nn3,5

Pyle, Sarah, xii, xiv, 17, 63, 128, 236n14, 238n26, 241n3, 247n14, 249n6

R

race and racism, 25, 32, 59, 38–39, 41, 71, 112–14, 119, 164, 175; and identity, 66, 116, 177, 179–80, 245n9; "modern racism," 65, 241n5. See also discrimination; segregation and self-segregation

railroad industry, 63, 66, 82, 129, 227

Rasmussen, Kai, 216, 217–18

religion: Buddhist-Christian feuds, 123; flexibility in, 120–25; religious affiliation, 6, 101, 120–25, 245n15; and resignation over wartime incarceration, 214. See also Baptist church; Buddhism; Buddhist temple (Tacoma); Buddhist temples; Christians; Konkokyo Shinto church; Methodist church; missionaries; Shinto; wartime incarceration: Buddhist and Christian divide during

"Research on Training Students in the Lower Primary Grades" (1931), 183, 188, 190, 191, 194

resistance and rebelliousness by Nisei children, 14, 175, 177–78, 198–201. See also Foucault, Michel

respect for elders, 10, 37, 174, 177, 179, 180, 184, 202, 212. See also ethics (shushin); filial piety (oyakoko); oyakoko (filial piety)

restaurants, 17, 76–78, 82, 83, 85, 88, 229

reunions, 58, 98–99, 203, 220, 236n7, 244n3

Rye, Mrs., 121, 245n16

S

Sakakida, Richard, 217

Sakamoto, Jimmie, 162–63, 171. See also Japanese American Courier (Seattle)

San Francisco, 44, 48, 216, 235n6, 239n11; school board segregation policies, 41

Sang, Yoko, 112

Sanitary Public Market, 65fig.

Sato family, 133, 242n15, 246n6. See also Hattori, Fumi Sato

sawmills. See lumber industry

School Support Society, 57, 58, 241n22

Seattle: FBI arrests, 205; hotels run by Issei, 80; Japanese community, 46, 47, 99, 108, 114, 244nn1–2; Japanese language school, 48, 49; as second city of Japanese America, 235n6

Seattle Immigration Service, 208

Seattle Star, letter "Plan to Oust Japs' Schools," 157

Second Sino-Japanese War (1937), 169

segregation and self-segregation, 7, 65, 96, 97–98, 114, 125, 173; race and discrimination and, 71, 112–16; reinforced by TJLS, 111–12; public school segregation in San Francisco, 41; and sports, 197; residential, 26; workplace, 71. See also discrimination; Issei: and discrimination/ racism; race and racism; religion

Semba, Hiroshi, 205

Semba, Mr., 133

Seto family, 218, 229

Seto, Joseph T. (Joe): campaign for high school diplomas, 214; family history, 229; on friendships outside the community, 114; papers in Tacoma Public Library xiv, 251n13;

on returning to Tacoma, 219; service in military intelligence, 218

Seto Misaki, xii, xiv, 238n26

settler period, 42, 48, 61. *See also* immigration of Japanese to the US

shame (*haji*), 39, 168; incarceration as, 215; instruction not to bring on family or community, 40, 89, 94, 113, 175, 176–77, 179–81. *See also* ethics (*shushin*)

Shibata, Kunio: class differences and comparison of himself with Ryo Munekata, 87; on contributing to the family financially, 178; family history, 230; on his father's employment, 85–86, 87; on incarceration, 87; on name change from Urushibata, 86–87, 239n7; on Ninomiya Kinjiro, 191–92; as oldest son, 87; on paternal discipline, 159, 184; on shame, 180–81; on sports teams, 197; on TJLS, 37, 110, 176, 193

Shidehara Kijuro, 45

shikataganai (it cannot be helped), 214

Shinto, 34, 187, 208, 245n5. *See also* Konkokyo Shinto church; religion

Shirasago, Sally Someko: family history, 227–28, 251n2 (app. A); on her parents' grocery store, 138–39; maiden name of, 246n12; memories of brother selling flowers along highway, 140–41; only member of family to attend TJLS and Buddhist temple, 140; on religious affiliation, 125; on TJLS and community closeness, 108

Shirozu, June Miyeko. *See* Hayashi, June Miyeko Shirozu

shushin. See ethics (*shushin*)

Sino-Japanese War (1894–95), 40–41

situated practices (Pred), 11, 113, 245n10; situated ignorance, 19;

situated, spatial, transnational analytic, 15, 20

Smith, Michael, "transnational urbanism," 10

Snyder, Electa A., 58, 158, 159, 234

Sone, Monica, *Nisei Daughter*, 108

South Tacoma: empty lot, 129, 247n14; highway markets, 19, 96, 128, 138–42; Japanese-owned businesses on South Tacoma Way, 139*fig. See also* tideflats

spatial approach and spatiality, 11–15, 17, 20, 26–27, 125, 202, 204, 236n12; community destruction as spatial, 204, 219–21; identity and community formation, 13, 26, 96–126, 174, 221, 224, 236n12; spatial stories, 7, 12, 96–97, 126, 221; topological, 15, 171, 236n9. *See also* bridging; mapping; Pred, Allan; situated practices (Pred); transnational approach; walking

Special Collections, UW Libraries, xiv, 7*fig.*, 23, 55*fig.*, 129, 130, 165*fig.*

Spickard, Paul, 49, 108, 239n10, 244n31

Spokane, 17, 46; Japanese language school, 49

sports, 70–71, 112, 196–98; baseball, 70, 122, 136, 197–98, 243n22; *undokai* sports days, 194–95

SS *Tacoma*, 40

St. Paul & Tacoma Lumber Company: allowed union privileges to Japanese, 77; archival records, 23, 69–70, 129, 131; employee housing, 129–34; employee social club, 132; Japanese employees of, 69–70, 73, 133–34, 225, 229, 243n26; general store and other benefits, 129; as key employer, 67, 68; as key lumber producer, 242n8; night shift, 1915, 69–70; workers'

St. Paul & Tacoma Lumber Company
(*continued*)
  memories of, 70–71. *See also* lumber
  industry; St. Paul Avenue; tideflats
St. Paul Avenue: Butsuda's description,
  131; hotels, 129–32; residents and
  residences, 130, 133–36, 246n9; St.
  Paul and Tacoma Hotel, 129, 132;
  tideflats, 142, 102*map*. *See also* St.
  Paul & Tacoma Lumber Company;
  tideflats
Stadium High School, 13, 58, 106, 160,
  206; baseball field, 197; paths to,
  102*map*
Standard Meat Market, 231
Stanley, George A., 157
State Cafe, 77–78, 88, 229
Steilacoom Beach, 129, 195; beach
  outing, 196*fig.*
streetcar, 103, 106, 138, 159
strikes and demonstrations, 77, 78
structural and systemic forgetting, 4,
  6, 19–20, 67, 95, 220, 221, 235n3;
  countering forgetting, 20, 67. *See
  also* Connerton, Paul; erasure; Pred,
  Allan; situated practices (Pred)
subject formation: as contingent,
  dynamic, contested, 8, 14–15, 29, 97,
  113, 170–71, 175, 205, 221, 245n9,
  249n3; and ethics education, 10,
  174–75, 177, 182–83, 202; micropractices of, 144, 174, 185, 192, 202;
  and race, 116; and resistance, 198–
  201; spatial aspects, 12, 22, 97,
  125–26, 174, 202, 221, 236n12; transnational aspects, 174, 202, 205, 215,
  221. *See also* bridging; Foucault,
  Michel; identity formation; Nisei;
  race and racism; spatial approach
  and spatiality; transnational
  approach

Sugiyama, Yoshiko Fujimoto: on going
  to public school after Pearl Harbor,
  206; on her mother's immigration,
  42; on her parents' helping the
  community, 94; on Mr. Yamasaki
  and cultural heritage, 181; on public
  behavior, 180; on school outings,
  195–96; on sectarian Japanese language schools, 101; on TJLS, 53–54,
  160, 189. *See also* Fujimoto sisters
Sullivan, Michael, 25, 238n27
Sumi, M. (employee at St. Paul &
  Tacoma Lumber Company, 1915),
  70
Sumner, 218
Sundquist family, 134; Iveldell (Ivy),
  132, 134
Superior Hotel: on Broadway, 229,
  251n4; on Market and 17th, 73, 133,
  242n15, 251n3

T

Tacoma: attraction of Issei to, 6; built
  landscape, 204; businesses, 64*map*,
  78–79; downtown area, 17, 19, 20,
  47, 48, 71, 115, 127–28; establishment
  of Japanese consulate in, 6, 46–47;
  expulsion of Chinese, 114, 117,
  245n13; Japanese Americans not in
  census, 238n27; maps of, 130; race
  relations, 7, 119; return to, after
  incarceration, 203–4, 219–20; as
  seaport, 6, 40, 47, 132, 137, 150; as
  site for Nisei research, 6–8; as terminus of Northern Pacific Railroad, 6; urban development, 12, 19,
  63, 94, 204, 221. *See also* community, Japanese of Tacoma; Nihonmachi (Tacoma); South Tacoma;
  tideflats

Tacoma Buddhist Temple. *See* Buddhist temple

Tacoma Daily Ledger: article and ad after Pearl Harbor, 210, 211; article from 1893, 40

Tacoma Japanese Association: archival materials on, 23; community events and meetings at TJLS, 37, 108; education committee, 53, 54–56, 240n19; establishment of, 43, 239–40n11; formal communications, 35; and founding of a language school, 51, 52–53, 57; functions of, 44–45, 240n12; leaders of, 150; political action of, 56–57; survey of children, 52; ties between community and Japan, 45; Yamasaki's membership in, 208

Tacoma Japanese Society, 43, 46–47, 239–40n11, 240n16

Tacoma Land Company Hotel, 58

Tacoma Times, 210–11

Taira, Junichi: on citizenship, 174; family history, 230; father's arrest, 206; father's employment and family tofu business, 82, 230; on friendships outside the community, 115; on Meiji, 28; on misbehavior, 199, 200; recruited for US military intelligence, 218; on shame, 181; on TJLS, 53, 155, 160, 186; on the Yamasakis, 147, 152, 186

Taira, Michie. *See* Hori, Michie Taira

Taira, Takayoshi, 230

Taiyo Club (baseball), 70

Takahashi, Jere, 162

Takahashi, Kumataro, 43, 53

Takaoka, Chizu Tomita: on boys' misbehavior, 200; on "clannishness", 106–7; comparison of Chicago with Tacoma, 107; on evacuation and storing goods at TJLS, 212; family history, 231; on financial difficulties, 93; on her teachers, 159, 201; on playing with children from the tideflats, 136; on proper behavior, 178, 185, 187; on religious affiliation, 120; on TJLS, 108, 156, 158, 192; on *undokai* sports days, 194–95; on walking to school in the snow, 104; on working in markets, 141; on the Yamasakis, 148, 149, 172

Takasugi, Misau, 230

Takasugi, Mitsuo: on the Depression, 93; on evacuation, 213; family history, 76–77, 230; on having to demonstrate calligraphy, 187; on his family's restaurants, 76–77, 243nn20–21; on self-segregation and discrimination, 96; on TJLS and Mr. Yamasaki, 52, 181; on traditional values and rules, 176, 183; on walking from public school to TJLS, 106

Takasugi, Robert Mitsuhiro (federal judge), 220–21, 230, 251n15

Takasugi, Terry, 230

Takoma jiho, 228, 248n6, 250n9; "men of distinction" selected by, 150–51

Takoma shuho (*Tacoma Japanese Weekly*), 210, 228, 238n3, 250n9; "Let's Hurry to Prepare for Evacuation," 211

Tamaki, Chiyoko, TJLS essay, 161

Tamaki, Shigeko Gay. *See* Yoshiwara, Shigeko Gay Tamaki

Tamaki, Ted, 218–19, 231

Tamura, Eileen, 158–59

Tamura, Linda, 57–58

Tanaka, S. (employee at St. Paul & Tacoma Lumber Company, 1915), 70

Tanaka, Tokichi, 50

Tanbara, Greg, ix-x, 247n5

Tanbara, Kimiko Fujimoto: at Capital Dry Cleaners, 84*fig.*; on closeness of Tacoma Japanese community, 100–101; on her parents' helping the community, 58, 93–94; postwar residence in language school, 247n5; on residing across from TJLS, 136; son Greg, 247n5; on TJLS, 58, 189, 190, 196, 199–200; on the Yamasakis, 148, 159–60, 167. *See also* Fujimoto sisters

Taniguchi, Taeko Hoshiwara: on boys from Hawaii, 100; family history, 226–27; on incarceration, 100; on Mr. Yamasaki, 154; on performing in plays at TJLS, 192–93; on reunions, 220; on *undokai* sports days, 194; on walking, 102

tanomoshi (money pooling), 27, 57, 62, 63, 65, 71, 94

Tatsumi, Henry S., 169

tideflats: childhood memories of, 19, 128, 133, 134–37; Japanese hotel, 130, 131–32; map, including residences of Japanese families and bachelors, 130*map*; in the 1980s, 242n7; residences, 17, 19, 132, 136, 229, 246n1; sawmills, 67, 129–31; walking to school from, 135. *See also* lumber industry; South Tacoma; St. Paul Avenue

Tjade, Donna May (Janis Page), 116

TJLS (Tacoma Japanese Language School): academic experience, 155; addressed by Nitobe Inazo, 169–70; as agent of segregation, 111–13; alumni association, 150, 236n7; archival materials, 23; arts festivals, 243n24; attended by Iveldell (Ivy) Sundquist, 132; building of, 4, 20–21, 23, 56–57, 58–60, 204, 226, 236n13, 237n20; calligraphy instruction, 155, 187, 198–99; ceremonies, 35, 52, 97, 185–87, 208; as Civilian Control Center, 204, 211–12; and community closeness, 107–10, 112, 120–21, 125; community events, 108, 110, 121, 186, 194–95; discipline, 184–85; in disrepair, 2004, 21*fig.*; emphasis on being American first, 167; English instruction, 158, 159; equipment and furnishings for, 59–60; establishment and opening, 26, 48, 51, 52–53, 56; ethics curriculum, 9, 37, 145, 165, 172, 174–77, 214; five students' daily paths to, 102*map*; funding of, 54–56, 57, 58; gardening, 190; graduation, 187; great hall, 59, 185–86, 186*fig.*; group portrait, ca. 1920–35, 144*fig.*; historic preservation reviews, 20–21; as hostel for returnees, 204; importance of the Yamasakis to, 6–7, 145–46; inaugural students, 240–41n21; instruction in ceremonial behaviors, 185–87; Issei role in, 57, 60; and Japanese identity, 124, 126, 180, 181–82; land for, 58; language instruction, 7, 100, 109, 152, 155–56, 158, 218; as lens for study of community, 23, 237n23; memorial sculpture, 220; notice soliciting funds, 55*fig.*; outings and field trips, 194–96, 196*fig.*; as preparation for bridge role, 26, 171; recitation of Imperial Rescript on Education, 30, 185; report cards, 155; reunions, 58, 220; school cleaning tasks, 148, 187–89, 247n3; school song, 163–64; School Support Society, 57, 58, 241n22; as secular, 6, 48, 53–54, 107–8, 109, 166, 174, 177;

standard of education, 7, 201–2; storage boxes for evacuees, 198, 204, 212; student essays in Japanese, 161–62, 164, 169, 173; students and teachers, 1927, 7*fig.*; students recruited for military intelligence, 7, 205, 216–19; as Tacoma's only Japanese language school, 100–101; teachers, 82, 90, 147, 152–53, 167, 176, 199–202, 225, 226, 227, 233–34, 246n9, 249n7; teaching of American democratic values, 26, 145, 165–67, 172, 174; temporary location of, 57; textbooks from Japan, 156–57, 248n10; and transnationalism, 60, 215; tuition, 58, 89, 166, 174; use of folk tales and plays, 190–93; varied memories of, 13. *See also* spatial approach and spatiality; subject formation; Yamasaki, Kuniko; Yamasaki, Masato; Yamasakis

tofu businesses, 82–83, 230
Tokugawa system, 34
Tokyo Beach, 19, 136–38, 142
Tomita family, 231. *See also* Takaoka, Chizu Tomita
Tommy's Produce Stand, 65*fig.*
Torimaru, Hanna Kae Nakagawa: as Christian friend of Chizu, 120; on clash between longshoremen and police, 77–78; family of, 229; recollections of mother's ideas on social class, 88; on walking, 104
transnational approach, 8–10, 14–15, 20, 22, 25, 27, 205, 221; versus "assimilation" and "bridge" 10, 14; and bridging, 8, 10, 14–15; and Nisei identity, 10, 29, 60, 174, 202, 215, 221; for understanding Issei generation, 28–29, 38, 46, 60, 145. *See also* bridging; ethics (*shushin*); spatial approach and spatiality

Traveler's Hotel, 80
Treaty of Portsmouth, 41
Tsuchimochi, Shigeyo, 234
Tsutakawa, Gerard, *Maru*, 220
Tule Lake Relocation Center, 87, 209–10, 213, 214

U

Ueno Senichi, 50
Ukaji, Waichiro, 240n19
undokai sports days, 194–95
unequal treaties, 33, 38
Union Laundry, 79, 228
Union Station, 13, 212–14, 220–21
University of Washington Libraries Special Collections. *See* Special Collections, UW Libraries
University of Washington, Tacoma: purchase and demolition of TJLS building, 20–21, 23, 226, 237n20; sculpture memorializing TJLS, 220; as urban serving university, 20
urban histories, 24–25
Urushibata family, 85, 230. *See also* Shibata, Kunio
Uyeda, Clifford, 117, 245n13

V

Vancouver, BC, 141; Chinatown, 236n12; language school, 217, 248n12; Seto family history, 229
vegetable peddlers, 13, 85, 86, 87, 230, 231
Vendome Hotel, 73, 88, 225, 242n16
victimhood, 14, 24–25

W

Wadland, Justin, 25
Wakabayashi, Kisa, 234

Wakabayashi, Mitsue, 234
Wakamatsu, Shigeo, with Eleanor
    Roosevelt, December 1941, 118*fig.*
Walker, Jonathan M., 58
walking, 11, 13–14, 17, 96–98, 101–6,
    113, 134, 135, 137, 183, 213, 220; daily
    paths, 7, 97, 113, 125, 128, 140; five
    students' daily paths to and from
    school, 102*map*; walkability, 17,
    26, 98–101, 107, 125. *See also* de Cer-
    teau, Michel; spatial approach and
    spatiality
War Relocation Authority, 219; incar-
    ceration locations, 251n10; policy of
    dispersing Nikkei, 203–4. *See also*
    wartime incarceration
wartime incarceration: Buddhist and
    Christian divide during, 109; com-
    parisons of Tacoma Japanese and
    others, 100; and the "dissembling of
    Japanese American heritage, 4; and
    enryo, 236n10; evacuation, 13, 26,
    212–14, 220; Executive Order 9066,
    13, 117, 203, 211, 214; FBI arrests, 172,
    205–8; feeling of shame, 215; and
    forgetting, 235n3; Fort Missoula
    detention camp, 172, 208–9, 250n3;
    of Hawaii Japanese, 100, 245n4;
    Minidoka Relocation Center, 210;
    Pinedale Assembly Center, 13, 213,
    214, 251n10; redress movement, 4,
    24; registration at TJLS, 212; studies
    of, 24; and sympathetic politicians,
    119; torture, 209; transnational and
    spatial view of, 204–5; Tule Lake
    Relocation Center, 87, 209–10, 213,
    214. *See also* Lordsburg Internment
    Camp
Washington Hotel, 243n19
Watanabe, James, *History of the Japa-
    nese of Tacoma*, 238–39n3

Watanabe family, 133
Wheeler-Osgood Lumber Company,
    67, 69
Whitney Memorial Methodist Church.
    See Methodist church
Williams, Duncan Ryuken, 145, 245n15
Wilson, Woodrow, 32

Y

Yanagita, Mr., 225
Yakima Fruit and Produce Company,
    138, 140*fig.*
Yamamoto family, 133
Yamane, Magoichi, 151
Yamane, Matsue, 234
Yamasaki, Kuniko: background in
    Meiji Japan, 146–47; daughters of,
    148; as founding teacher of TJLS, 6,
    56, 143, 147, 149; internment at Tule
    Lake, 210; students' memories of,
    147–49; students' terms for, 145; as
    teacher of calligraphy, 146. *See also*
    Yamasakis
Yamasaki, M. (employee at St. Paul &
    Tacoma Lumber Company, 1915), 70
Yamasaki, Masato: as adopted son-in-
    law (*mukoyoshi*), 149; arrest and
    incarceration, 172, 205, 207–10;
    background in Japan, 106, 149; and
    Central School students' English
    ability, 157–58; on ceremonial occa-
    sions, 35, 52, 187; commendation
    from Japanese Foreign Ministry,
    151, 208; as community leader, 150–
    52, 172, 207; death at Lordsburg,
    172, 205, 209–10; educational phi-
    losophy, 144, 145, 154, 161–62, 163,
    166, 176, 183, 248n7; emigration to
    Seattle, 149; emphasis on American
    values, 26, 167; emphasis on ethics

and proper behavior, 10, 37, 181, 183; guidance to Issei parents, 159–60; instruction in ceremonial behaviors, 186–87; as liaison with public schools, 160; memorial service announcement, 210; presumed author of "Research on Training Students in the Lower Primary Grades," 183, 188; relief mission in Japan in 1939, 207–8, 249–50n2; remembered as strict, 152–54, 186; role in community, 26, 150; selected as "man of distinction," 150–51; students' terms for, 145; students' views on, 144, 152, 190; and Tacoma Japanese Association, 35, 150, 208; talk "The Races of Ancient Japan," 150; use of stories and plays, 191–93; wrote TJLS school songs, 163–64, 194. *See also* Yamasakis

Yamasakis: children of, 107, 148, 149, 153; as community leaders, 143; educational philosophy, 26, 163, 165–67, 172; and field trip accident, 154–55; influence on students, 170, 172, 182; residence of, 59, 143, 149–50; as TJLS core, 6–7, 143, 146; use of bridge concept, 15, 171, 172

Yanagisako, Sylvia, 249n2 (chap. 6)

Yanagizawa, Motozo, 205

Yano, Hiroshi, 53

Yano, Perry Yoshiaki: family history, 231; on his father's employment, 75; lessons with Mrs. Rye, 245n16; on TJLS and Mr. Yamasaki, 153, 182, 195

Yoo, David, 43, 114, 123, 125, 161, 164, 166, 237n16

Yoshida, Fusae Fujii: on arrest of her grandfather, 209–10; family history, 225; on Kenkichi Honda as sawmill boss, 69; on sports teams, 197; on TJLS, 159, 185–86

Yoshida, Keisuke, 70

Yoshida, Naoshi, 53

Yoshide, K. (employee at St. Paul & Tacoma Lumber Company, 1915), 70

Yoshioka, Fusako, 240–41n21

Yoshioka, Hiroko Betty Fukuhara, 74, 116, 226

Yoshiwara, Shigeko Gay Tamaki: on after-school activities versus Japanese school, 112; on evacuation, 212; family history, 231; on meeting with Eleanor Roosevelt, 117–18, 118*fig.*; on plays at TJLS, 193

Yueta, K. (employee at St. Paul & Tacoma Lumber Company, 1915), 70

Yukino Eijiro, 44, 46

THE SCOTT AND LAURIE OKI SERIES
IN ASIAN AMERICAN STUDIES

From a Three-Cornered World: New and Selected Poems, by James Masao Mitsui

Imprisoned Apart: The World War II Correspondence of an Issei Couple,
    by Louis Fiset

Storied Lives: Japanese American Students and World War II, by Gary Okihiro

Phoenix Eyes and Other Stories, by Russell Charles Leong

Paper Bullets: A Fictional Autobiography, by Kip Fulbeck

Born in Seattle: The Campaign for Japanese American Redress,
    by Robert Sadamu Shimabukuro

*Confinement and Ethnicity: An Overview of World War II Japanese American
    Relocation Sites*, by Jeffery F. Burton, Mary M. Farrell, Florence B. Lord,
    and Richard W. Lord

Judgment without Trial: Japanese American Imprisonment during World War II,
    by Tetsuden Kashima

Shopping at Giant Foods: Chinese American Supermarkets in Northern California
    by Alfred Yee

*Altered Lives, Enduring Community: Japanese Americans Remember Their
    World War II Incarceration*, by Stephen S. Fugita and Marilyn Fernandez

Eat Everything before You Die: A Chinaman in the Counterculture,
    by Jeffery Paul Chan

Form and Transformation in Asian American Literature, edited by Zhou Xiaojing
    and Samina Najmi

Language of the Geckos and Other Stories, by Gary Pak

Nisei Memories: My Parents Talk about the War Years, by Paul Howard Takemoto

Growing Up Brown: Memoirs of a Bridge Generation Filipino American,
    by Peter Jamero

*Letters from the 442nd: The World War II Correspondence of a Japanese American
    Medic*, by Minoru Masuda; edited by Hana Masuda and Dianne Bridgman

Shadows of a Fleeting World: Pictorial Photography and the Seattle Camera Club,
    by David F. Martin and Nicolette Bromberg

Signs of Home: The Paintings and Wartime Diary of Kamekichi Tokita,
    by Barbara Johns and Kamekichi Tokita

Nisei Soldiers Break Their Silence: Coming Home to Hood River, by Linda Tamura

A Principled Stand: The Story of Hirabayashi v. United States, by Gordon K.
    Hirabayashi, with James A. Hirabayashi and Lane Ryo Hirabayashi

Cities of Others: Reimagining Urban Spaces in Asian American Literature,
    by Xiaojing Zhou

Enduring Conviction: Fred Korematsu and His Quest for Justice,
  by Lorraine K. Bannai
Asians in Colorado: A History of Persecution and Perseverance in the Centennial State,
  by William Wei
The Hope of Another Spring: Takuichi Fujii, Artist and Wartime Witness,
  by Barbara Johns
Becoming Nisei: Japanese American Urban Lives in Prewar Tacoma,
  by Lisa M. Hoffman and Mary L. Hanneman